The Futile Crusade

The Futile Crusade

ANTI-COMMUNISM AS AMERICAN CREDO

by Sidney Lens

QUADRANGLE BOOKS — *Chicago*

Library of Congress Catalog Card Number: 64-14137

Manufactured in the United States of America
Designed by Joan Stoliar
First Printing

To SHIRLEY LENS
my beloved back-seat driver,

and A. J. MUSTE
*whose contribution to our times
has not yet been properly evaluated*

Acknowledgment

SELDOM is an author privileged to have four such eminent scholars read his manuscript and offer suggestions for improvement. Though the views herein are exclusively my own, I am deeply grateful to D. F. Fleming, Erich Fromm, Fred Warner Neal, and William A. Williams for the hours they spent with this work and the many helpful ideas they gave me for strengthening it. My thanks, too, to Ivan Dee, managing editor of Quadrangle Books.

Introduction

THE LAST fifteen years have seen greater waste of the natural resources of the earth and of the results of man's labor than the whole of previous history. During this decade and a half the great nations, in the course of the Cold War, have expended nearly a thousand billion dollars on militarism. The United States and the Soviet Union have built up stockpiles of nuclear weapons and vehicles for delivering them such that each nation could, in a great nuclear war, completely destroy the other, and neither could prevent its own destruction.

I have estimated that the nuclear weapons now in existence total 320,000 megatons. The Second World War involved the use of six megatons of weapons, over a period of six years. The present nuclear stockpile would permit a six-megaton war, equivalent to the Second World War, to be fought every day, day after day, for 146 years.

For several years the United States (and the Soviet Union) have lived under the shadow of the possibility of complete destruction. We are still in great danger—tomorrow, or the day after tomorrow, the psychological or technological accident might occur that would initiate a nuclear war that might mean the end of civilization.

It is hard to understand how the American people, who are sensible human beings, and the Russian people, who are sensible human beings, could have been led to permit the wasteful expenditure of a large fraction of their national income to achieve a goal that is itself irrational and almost inconceivably perilous. One factor that has operated is that the danger that a nuclear war would be initiated by design has been thought to be smaller if the destructive power of the Soviet Union and that of the United States were approximately equal, than if one nation were to fall far behind the other.

During most of the Cold War the United States has led in militarism, and the Soviet Union has followed our lead. We made and exploded the first atomic bombs and built up the first atomic stockpile. Three years later the Soviet Union followed our example. We made and exploded the first modern bomb—the three-stage fission-fusion-fission bomb, with explosive energy enough to destroy any city on earth; the Soviet Union was one year behind. We built up the first nuclear stockpile great enough to achieve the annihilation of an enemy country. The Soviet Union followed.

Only in the pollution of the atmosphere with radioactive materials has the Soviet Union taken the lead. By testing a large number of nuclear weapons during the year beginning in September 1961, including a sixty-megaton bomb, the Soviet Union assumed the onus of responsibility for two-thirds of the radioactive pollution, and for two-thirds of the millions of genetically damaged children who are the sacrifices of future generations to the nuclear militarism of our generation.

Why did our national leaders decide upon this policy of increased nuclear militarism? I do not know the answer, but I surmise that some arguments relating to the control of communism were involved. And why did the sensible American people permit it to be done? Why did the scientists, who during the years immediately following the use of atomic bombs to destroy Hiroshima and Nagasaki were, by the hundreds, active all over the United States in informing their fellow American citizens about the nature of nuclear weapons and nuclear war and the possibilities of devastation unless war were abolished and replaced by international law, not continue their vigorous campaign for peace and reason in the world?

I believe that the answer to these questions is to be found in this book by Sidney Lens. I hope that very many Americans will read the book and think about its relation to the plight of the world today, and the need to continue the move toward the abolition of war that was initiated in 1963 by the test-ban treaty. In his address to the United Nations General Assembly in September 1961 our late President John F. Kennedy said, "The goal [of disarmament] is no longer a dream. It is a practical matter of life or death. The risks inherent in disarmament pale in comparison to the risks inherent in an unlimited arms race."

I believe that we need to understand the important aspects of our recent history that are discussed by Mr. Lens in this book, in order that we may be helped in the effort to achieve the goal of the abolition of war and its replacement by world law. I am confident that the intelligence and good sense of the human race are equal to this task, and that we shall be able in the course of time to build a world characterized by economic, political, and social justice for all human beings, and a culture worthy of man's intelligence.

LINUS PAULING

Contents

	INTRODUCTION	7
I	A Half-Century of Fear	13
II	The Anatomy of Anti-Communism	21
III	Cold War and New Credo	41
IV	The Alliance of Conservatives and Ex-Radicals	64
V	Pax Americana in Europe	79
VI	Nationalism and Communism in Asia	94
VII	Their Side and Ours: People Versus Arms	113
VIII	Burma: Case History of a Positive Policy	136
IX	Anti-Democracy at Home	143
X	Anti-Communism Hardens Communism	161
XI	Latin America: The Final Disaster?	183
XII	The Futile Crusade	216
	NOTES	237
	INDEX	251

I

A Half-Century of Fear

FEAR OF communism has persisted in American life with varying intensity ever since the Russian Revolution a half-century ago. It has been a unique type of fear, not easy to classify.

It has not been, for instance, a "fear of the unknown," for in point of fact the study of Russia, China, Yugoslavia and other communist nations has been elevated to special status, occupying the energies of thousands of professors and specialists. The "science" of Sovietology, indeed, is now a specific branch of learning. Nor has it been a simple reaction to what we normally refer to as "power," for at all times since 1917 the Soviet Union has been inferior to the West, both economically and militarily. Bolshevism inherited an army that had disintegrated—76 per cent of the Czar's twelve million soldiers had either been killed, wounded, taken prisoner, or deserted. It inherited an economy— on which militarism normally rests—that was a shambles, its railroads and industries out of operation, its people hungry, its bread in short supply. Even today, when Russia has surpassed the levels of European nations, its production of goods and services is only 50 to 60 per cent that of the United States. All the communist nations together, as published statistics prove incontrovertibly, are still far behind the productive potential of the advanced nations in the free-world bloc. As for Soviet military force, it is of course formidable, but its stockpile of nuclear weapons is one-third that of the United States.

Nor has the fear been based on a reasonable concern over the activities of local communist parties—certainly not in the United States. At its peak in the 1940's, the American Communist party claimed 100,000 members. In 1954, FBI chief J. Edgar Hoover estimated its strength at 54,000. "To suppose," writes Alan Barth, editorial writer of the *Washington Post*, "that in peacetime 54,000 or 540,000 communists, however disciplined, however enthusiastic, could overthrow the United States government and make

13

the American people accept them as masters is as rational as a belief in sea serpents or dragons. Americans are not docile, our country is not in a state of chaos; we have law enforcement agencies, not counting the Army, the Navy, the Air Force, and the Marines, quite capable of putting down any uprising so fantastic." [1] The party today is less than a fifth as strong as it was in 1950.

The fact is that communism has caused so pervasive an anxiety because it has altered not only the balance of power among nations, but the very *character* of our epoch and the long-established rules by which nations defend their security.

Before the Russian Revolution, the political world, by contrast with the geographical one, was flat and two dimensional. There existed, on the one hand, a small number of dynamic, vigorous, and relatively advanced capitalist states, and on the other an assortment of feudal and tribal countries that were stagnant, helpless, and easy prey for the stronger powers who invaded, occupied and threatened them with impressive impunity. The world, then as now—and perhaps as always—was turbulent, given to wars and self-aggrandizement, but it was simple in its make-up. Its international conflicts were confined, for the most part, to rivalries between nations of near-equal strength for the bounties of commerce and spheres of influence. The colonial peoples, as well as the working masses, were latent forces rather than immediate challenges. The so-called backward countries were pawns in a game over which they had no control. If they dreamed of national liberation, they could not depend on aid from any major power, or play one off against another as they were to do after World War II. They slept the slumber of hopelessness.

The Russian Revolution added a new dimension to international affairs—much as the American and French Revolutions did in the nineteenth century. Here, finally, was an organized state that could—and did—offer moral encouragement, material aid, and organizational support to radical nationalists in Asia and working class revolutionaries in Europe. By its very nature it came to be a "third force" in class and colonial conflicts. Whether it gave direct aid to rebellious forces or played a passive role as an example to be emulated, it was an inevitable encouragement to revolutionary aspiration. From 1917 to 1924 its influence appeared awesome. Sailors in Kiel, Germany, formed soviets; revolutionaries seized Bavaria; the communist leader, Bela Kun, gained control in Hungary; revolution and counter-revolution wracked Finland, Latvia, and, above all, Germany. Where there were no soviets or uprisings, large scale strikes threatened the ancient structures of war-torn Europe.

For the proponents of the established order these were traumatic circumstances. Young Winston Churchill, a few years after the Soviet victory, warned Lloyd George that unless something were done about Russia "we may well be within measurable distance of universal collapse and anarchy throughout Europe and Asia." [2] His sentiments were echoed by many.

The emergence of a leftist regime in Russia was not just *another* problem for Western statesmen, but a problem of a different *kind*. In a two dimensional world there was little need to worry about stagnant feudal and tribal societies. The only possible adversary for a great nation was a rival capitalist state, bent on expanding its sphere of influence. Only one menace threatened the equilibrium of the great powers—war. The emergence of Bolshevism in the Soviet Union, however, heightened and made more realistic a second possible threat: revolution. Western leaders would now be forced to protect their security on two flanks, rather than one as previously. Facing them was an unwelcome choice. They must either adopt a new strategy, based on changing social relationships in the world, or cling stubbornly to precepts of the past, on the theory that Bolshevism was an episodic phenomenon and revolutions could be checkmated by force of arms.

They chose the latter course.

The first reaction of the West to Soviet communism revealed little new insight. In its frustration it could think of no more imaginative policy than the one it had used so frequently in the colonies, military intervention. From 1918 to 1920, fourteen foreign armies occupied parts of the Soviet Union, and Britain and France donated hundreds of millions of dollars to former Czarist officers engaged in civil war against the red regime.[3] It proved, after two and a half years, a futile effort.

Equally inept was the wave of repression in the United States that followed the Bolshevik Revolution. Fear of communism converted itself to exaggeration, deception, red-baiting, arrests, deportations. In the two years after the Bolsheviks came to power, according to Walter Lippmann and Charles Merz, there were ninety-one reports in the *New York Times* that " the Soviets were nearing their rope's end, or actually had reached it." [4] Prior to May Day, 1920, Attorney General A. Mitchell Palmer predicted that hundreds of thousands of American Bolsheviks would that day try to overthrow the government and plant the red flag on Capitol Hill. Though the day passed without incident—not even a fist fight—the dire predictions did not cease.[5]

Those who counselled moderation were labelled "reds." Senator Robert M. La Follette of Wisconsin was called a "Bolshevik spokesman in America" because he proposed that U. S. troops be withdrawn from the intervention at Archangel. Colonel Raymond Robins was denounced as a "red" when he insisted that Lenin and Trotsky were not, as rumor had it, "German agents." [6] Such moderate organizations as the National Council of Churches and the Foreign Policy Association were painted with the same brush—"red."

On November 7, 1919, the second anniversary of the Russian Revolution, the Department of Justice conducted a national raid against foreign and native-born communists, as well as other radicals. Five hundred men and women were arrested in Boston, shackled, and marched through the streets, and three thousand were herded into trucks and paddy wagons in New York. For the next few weeks communist and other leftist headquarters were overrun in New York, Chicago, Philadelphia, Detroit, St. Louis, Newark, Jackson, Michigan, and elsewhere. In a single foray the communists were decimated from 75,000 to 16,000 members. Hundreds of foreign-born radicals were deported. The mood of repression spilled over to include non-communists as well. On January 7, 1920, five Socialists elected to the New York legislature were expelled because their views were "inimical to the best interests of the State."

Intervention and the Palmer Raids were the high water mark in this first period of Anti-Communism. By the early 1920's the mood had spent itself. The Soviet spark had failed to ignite revolutionary successes in Germany, Asia, or the Western Hemisphere. The West relaxed; its apprehensions allayed. Communism remained a major concern for middle-of-the-road and rightist politicians in France and pre-Hitler Germany, but it slipped from its status of priority for most other nations. The United States recognized the Soviet Union in 1933.[7] The communist state joined the League of Nations (Lenin had called it the "League of Bandits"), signed collective security pacts with France and Britain, and adopted a program of popular fronts with socialist and liberal bourgeois parties.

For Americans, in particular, communism became a peripheral issue, far removed from the epicenter of their deliberations. The nation retreated to a familiar isolationism, and any thought about Soviet Russia was a mental exercise about her progress, rather than an urgent reaction to danger. The American Communist party, to be sure, was vocal and worrisome because it often pinpointed blemishes in the democratic process which many preferred to overlook. But it was of little import as an organized political force. It never won a popular following to compare to its sister movements in Europe; it never emerged as a serious challenge to state power.

Any lessons which might have emerged from the 1917-1924 period were lost because the tide of social upheaval had been contained. The West, particularly the United States, unaware of the darkening clouds, lived in a false sense of security.

The situation changed in the most drastic manner after the end of World War II. The wartime ally, Russia, turned rapidly into the most hated enemy in our history. The balance of power it had disturbed a generation before was then not "our" balance of power, but one which primarily shielded Britain and Western Europe. Now the United States was itself the undisputed leader of a postwar world, charged with helping it to its feet. Any threat to international stability was a threat against American stability, and Russia's expansion in Eastern Europe, through military occupation and controlled governments, was considered such a threat. It excited passions and raised fears and anxieties that in some respects exceeded those of the first Anti-Communist period. Certainly they have lasted much longer—two decades.

As the Russian sphere of influence expanded into China, Indochina, Cuba, and elsewhere, those passions endured and flamed. The rockbound Western strategy of 1918-1920 had left only minor scars; communism had been isolated in a single bastion. But continuation of the previous strategy after World War II resulted, as we intend to show in these pages, in a spate of defeats for the West, each one increasing tension and decreasing self-assurance.

Now two continents—Asia and Africa—were in volcanic eruption. The revolutions were primarily nationalist and neutralist, rather than communist, but each one affected the balance of power and catered to anxiety.

By the 1960's, an entire generation of Americans has been born into the belligerency of Anti-Communism, guided by maxims a millennium apart from those of the 1930's and early 1940's. The preoccupation with communism had become all-consuming, to the point where tens of millions of people today believe that it is either "we or they." Senator Thomas J. Dodd told a Hollywood rally in October, 1961, that "the only alternative to total defeat in the struggle with communism is total victory." [8] Few people in the 1930's would have thought in such absolutist terms. Anti-Communism today is no longer a stance, but a credo.

Periodically, the negative approach of American policy is questioned by a prominent political leader. "Our foreign policy," said Senator J. W. Fulbright in 1958, "is inadequate, outmoded, and misdirected. It is based in part on a false conception of our real, long-term interests and in part on an erroneous appraisal of the state of the world in which we live . . . If there is a single factor which more than any other explains the predicament in which we now find ourselves, it is our readiness to use the specter of Soviet communism as a cloak for the failure of our own leadership." [9]

Periodically, too, government officials inadvertently cast doubts on their own course. Secretary of State Dean Rusk told the New Hampshire Council on World Affairs in 1962 that the United States as well as its fellow members in the arms race are caught in a paradox. While "pouring more and more resources and skills into improving armaments, they are, on balance, enjoying less security." [10] Defense Secretary Robert S. McNamara, in presenting the case for a nuclear test ban treaty in August, 1963, listed such an imposing array of American armaments— "tens of thousands" of nuclear warheads—that Americans might ruminate on why, with this overkill capacity, more are needed.[11]

But the mood of the United States has been frozen rigid. Logic yields to emotional anxiety, self-assurance to fear. British historian D. W. Brogan has observed that while in the past "America developed a self-confidence that the outside world marvelled at more than it admired," there is now an "alarming . . . combination of irritation and resentment that reflects a growing discomfort in the face of some painful aspects of the modern world . . . This is an awful situation and it produces dangerous reactions. . . . If America is in danger, it can only be through treason or incompetence verging on treason. If 'commies' and 'reds' could be rooted out, there would be a speedy return to the good old days when America's defeat was as inconceivable as the earth going around the sun the wrong way." [12]

As with a child who brushes aside his fears by wish-fulfilling dreams, so America brushes aside the complexities of the mid-century by looking back to the "good old days" before communism and world revolution disturbed its tranquility. Overawed by communism's expansion, America has begun to question not its strategy, but its values. Such extremists as Robert Welch of the John Birch Society argue that "democracy is a deceptive phrase, a weapon of demagoguery, and a perennial fraud." [13] An overwhelming majority of Americans would deny this, but, reinforced by the old frontier tradition, they have grown to believe that we must be "tough," that we must "fight fire with fire," and that we must accept transgressions on the democratic process, such as Congressional investigations into beliefs and political affiliations, as necessary expedients in the war against communism.

In affairs of state there is a tendency to judge the friendship of foreign nations by their attitude towards communism, and increasingly to overlook their demerits in other areas. The roster of America's friends and near-friends—such as Chiang Kai-shek and Francisco Franco—is disturbing to many, but it is rationalized as a lesser evil in the face of a greater one.

The United States is caught in the vise between a persistent uneasiness and an unwillingness—for fear it will puncture our self-esteem—to re-evaluate the past. Despite an expenditure of $650 billion for armaments since the end of World War II and $100 billion for foreign aid, there is an unformulated feeling that America is on the defensive, no closer to security than when the Cold War began. The Marshall Plan, to be sure, was able to revive Europe. Elsewhere, however, whole continents have resigned from the Western sphere in a torrent of nationalist revolution unequalled in history. This radical nationalism is surprising and confusing to a nation that is stable and affluent. Americans cannot understand why at times nationalism can be friendly to a system which they consider totalitarian. They have watched dozens of countries turn to neutralism and communism, but they have seen no communist countries turn capitalist. They suspect, vaguely, that more adverse changes impend—perhaps in Latin America—but they have no clear concept of how to meet the problem.

Under such circumstances, after eighteen or twenty years, a re-evaluation of American policy—a probing of indefinite fears— is long overdue. By now we should have experienced an end to anxiety. Is it possible that somewhere along the way America has taken the wrong fork in the road? Has its analysis of world problems, perhaps, been faulty? Is it possible that communism has been misjudged as the cause of Western travail, when in fact it has been its effect? Is it possible, as James P. Warburg insists, that "we are not being defeated in the Cold War by our communist adversaries. We are defeating ourselves."? [14]

II

The Anatomy of Anti-Communism

DURING a discussion at the Yalta Conference early in 1945, Winston Churchill pointed out with obvious saisfaction that the right of veto in the projected United Nations Security Council would adequately protect Britain's colonial claims—for example, over Hong Kong. If China, he said, were to ask for the return of this British colony, it should be given the fullest opportunity to "make a broad submission to the opinion of the world," to be followed by a British reply—and there the matter would rest. "There is no question," he said, "that we could not be required to give back Hong Kong to the Chinese, if we did not feel that was the right thing to do." In reply to a question by Stalin as to what might happen in a somewhat different circumstance, if "Egypt should raise the question of the return of the Suez Canal," Churchill noted that the same procedure would apply. The final arbiter on the British Empire was to be Britain. If it chose to liberate a dependency or turn over the operation of a Canal to a dominated nation, it would; if it did not, it would not.

No machinery was contemplated for the United Nations by which colonies could secure freedom, and the Soviet Union, for its own reasons, was no more anxious to add to the prerogatives of the world body than was Britain. But Stalin's rejoinder indicated the different approaches which the two leaders brought to the future, and posed, in guarded terms, the problem with which the nations would be wrestling for decades to come. "Mr. Churchill," he said, "thinks that China, if it raises the question of Hong Kong, would be content only with expressing opinion here. He may be mistaken. China will demand a decision in the matter and so would Egypt. Egypt will not have much pleasure in expressing an opinion that the Suez Canal should be returned to Egypt, but would demand a decision in the matter." [1] The divergence here was seemingly small, but as history was to prove, it could be widened into a Cold War.

I

In the background of this exchange, far behind its unruffled po-
liteness, were the seeds of disintegration growing out of wartime
dislocation in Europe, and even more foreboding, the burgeoning
nationalism in underdeveloped and dependent countries. Radical
nationalism, with increasing vigor, would soon press its three
main goals: to secure independence, both political and economic
from foreign rulers; to weld disparate peoples into a common
culture with a common language and common history; and to
establish a viable economy, through such measures as land reform and industrialization, so as to relieve poverty. The second
and third were long term projects, but the first was within
purview.

Thousands of young cultured minds were seizing on the war
as an opportunity to gain liberation. The colonial powers were
in a crisis of their own, shooting at each other over the length
and breadth of three continents, seeking allies in their travail
wherever they could find them, even amongst the harassed
people of the colonies. The opportunity for the colonial peoples
was made to order: to pit one side against another, as in an
auction, for their own benefit. If Japan wanted Burmese or
Dutch East-Indian nationalists to help purge Britain or Holland
from their territory, it was asked to give in return an ironclad
promise of independence. If Britain wanted African youth to
join the Allied colors, it must reassure them with the words of the
Atlantic Charter pledging self-determination. Most of the powers
in both camps were merely sparring for time; men like Nehru
spent most of the war years in jail, and nationalist leaders in
Burma, who welcomed collaboration with Japan to begin with,
soon turned to resistance. But nationalism took heart nonetheless; the war gave it momentum.

Looking back to Yalta and the later conference at Teheran, it
must seem odd that while the three powers could discuss at
tedious length matters of military strategy or the spoils of victory
—who would get what, in territory or spheres of influence—there
was no specific discussion of how shackled nations might relieve
themselves of their shackles. The Big Three could agree that

Russia would occupy Poland or that Britain would be responsible for the reorganization of Greece and Italy, but the question of how and when Kenya or Syria might gain independence was left hanging—swept, if you will, under the rug.

The reason for this is painfully apparent. Britain, Russia, and the United States were joined together in the conviction that Hitler must be stopped, but each had additional, simultaneous goals. For Churchill, the aim of the war was to restore as much of the old balance of power as possible, especially insofar as colonialism was concerned. As a corollary it was necessary to contain the Soviet Union, so that its influence and material aid would not be joined to a potential wave of revolution. To effectuate these goals the British Tory argued ceaselessly that the second military front should run north from Italy into the Balkans and then into Germany, rather than west across the channel into France. General Dwight Eisenhower pointed out with an abundance of data that this strategy would be costlier in men and material, but the irrepressible Churchill was not appeased. If American and British armies could be placed flat against the Soviet borders, or close to it, Russia would be checkmated, and the prewar status quo would have a far better chance of restoration.

For Stalin, the defeat of Hitler was one facet of a strategy which included the demolition of the very balance of power Churchill cherished. For it had been this policy that had isolated Soviet Russia for decades and had forged a *cordon sanitaire* around its periphery. If the defeat of Germany and Japan were to be accompanied by a fragmentation of the British, French, Dutch and other empires, their resulting weakness would offer the Soviets not only a breathing spell, but an opportunity to create a buffer area in Eastern Europe between Russia and an Anglo-French Europe.

Roosevelt's approach was more subtle, but equally two- or three-sided. He looked on himself partly as mediator between Churchill and Stalin, and partly as the architect of a stable world in which American commercial interests might expand. The demise of the British Empire would further these objectives, first because it would remove colonialism as a festering sore threatening the peace, and second because it would expand America's opportunity for trade and investment. "We've got to make clear to the British from the very outset," he told his son Elliott, "that we don't intend to be simply a good-time Charlie who can be used to help the British Empire out of a tight spot, and then be forgotten forever. . . . I think I speak as America's President when I say that America won't help England in this war simply so that she will be able to continue to ride roughshod over colonial peoples." [2]

Insofar as Russia was concerned, Roosevelt's eyes were fixed on postwar equilibrium. An American intelligence report, handed to Roosevelt and Churchill during one of the wartime conferences, concluded that "with Germany crushed, there is no power in Europe to oppose her [Russia's] tremendous military forces. . . . The conclusions from the foregoing are obvious. Since Russia is the decisive factor in the war, she must be given every assistance, and every effort must be made to obtain her friendship. Likewise, since without question she will dominate Europe on the defeat of the Axis, it is even more essential to develop and maintain the most friendly relations with Russia." [3] The issue here is put in terms of power politics, but whatever its motivations it supported Roosevelt's view that Russia must be kept as an ally far into the future.

Roosevelt, like most Americans, disliked Stalin's communism, but he had no pathological fear of it. He recognized its pliability. The American communists had once called him a reactionary, but after he recognized the Soviet Union in 1933 they looked upon him as a solid progressive, meriting support. After Hitler invaded the Soviet Union in June, 1941, American communists became the most fervid advocates of the no-strike pledge, national unity, and class peace. The chances were good that if Russia were offered a measure of security, a soft communist line, everywhere in the world, might endure for decades.

What appeared to the world as unshakeable unity among the three great powers, therefore, was a tenuous relationship, to be sundered quickly if underlying differences were not resolved. Behind the secondary strategies of Churchill, Stalin, and Roosevelt, lurked portentous questions for the aftermath of war, more important than the war itself. What would the world look like, after hostilities? Would the old order be revived? Would Europe, drained and prostrate, be able to resist an avalanche of unrest similar to that after World War I? Would the nationalist revolution take wing, or would it be interrupted once more as it had been a generation back? Was it possible to *manage* the pace of revolution? Would communism be contained, appeased, moderated? And—if a grand nationalist upheaval were inevitable— what measures were needed to assure the security of the three Allies so they might continue collaboration?

It is doubtful that any of the three leaders fully anticipated the impending whirlwind or had definitive answers to these questions. They planned a United Nations as a forum for disputes *between* nations, but they fashioned no mechanism for handling the popular aspirations *within* semi-independent nations or colonies.

"The nearer we come to vanquishing our enemies," Roosevelt told Congress on January 6, 1945, "the more we inevitably become conscious of differences among victors." [4] It was relatively simple to hold the wartime alliance together, for the Allies could find a common denominator—defeat Hitler. What was to be the common denominator, however, for the postwar? In the womb of history was a colonial revolution that in two decades would result in five dozen national liberations. If the Allies could agree on the necessity of helping this revolution reach democratic fruition, they could continue their alliance—despite ideological competition—after hostilities were over. But if one or two were bent on delaying or subverting the revolution, while a third accepted or accelerated it, then normal relations between the three powers would become impossible. The strategy of competitive coexistence demanded joining the revolution of rising expectations, just as defense of the old order would inevitably sever the wartime alliance.

For Stalin there was little choice. His communism admittedly was insular, concentrating on "socialism in one country" rather than the need for world revolution. But Stalin had relied for two decades on leftist pressures both in advanced countries and in colonial areas, as a bargaining weapon to achieve Soviet foreign policy objectives. If those pressures created full scale revolution—as they were about to do—Stalin could not disregard them. He was bound to seek a *modus vivendi*.

For Great Britain, the choice was much more difficult because her wealth and power were tied to colonialism and empire. A *volte face* would require fundamental reorientation both of policy and national élan. For the United States, though it had a large sphere of influence in Latin America and a few colonies, adjustment to the impending social upheaval would be simpler. But it must determine in advance where its destiny lay—with the prewar status quo or with the rising tide of revolution. If it decided on the latter, it must inevitably strive to keep intact the wartime alliance, and under any circumstances, co-exist with the Soviets. If it decided on the former, it must inevitably sunder the alliance and embark on a new phase of Anti-Communism.

II

The dilemma of America, as hostilities ended, was best apparent among the liberals. For conservatives and rightists, Anti-Communism was a natural stance. They were Anti-Communists long before the war precisely because they opposed social change. A conservative spoke of the New Deal as "creeping socialism" and of socialism as a cousin to communism, because he eschewed social reform in principle. Rightists in California pasted slogans on auto bumpers that "Socialism is Communism" because they felt that any basic modification of the old order—anywhere—was repugnant. For such elements antipathy to communism was the obverse of a schematic defense of "free enterprise."

By contrast, the liberal was an avowed proponent of social change. The war, for him, was fought so that out of its ruins could emerge systems of social justice. He was willing to experiment with and propound new ideas. Liberal writer Irwin Ross, by way of example, advocated a "Mixed Economy" for the U. S. which he defined as "a blend of capitalist, socialist, and cooperative elements . . . [which] would promote planning, abolish depression and unemployment—without threatening anybody's freedom." Probably a majority of liberals subscribed to that proposal. They were partisans of a Welfare State, offering the citizen cradle-to-the-grave security, and they espoused with utmost sincerity the cause of anti-colonialism.

But liberals could not bypass the issue of Russia and communism. It drove deep wedges into their ranks, disuniting them, until the segment which inclined toward collaboration with the Soviets and tolerance toward local communists disintegrated, while another, which elevated communism and Russia to primacy among a spectrum of enemies, found its goals blurred, compromised, and finally perverted.

A Win-the-Peace conference in 1946, sponsored by the National Citizens Political Action Committee and the Independent Citizens Committee of the Arts, Sciences and Professions, called for unrestricted U. S. aid to Russia, but opposed loans to Britain "until sufficient guarantees have been made that these materials and funds will not be used for the exploitation and oppression of the colonial peoples." [5] Admittedly, this conference, chaired by Paul Robeson, was infiltrated with communists and their sympathizers, but there were many highly respected non-communists present as well, such as former Secretary of the Interior Harold Ickes, who was chairman of one of the participating groups, ICCASP. When the two organizations, plus the political action committee of the Congress of Industrial Organizations, sponsored a broader conference for progressives a few months later, they attracted such prominent liberals as James Patton, president of the National Farmers Union, A. F. Whitney, president of the Brotherhood of Railroad Trainmen, Walter White, secretary of the National Association for the Advancement of Colored People, and two former members of Roosevelt's cabinet, Ickes and Henry Morgenthau, Jr. The dominant figure behind the scenes was Henry A. Wallace, Vice President of the United States during Roosevelt's third term, and former Secretary of Commerce under Truman. That the "progressives" could attract the CIO, without which no liberal movement had any possibility of exerting significant influence on the American public, indicated their appeal to a decisive cross-section of liberalism in 1946.

At the other end of the liberal spectrum, perhaps half the size of Henry Wallace's Progressive Citizens of America, but similarly studded with such prominent names as Eleanor Roosevelt, Chester Bowles, Walter Reuther, and Wilson Wyatt, was the Americans for Democratic Action. Where PCA considered the problem of communist Russia subordinate to that of imperialism and the need for social change, ADA assigned a schematic, co-equal place to both.

The nucleus of ADA was a group of dissident former socialists whose disillusion with purge trials, forced labor camps, secret police, and the lack of elementary civil liberties in Russia, convinced them they must fight a "two-front war for democracy." Their leader, James Loeb, in a May, 1946, letter to the *New Republic* decrying the Win-the-Peace conference, advised liberals that they must decide "whether they believe the present critical tension in international affairs is due *exclusively* to the imperialistic, capitalistic, power-mad warmongering of the Western democracies and whether it is their conviction that the *sole* objective of the progressive movement is economic security or whether human freedom is a co-equal good." The menace to peace, in this view, was not exclusively from imperialists and reactionaries, but at least as much from the Soviets. Alienated by such incidents as Stalin's murder of Jewish socialist leaders Henryk Erlich and Victor Alter, and disturbed by exposés of Soviet forced labor camps, ex-socialists like Loeb saw in the export of Stalinism to Eastern Europe a threat to postwar freedom and international stability. Their justified revulsion became so overpowering, however, that they overlooked other factors in the world equation and ultimately made communism the main enemy.

The choice for America—and the West generally—in 1946-1947 was not between "pro-communism and anti-communism," or "pro-imperialism and anti-imperialism." These were static concepts, far too simple for the complex turbulence that was beginning to shake the planet. Nor was the formula "down with both communism and imperialism" any more satisfactory, for it too was a static thesis. The world was in a many-faceted crisis, with many interacting forces—capitalism, communism, imperialism, neutralism, feudalism, tribalism. The true choice was between co-existence with Russia while guiding all advanced countries into an accommodation with the world revolution, or a schism of the wartime alliance in which two blocs would fight for the allegiance of the mass of humanity. If the latter were to be our course, then we must carry the burden of those in the Western camp who wished to preserve as much of their empires and the status quo as possible. And we must find allies in the underdeveloped world who did not exist: decent nationalists who were both anti-communist and anti-imperialist at the same time. There were, to be sure, innumerable non-communists at the head of genuine nationalist movements, but not *anti*-communists. Their enemy for more than a century had been imperialism, and though they might disagree with communist ideology for religious or other reasons, they considered communists as fellow-fighters in the struggle against imperialism.

Whether or not we could co-exist with Russia—despite our aversion to communism—was bound to determine our approach to radical nationalism as well. If the wartime unity could be sustained, there was a possibility of a common formula to meet the revolution of rising expectations, with each power slowly modifying its concepts of security, shifting gradually from power politics toward the implicit goal of the United Nations—one world. But if the alliance were to be severed and blocs formed, the colonialist pressures on America by her allies would increase considerably. Security would again be formulated in terms of the power politics of a flat, two-dimensional world.

What is more, if the conflict with communist Russia for the allegiance of humanity were to take on the form of a life and death struggle, instead of the controlled competition of co-existence, then the West must find means of containing and reducing Soviet power. If you viewed Russia as an ally in a managed effort at social change, that was one thing; but if you viewed her as the fountainhead of instability, every revolution which upset or threatened stability elsewhere would accentuate the need to check Russia, too.

But how? We could declare war—there were many in the late 1940's who cried for "preventive war." Or we could employ measures short of war, encircling the Soviets with military bases and using our atomic bomb monopoly as a permanent threat. In either case, our strategy toward Russia must affect our strategy toward radical nationalism and social change. If containment of Russia required renewal of the arms race, then in the end we must militarize our allies and our potential friends in Asia and Africa as well. We must lean on governments receptive to placing American military bases on their soil, and willing to join with us in military pacts to isolate Russia. Such governments were not likely in the new developing nations of Asia or Africa, for they were concerned with positive improvements, land reform, education, roads, dams, factories, rather than with dissipating meager resources on weaponry. Like the United States itself in its formative years, they would tend to neutralism and non-involvement in arms races. They would eschew military alliances. The only likely allies in underdeveloped areas were dictators disinterested in social change, who would accept American arms and bases to enhance their authority and add to their profits. The road away from co-existence with Russia could lead only to militarism, alliances with unsavory political figures abroad, and a proclivity to accept the status quo.

There were many liberals who saw this in 1946-1947. Sumner Welles, Under-Secretary of State under Roosevelt, wrote: "The success of the United Nations is predicated upon the ability of the United States and the Soviet Union to resolve their differences and to work together at least during the initial period of the new world organization. . . . The alternative is only too apparent. If agreement becomes impossible all hope of a peaceful and stable world order breaks down. The result will be two worlds rather than one. The United States, to guard its own security, will be compelled to engage in an armament race, especially in the fields of aviation, of atomic weapons, and of scientific and biological warfare. The manner of living of the American people will have to be radically transformed. An American trend toward imperialism will be inevitable." [6]

But the men whom Arthur Schlesinger, Jr., has called "pragmatic liberals"—as opposed to "utopian liberals"—were unable to grasp the logic inherent in their position. If they repeated over and over again—as they did—that there was little difference between communism and fascism, then even colonialism, as much as they disliked it, must become the lesser evil. And if, in any situation—such as Korea or Indochina—communism and nationalism were found in alliance, it would be incumbent on them to turn their backs on radical nationalism for fear it might strengthen the greater evil, communism. The decision was always difficult and soul-searching, but inescapable once the defeat of communism and Russia become the primary objective.

The logic of their course did not impress itself on the pragmatic liberals immediately. They were neither venomous nor dishonest, and there were sometimes inconsistencies in their behavior; but their *direction* was already set by the flaw in their analysis. Two political events in the mid-1940's helped the process along. One was the death of Roosevelt. President Truman was more middle-of-the-road than his predecessor, unwilling to keep the more outspoken liberals on his team. One by one such people as Ickes,

Frances Perkins, Wallace, Morgenthau, Bowles, and Wilson Wyatt were separated from the new administration. The second was the sizeable Republican victory in the 1946 Congressional elections. The American political scale tipped drastically to the right, disorienting those liberals who had felt entrenched during three terms under Roosevelt. To achieve their victory, the Republicans had relied essentially on Anti-Communist propaganda. It evidently had an appeal to the American public, causing some liberals to conclude that it had to be appeased.

For a long time thereafter, many pragmatic liberals felt it necessary first to present Anti-Communist credentials of their own for fear the public would label their reform proposals "communist."

The first plank in an ADA circular in the 1950's read: "Effective American mobilization for the security of the free world against Communism." [7] The sub-head of Walter Reuther's pamphlet for "A Total Peace Offensive" called it a plan "to stop communist aggression by taking the initiative in the world contest for men's minds, hearts and loyalties," and the first paragraph of the foreword began: "In view of the character of world communism . . ." [8] Put on the defensive by constant attack from the right, Senator Hubert Humphrey, an ADA leader, explained to the Senate that "in policy, platform, and performance ADA has opposed the Communists on all the important issues of our time. . . ." [9]

The decisive moment for the pragmatic liberal came in 1947 when Harry Truman promulgated the Truman Doctrine. The Cold War was now formalized. The Progressive Citizens of America immediately denounced the plan as an "invitation to war," replacing the "American policy based on one world" for one which "divides the world into two camps." The *Nation* decried the Doctrine as "a plain declaration of political war against Russia," and the *New Republic* said "the U. S. is now ready to excuse unholy alliances of its own by adopting the apology that the end might justify the means." But the ADA, sorely torn internally, was silent for two long weeks on what Freda Kirchwey, editor of the *Nation*, called "the greatest issue before the country." [10] In the end, against bitter opposition within its ranks, it endorsed the Doctrine. From this point on, it would go along with most of its implications. There were then and there are today not a few liberals in ADA who reject Anti-Communism. But most who remained associated with it linked themselves to the Cold War. On this, the decisive issue of our time, the gap between the ADA and the conservatives narrowed to derivative and peripheral issues, such as the extent of economic aid.

If Henry Wallace's movement had shown a spirit of independence, it is possible that American liberalism might yet have rallied as an effective counterfoil to the Cold War. The Progressive Citizens of America—soon to become the Progressive party—was as confused on the question of co-existence as the ADA was on communism. Properly interpreted, "living with Russia" did not mean agreement with it on all points or adopting a parallel policy. Implicit in true co-existence is an inevitable element of competition. Each nation goes its own way, furthering its own interests, but pledges not to use war or the threat of war as a means of resolving international disputes. It is to live together, differ if need be, but without an arms race. In such an atmosphere, compromise and accommodation are possible, and the rigid tensions of bloc politics are averted.

But Wallace and his friends, beholden to the communists who were PCA's most active organizers, tended to trim policy to the Russian pattern. For instance, when the Marshall Plan was proclaimed, Wallace first endorsed it as "a great advance over the Truman Doctrine . . . [embodying] many of the things I have been saying in recent months." But later, after Russia had refused to participate in the Plan, he denounced it as "too little and too late." [11] To the majority of liberals, the Progressive party appeared to be a carbon copy of the Communist party, subservient to Soviet needs, rather than independent of it. They wanted peace with Russia, but as Americans concerned with *American* interests, not those of the Soviet Union. The Progressives nominated Wallace for President in 1948, but the stigma of "communist front" could not be erased. He received less than a million votes, and both he and the organization he led passed into oblivion. Since then, and until a peace movement began to emerge in the late 1950's (led, incidentally, by "utopian liberals" who, for the most part, refused to buckle to Anti-Communism), this segment of liberalism has been homeless and disoriented. What might have been an effective barrier against the futility of Anti-Communism was broken and dispersed.

III

The dilemma of the pragmatic liberals and all others who embraced Anti-Communism rests primarily in a failure to understand the relationship between communism and nationalism. The communist upsurge, good or bad, aborted or not, is not an isolated phenomenon but an intrinsic link in a chain of events that began four hundred years ago, and is part of the same chain as capitalism itself. It has grown out of and has fed on the same seed of social disintegration which was responsible for the bourgeois revolutions of yesterday, or the non-communist revolutions of today.

Ever since 1573 there has been a wave of nationalist upheavals against un-free and stagnant social systems, such as feudalism. In Holland, Great Britain, France, and Scandinavia, and later in Germany, Italy, and Japan, feudalism was uprooted; viable, nationally unified societies rose in its place. Had this process continued without interruption, it is more than likely that the world would never have known either Leninist, Stalinist, or Khrushchevist communism. But the very nations which liberated themselves during the sixteenth, seventeenth, and eighteenth centuries prevented the spread of nationalism and capitalism to other areas—China, India, Russia, Egypt, etc.—during the nineteenth century. This self-aggrandizing folly, in which Britain was to play the major role, has become known in history as "imperialism." In their own interests, the Western nations restored the power of feudal lords when that power was tottering. If it were not for the throttling effect of imperialism, the nationalist revolutions we confront in the twentieth century might very well have been completed in the nineteenth.

History has caught up with popular frustration in the underdeveloped areas. Whether Marx or Lenin had ever been born, this wrong was bound to be righted. Indeed, the first twentieth-century revolutions were not in Russia, but in Mexico in 1910, and in China in 1911. In Russia itself there were innumerable uprisings against the Czar—long before Lenin. Beginning with the Decembrists, who in 1825 refused to swear allegiance to a new Czar, countless insurrectionaries, imbued with nationalist pride, sought to topple the regime. The defeated revolution of 1905, in which humble peasants had petitioned their "Little Father" for relief from hunger and had been unceremoniously slaughtered, was, as Lenin himself argued, "bourgeois" in character. In its first phase, from March to November, 1917, before Bolshevism seized power, the Russian Revolution introduced a liberal democratic government with a mild socialist flavor, not too dissimilar from the Austrian coalition of Social Christians and Socialists today.

Marx and Engels talked of a "proletarian" revolution, but in point of fact the communist revolution has been a movement *away from* feudalism, slavery, and tribalism, just as the early capitalist revolutions and the present nationalist revolutions are links on the same historical chain.[12] To be sure, communism differs in ideology, in methods, in perspectives; but it is a medicine for the same type of social disease. Its answer may be right or wrong, progressive or reactionary, or it may be some of both, but it is a response to the same challenge as the French Revolution of 1789, or the British Revolution of 1642, or the Indian Revolution of 1947. It is part of a cycle much broader than itself, and if it had not occurred under Bolshevik leadership it would have found some other radical force to guide it to its destiny.

In an article in September, 1905, Lenin wrote that "we shall with all our might help the whole of the peasantry to make the democratic revolution *in order that* it may be *easier* for us, the party of the proletariat, to pass on, as quickly as possible, to the new and higher task—the socialist revolution."[13] Until 1917, the father of modern communism believed there would be two separate revolutions, one bourgeois and national in character, the other proletarian. It was the duty of Bolshevism to support the former in order to pave the way for the latter. By 1917 he had convinced himself it was possible to combine these revolutions, and, so to speak, skip a stage in history.

When Stalin became the guiding spirit of world communism he discarded the 1917 Leninist theory of a "double revolution," in which the working class would accomplish the tasks of the peasant revolution simultaneously with its own, in favor of the older Leninist concept of two revolutions, separate from each other. By now Stalin had lost hope in the possibility of "proletarian revolution" in the advanced countries, but he allied himself to nationalist movements. He ordered the Chinese com-

munists, for instance—against the shrill opposition of Trotsky—
to bury their identity as a separate organization and join as
individuals the Kuomintang. He supported the Spanish Republicans during the 1936-1939 Civil War.

Communism, clearly, is not a threadbare espousal of the "dictatorship of the proletariat," but an on-going strategy which
recognizes non-communist nationalism as a lineal relative. To
edge close to that relative, to embrace him, to urge him on, is
the epitome of policy; and once the nationalist has completed the
first period of revolution, the task becomes to ease him steadily
toward a second, socialist period. Communist tactics, as we shall
see, have often been sectarian and only partially effective, but
they mesh with an overview of two *associated* revolutions.

The theoreticians of Anti-Communism refuse to recognize the
implicit affinity of communism with nationalism. For them, communism is merely a function of Soviet power politics, nothing
more. "The communist ideology," writes Sidney Hook, "like the
Nazi ideology *but for different reasons,* impels those who hold it
to embark on a program of world conquest." [14] "Conquest" implies power politics, control either through military threat or
military occupation. The Soviets have engaged in their share of
power politics—for example, in Eastern Europe. But side by side
with this, and more characteristic, is a different *kind* of politics,
which may be called neo-revolutionary. The position of Hook
and other Anti-Communists is no minor misunderstanding, for
wherever a nationalist revolution has communist support it can
be labelled a Soviet effort for "conquest" rather than a revolutionary effort for liberation. Thus, fear of communism leads,
ultimately, to hesitancy about genuine nationalism. Where communism seeks to draw closer to nationalism, Anti-Communism,
though it abstractly recognizes nationalism's progressive character, all too often shies away. In practice, this hesitancy is frequently converted into a policy of anti-revolution.

The intimacy between communism and nationalism forces the
Anti-Communist, whether he is a pragmatic liberal or a conservative, to an impossible choice. In each critical situation he
must weigh his moral commitment to national independence
against his hostility to communism. Either he must support
nationalism, despite its tolerance toward communists or its communist tinge; or he must oppose both as one. He cannot accept

the first alternative, because communism is *the* enemy, out-weighing even the menace of imperialism or social stagnation. He chooses therefore the latter course—for instance, to aid imperial France against a nationalist-communist alliance in Indochina under Ho Chi-minh.

To allay a sense of guilt, the Anti-Communist devises a crude formula. For the moment, he says to himself, we must concentrate on containing or defeating communism. But after we have set it back, we can then begin to implement our programs of anti-colonial and social reform. We are "postponing," not forgetting, social progress.

No one expresses this thesis so candidly as Senator Barry M. Goldwater. "Victory over communism," he writes, "must be the dominant proximate goal of American policy. . . . Peace is a worthy objective but if we must choose between peace and keeping the communists out of West Berlin, then we must fight. Freedom, in the sense of self-determination, is a worthy objective, but if granting self-determination to the Algerian rebels entails sweeping that area into the Sino-Soviet orbit, then Algerian freedom must be postponed. Justice is a worthy objective but if justice for Bantus entails driving the government of the Union of South Africa away from the West, then the Bantus must be prepared to carry their identification cards yet a while longer. Prosperity is a worthy objective, but if providing higher living standards gets in the way of producing sufficient weapons to be able to resist communist aggression, then material sacrifices and denials will have to be made." [15]

First, according to Goldwater, we must defeat communism, *then* we can devote our energies to peace, self-determination for Algeria, justice for the Bantus, prosperity for America's underprivileged. In the meantime, those who wait for deliverance must wait.

The pragmatic liberal is caught in the same quandary. Unlike the rightist, he pays obeisance to the need for social change. He recognizes the "revolution of rising expectations" as an irreversible phenomenon. But such is his fear of communism and his anxiety over a shifting balance of power that in the critical moment he too chooses the lesser evil. He too is willing to postpone the very reforms he espouses. Though the rhetoric of the pragmatic liberal and that of the extreme right are as wide apart as the poles, in deed they share an uneasy alliance.

For both, communism is the permanent enemy that cannot be assuaged but must be beaten. "The only hope of survival against such a foe," say the editors of *Fortune*, "is to take an equal and opposite resolve against his existence." [16]

IV

In rhetoric the pragmatic liberal has doubts about militarism as the means of "containing communism," but in deed he finds a *modus vivendi* with the rightist and the conservative. He too votes for $50 billion defense budgets. He abhors, in theory, the "big stick" and "interference in the internal affairs" of other nations. But he utters little protest when American troops land in Lebanon to "protect American interests" against a revolution in Iraq, and he sees nothing wrong in shipping troops to Thailand as a measure against civil war in Laos. He is silent when the CIA finances and guides rightist revolts against sovereign regimes in Guatemala and Iran. Though he hates dictatorship, he finds it expedient to continue relations with Fascist Spain, apartheid-ist South Africa, and the dozen other tyrannies that are called part of the "free world." He votes continued aid to Paraguay, Guatemala, Nicaragua, South Viet Nam, Pakistan, Jordan, and Saudi Arabia, though their regimes are reactionary or have come to power through illegal coups d'état or rigged elections. In the myopia of Anti-Communism, he will not openly propose recognition of Red China, but on the other hand he does not suggest strongly that we sever relations with rightist regimes such as Franco Spain. The pragmatic liberal punctiliously respects all treaties and all law—in theory—but he blinks capriciously when the United States violates the United Nations Charter, the Organization of American States treaties, and our own neutrality laws to arm an exile force and send it into Cuba. Where communism is concerned, the rules are suspended. We are in a permanent war. We must win—no matter how distasteful the means we use.

Consider, for example, Truman's policy toward China. Certainly, the United States was disenchanted with Chiang Kai-shek. On April 10, 1947, President Truman sent Chiang a note expressing his deep concern that Chiang's government resorted "to force, military or secret police, rather than democratic processes to settle major issues." The President was alarmed that the "hopes of the people of China are being thwarted by militarists and a small group of political reactionaries." [17] General George C. Marshall was sent to China not to suppress social change, but to convince Chiang that he ought to invite communists into a coalition government and institute much-needed reforms.

But here began the dilemma. What policy should the United States pursue if Chiang *refused* to effectuate democratic changes, if he refused to thwart "militarists and political reactionaries"?

Nathaniel Peffer, professor of international relations at Columbia University, reported in May, 1947, after a stay in China, that the power elite of that country "listen respectfully to American exhortations to reform, to institute democracy, whether made by President Truman, General Marshall or Ambassador Stuart, but they have no intention of giving heed to them. They do not believe they have to. Whatever they may say openly, they believe America has to support them anyway. They believe they are in a position to blackmail America. The reason is Russia. Privately men of that class tell a visiting American . . . that America is going to fight Russia. Therefore, America needs China, and it must and should stiffen up the national government. It must support the Kuomintang Government against the Chinese communists, because the communists are the vanguard of Russia. . . . What they say . . . to each other is why, then, make any concessions by way of reform that will cost them the prerequisite and profits of monopolistic power?" [18]

In the face of this callous attitude, the United States had three choices: to support the communists, to withdraw entirely and let history take its course, or to accept the Chiang regime "warts and all." Since the war with communism was overriding and permanent, there was really no choice. Truman yielded to Chiang's blackmail, in the hope that after the Chinese communists had been defeated or fought to a stalemate, some other solution would be possible. History was to prove this a vain hope.

Consider a somewhat different example of how the pragmatic liberal is drawn into the maw of Anti-Communism. "I am frankly of the belief," said *Senator* John F. Kennedy on April 6, 1954, "that no amount of American military assistance in Indochina can conquer an enemy which is everywhere and at the same time nowhere, 'an enemy of the people' which has the sympathy and covert support of the people." [19] Eight years later, however, *President* John F. Kennedy sent in to a sector of Indochina, South Viet Nam, 16,000 American military "advisers" and $400 to $520 million a year in military aid. The opponents of the late Ngo Dinh Diem were the same nationalists and communists who have the "sympathy and covert support of the people." But Kennedy in power followed only a slightly different course from the one he criticized in 1954, bolstering a rightist regime because it "fights communism."

The inconsistency here is not the result of deception, but a coefficient of the different set of pressures experienced by the late President in the White House and as Senator. As President he had to deal with an army, clamoring for an opportunity to try out its paramilitary techniques, and with an impatient public, hiding its anxiety behind a demand for "action." Under such circumstances the "easy" way out of the dilemma was to yield to the accepted Anti-Communist pattern.

The pragmatic liberal would like to defeat communism and effectuate social change simultaneously; he always emphasizes this in his rhetoric. But in the moment of crisis he jettisons reform and revolution in favor of expediency. First . . . we prop Chiang Kai-shek with $3 billion in military aid; later we will press him more vigorously for internal reform. First . . . we must ship large stores of weapons to France, fighting communism in Indochina; later we will strive to end colonialism. If there is a danger that communism will benefit by a revolution we must be ready to intervene, militarily if necessary, against it. Since that danger is ever-present, our policy is ever-militaristic and almost always anti-revolutionary. There are a few notable exceptions— Indonesia and Bolivia, for instance—but in the main this has been the general line, adopted by pragmatic liberal and conservative, as well as rightist.

The *policy* of Anti-Communism must not be confused with *opposition* to communist theory or practice. The lack of dissent in the Soviet orbit, the manipulation of its citizens, and many other features are abhorrent to most people, including this author. To criticize these is one thing. But to elaborate from them a policy which makes communism *the* enemy, whose disappearance is a prerequisite for American security, and to seek to contain it by military threat while postponing necessary social change, is something else again. Involved is not just a clash of ideas but two different pathways of strategy.

One strategy recognizes a resurgent nationalism throughout the new world being born in the ashes of yesterday's war. The other, implicit in Churchill's comments to Stalin in 1945, envisions a postwar world that is socially static and which, with minor changes, can be kept that way so long as the West is militarily predominant.

A few decades ago this latter policy might have succeeded. The backdrop of power then was military strength. This is no longer the case. Time after time since 1945 it has been made all too apparent that great armies are immobilized against nationalist liberation movements. Superior arms failed to defend the Western colonial systems. Superior arms failed to prevent communism from sweeping China, North Viet Nam, or Cuba. Only twenty years ago the West dominated Asia, Africa, Latin America, Eastern Europe. But in spite of an impressive superiority in guns, atom and hydrogen bombs, and economies, it has yielded most of these bastions to neutralism or communism.

To ascribe so momentous a setback to guile or conspiracy is naive. All nations and all political movements rely on conspiracy and secret activity to some extent. Our Central Intelligence Agency doubtless can match the Soviets spy for spy, and it dispenses dollar for dollar as much "Washington gold" to those in other countries whom it considers friendly and useful, as the Russians dispense "Moscow gold" to their communists. But the Russians and Chinese seem to build large mass movements, with millions of dedicated followers, and our side does not.

The question is WHY? Whether or not we reach a detente with Russia, we will still have to answer this. What is the *source* of Soviet and Chinese power, and why, by contrast, has the West been quagmired, so often, in impotence? The fact is that, despite all the features Americans dislike in communism, it has adroitly exploited historical forces working in its favor, while the Western world, despite its political democracy, has been unable to join that stream.

III

Cold War and New Credo

THE FIRST casualty of war, someone once observed, is truth. It would be more accurate to say "perspective," since apologists rarely resort to outright falsification. Usually the truth is slanted by failing to give the enemy's position, by leaving out pertinent information, by altering the sequence of incidents, or by exaggeration. The reader or listener has valid "facts" at his disposal, but they are hopelessly out of perspective.

As might be expected, the Cold War, just like many hot wars before it, has been given precisely this kind of treatment.

Popular legend in the West lays the entire blame on the Soviet Union. The Cold War began because untrustworthy leaders in Moscow violated solemn pledges given at Yalta, Teheran, and Potsdam. In 1948, President Truman charged the Soviets had reneged on thirty-seven pledges.[1] A House Foreign Affairs Committee in 1961 listed thirty-three pages of "Soviet violations of international treaties and agreements." Russia violated its promise, Americans contend, of free elections in Poland and Eastern Europe. It engineered a coup d'état against the coalition government of Czechoslovakia. It carved out an East German state to thwart German unification.

In the East, the *bête noire* is the United States, or at least those "imperialistic circles" in America whose interests lie in a war economy. The Cold War, they say, began when the West refused to honor understandings that assigned most of Eastern Europe as a Soviet sphere of influence, to bolster its security. It was aggravated later by the scrapping of an inviolable agreement to demilitarize Germany forever. While Roosevelt was alive, say the Russians, the United States committed itself to collaborate with the Soviets far into the postwar era; instead, under Truman, Eisenhower, Kennedy, and Johnson, it has formed a military alliance against her and forged a frightening ring of bases around her periphery.

If the conflict is viewed in terms of power politics—in a

41

vacuum, that is—there is no question that each side gave more promises than it kept, and there is a measure of truth to all the charges. The United States, whatever the sequence of events, whether before or after provocation, *did* remilitarize Germany. The Soviet Union, again whatever the sequence of events, whether before or after the West had decided to isolate her, *did* conduct fraudulent elections and engage in severe repression in Poland against resistance elements who were controlled by Britain and a London government-in-exile. Sixteen leaders of this resistance movement, including two socialists, Puzak and Pajdak, were invited for consultations by Soviet military authorities in Poland, under the assurance of absolute safe conduct; they were then bundled off to Moscow in a military plane, tried, and, all but three, sentenced to prison terms. Fifty thousand members of the Home Army were disarmed and sent to Siberia. In November, 1946, three hundred socialists were arrested. During the 1947 election period, 149 Peasant party candidates for office were jailed, eighteen of them executed.[2]

Repressions by Britain, France, Holland, and others in Greece, the Dutch East Indies, Indochina, the Gold Coast, Cyprus, Malaya, and elsewhere were equally harsh. Each side's charges and criticisms can be rebutted and re-rebutted endlessly, for they are meaningless out of context. It is impossible to unravel the knotted threads of Cold War history without recourse to fundamentals. At this level the story is not merely a saga of diplomats, but of peoples; not merely of shattered agreements, but of social strains. The focal point is not what the statesmen promised, nor even their moral integrity, but how close they came to the necessities of a new era.

I

The thread of discord unravels back not to 1945 or 1946, but to August, 1941. Four months before Pearl Harbor, Churchill and Roosevelt met secretly "somewhere in the Atlantic" aboard the ship *Argentia*. Britain's plight was desperate. Her citizens were training with pitchforks and shovels for an expected German invasion. Her ally, France, lay prostrate under the Nazis. The Red Army was being pushed steadily toward the Urals. It was a propitious moment to kindle idealistic spirits by elaborating the principles that would guide the Allies after victory. The Atlantic Charter, proclaimed by the two leaders, was a document of high resolve, saturated with nobility, promising a beautiful tomorrow dramatically different from the ragged yesterday. Like Wilson's Fourteen Points a generation before, unfortunately, it was destined for the dustbin.

Point One of the Charter pledged the two powers to "seek no aggrandizement, territorial or other." Point Two bound them to "no territorial changes that do not accord with the freely expressed wishes of the peoples concerned." Point Three—most important of the eight statements of purpose—promised "sovereign rights and self-government restored to those who have been forcibly deprived of them."

History would certify that on Churchill's part, as Robert Sherwood has written, the document was "not much more than a publicity handout." He had much bigger fish to fry, namely involving the United States in actual hostilities. He was ready to sign almost anything to gain that objective. Later he argued that the rights of sovereignty and self-government, promised in Point Three, were meant only for "the states and nations of Europe now under the Nazi yoke"—not for the colonies under the British, French, Dutch, Belgian, or American yoke.[3] The Empire was sacrosanct; that was indeed what the war was being fought to save.

For Roosevelt, however, the Charter had deeper meaning. Whatever his motive—whether idealism or an effort to enhance American influence at the expense of Britain—the President foresaw a different type of international community arising after the maelstrom. Roosevelt's bias was so obvious that at one point Churchill remarked churlishly: "Mr. President, I believe you are trying to do away with the British Empire. Every idea you entertain about the structure of the postwar world demonstrates it."[4] Roosevelt was not deterred. He felt affection for Churchill as a wartime leader, but he did not believe he was meant to supervise future reconstruction. Subsequently, F. D. R. met with the Sultan of Morocco to give further assurances that the right of self-determination would be respected after hostilities were over. All over Africa and Asia young men joined the Allied colors believing they were fighting not merely against Nazism—which they knew only slightly and indifferently—but for the final liberation of their own countries from imperialism. Within Europe, too, hundreds of thousands of men and women, formed into guerrilla contingents to resist Hitler, felt they were building a life radically different from the past.

The Cold War grew from the seed of their disillusionment—not merely from broken treaties. "The path of history is littered," says Secretary of State Dean Rusk, "with broken treaties. . . . Where vital interests are concerned a nation by and large felt that it must take care of its vital interests and not give top priority to its . . . strictly legal commitments." [5] Senator Fulbright notes "there are other countries . . . with whom we have very intimate relations . . . [which] have failed to honor their undertakings . . . So that [Russia's behavior] isn't a unique record." [6] The Soviets, contrary to public belief, kept most of their pledges. They had agreed that Greece be a British sphere of influence and they adhered scrupulously to this even while Greek communists were being arrested and killed; they kept their word—begrudgingly—to leave Iran; they abided by agreements on entering the war against Japan; on granting France a zone of occupation in Germany; on including France and China in the Security Council of the United Nations and many other U. N. terms. They tried to live up to promises relative to Yugoslavia and China, though these were repudiated by Tito and Mao.

Under any circumstances, the conduct of the Soviets must be judged against the background of a Western alliance seeking to restore the old order in Europe and the colonial areas. To accomplish this, the West would not only turn its back on the Atlantic Charter, but it would inevitably come into conflict with Soviet "vital interests" and seek to isolate Russia once again. Neither side lived entirely by the principles of the Charter. But the West flouted it at least as much as the East, for a Western dominated world was being uprooted. Social uneasiness accompanied the post-World War II period just as it had the period after World War I, but on a vastly larger scale. With each attempted suppression of nationalist and other social strivings, with each effort to return to the status quo, suspicion corroded East-West relations until the principles of power politics became once more the underpinning of policy. The West returned to the practices of Anti-Communism, so ineffective in 1918-1920; the East adjusted to the revolutionary eruption and broke out of its isolation.

One of the first signs of the times was the re-investment of monarchies in Italy, Belgium, and Greece, where, after the Axis forces had been ousted, British troops had the primary responsibility for maintaining order. After the collapse of Mussolini in June, 1943, Churchill insisted that King Victor Emmanuel be returned to his throne. Reforms were held in abeyance, and resistance fighters who had played a heroic role in the north were disarmed without any concessions to their political demands for change. "It seemed," writes Robert Sherwood, "that Britain was backing the more conservative elements . . . as opposed to the liberals or leftists who had been the most aggressive in resistance to the Germans and Fascists." Britain argued its actions were determined by military necessity, "but American liberal opinion had already heard too much of this explanation in connection with the various 'temporary expediency' arrangements or deals and was impatient for some proof of the establishment of democracy and application of the Four Freedoms in all liberated areas. This liberal opinion . . . was becoming increasingly suspicious of Churchill's apparent determination to restore the unsavory status quo ante in Europe." [7] Some time later Britain vetoed Count Sforza, a leading liberal who had lived in exile and was popular in the United States, for membership in the Italian cabinet. Washington was so alarmed that Secretary of State Edward Stettinius issued a public statement that "the composition of the Italian government is purely an Italian affair . . . [and that] this policy would apply in an even more pronounced degree with regard to governments of the United Nations in their liberated territories." [8] Relations between Churchill and Roosevelt, as Sherwood points out, "were more strained than they had ever been before," but Churchill continued on his course.

In Belgium and in Greece, Britain similarly resuscitated discredited monarchs and conservative politicians. Its troops mercilessly battered the leftist EAM (National Liberation Front) out of Athens, even though EAM had been the backbone of resistance to Hitler and Mussolini. EAM, according to L. S. Stavrianos, professor of history at Northwestern University, "represented the people of Greece as much as any organization could during the period of occupation. . . . Under it for the first time the average Greek felt a sense of belonging, a sense of working toward a common goal." [9] For four years EAM and its military arm, ELAS, had fought with vigor and self-sacrifice against the Nazis and fascists, only to be greeted by Churchill's soldiers with sixty-three days of machine gun terror. Elliott Roosevelt reports that his father was appalled by this development. "How the British can dare such a thing! The lengths to which they will go to hang on to the past!" [10] But Churchill was single-minded in his determination. In the process thousands of Greeks were killed, a quarter of a billion dollars of property destroyed.

What was remarkable in this pre-Cold War era was not Stalin's bellicosity, but contrariwise, his adherence to so many understandings. Churchill himself alludes to it in discussing a second British repression. "We have been hampered in our protests against elections in Eastern Europe," he wrote, "by the fact that in order to have freedom to save Greece, Eden and I at Moscow in October [1944] recognized that Russia should have a largely preponderant voice in Rumania and Bulgaria while we took the lead in Greece. Stalin adhered very strictly to this understanding during the thirty days fighting against the communists and ELAS in the city of Athens, in spite of the fact that all this was most disagreeable to him and those around him." [11] Not one word of criticism appeared in Soviet newspapers against the terror in Greece.

Another sign of the times, more portentous than Churchill's acts in Europe, was the suppression of nationalists in Madagascar, an island in the Indian Ocean that belonged to France. Britain had occupied Madagascar at the outset of the war to prevent it from falling into the hands of the Nazis or the Nazi-controlled French government at Vichy. But in 1943, by agreement with de Gaulle, Free French troops replaced the British. The Malagassy nationalists demanded self-government and freedom. De Gaulle offered them a transparent scheme that would continue ancient domination: Madagascar was to become part of a French union, with the four million Malagassy represented by three elected members in the French Parliament, and the fifty thousand French colonists also alloted three members. The native delegates arrived in Paris sometime later, and, instead of taking their seats, denounced this plan as a sham. It was not the "sovereign rights and self-government" pledged by the Atlantic Charter, but a ruse for colonialism.

Quai d'Orsay rejected the pleas of the Malagassy. Tempers flared, "incidents" occurred. The Malagassy attacked a military camp at Mouramanja. When the clouds had lifted the three native members of parliament were in jail, sentenced to death— though later commuted to life imprisonment in the Comores Islands. Thousands were arrested, and by official figures eighty thousand Malagassy and two hundred French were killed in bitter fighting. The nationalist council claimed that 220,000 died, some thrown from airplanes without benefit of parachute, others buried alive.

Similar outbursts occurred in Algeria, Tunisia, and Morocco for the same reasons and with the same results. The native peoples demanded independence; de Gaulle, with the assent of Churchill, answered with machine gun fire. Forty-five thousand Moslems died in Algeria in 1945, and seven thousand in Tunisia. Had it not been for the intervention of an American consul in Tunis, Hooker Doolittle, the figure might have been higher.

Such occurrences received scant attention in the American press and are seldom considered today in studies of how the Cold War began. For Churchill and his friends on either side of the ocean, World War II strategy was two-pronged: to defeat Hitler and to preserve the old, highly favorable, balance of power. This too, like the Soviet reneg on elections in Poland and its harsh policy in Eastern Europe, is part of the calculus of the Cold War.

II

After the Yalta Conference, *Time* magazine could say, what it must since have forgotten, that "all doubts about the Big Three's ability to cooperate in peace as well as in war seem now to have been swept away." James Byrnes, later to become Truman's Secretary of State, comments that this "was how I felt about it." [12] They were both wrong.

Had the Allies shared a common belief that the prewar world could not be put together again, they might have found a conjunction of interests into the postwar era. If colonialism and feudalism were finished, the intelligent policy would have been to collaborate in interring it, while moderating the effects on powers like Britain through enonomic aid and other devices for their security.

Had Roosevelt lived, this strategy might have prevailed. "The Soviet leaders, and Stalin in particular," writes former Assistant Secretary of State Sumner Welles, "had as a result of many years of direct dealing with President Roosevelt finally convinced themselves that the policy he pursued had no ulterior motives. With his death, and with control of American foreign policy vested in new hands, the confidence vanished." [13]

The late Harry Hopkins, F. D. R.'s closest adviser, said: "We really believed in our hearts that this was the dawn of the new day we had all been praying for and talking about for so many years. . . . The Russians had proved that they could be reasonable and far-seeing, and there wasn't any doubt in the minds of the President or any of us that we could live with them and get along with them peacefully for as far into the future as any of us could imagine." [14] Stalin had made quite a few concessions to the American position—the inclusion of France in the Control Commission for Germany, reduction of Soviet requests for representation at the United Nations from sixteen to three, a modification of the Security Council veto in line with the American position, and a promise to enter the war against Japan. In hindsight today, the Soviet concessions of 1945 seem either minor or duplicitous. But the evidence of the war period, and for a short time thereafter, indicates that Stalin gave at least as much as he received. In return for American support, the communist world movement slowed the pace of revolt—and sometimes reinforced the status quo. Stalin naturally favored revolution in theory, but he was also a Russian nationalist. Communist parties were therefore pressured to subordinate their anti-capitalist and anti-imperialist goals to the wartime objectives of Soviet Russia.

The communists in India, for instance, endorsed the war unconditionally and joined the British colors, while Mahatma Gandhi insisted that Britain must "quit India" first. American communists not only gave no-strike pledges in the unions they controlled, but urged workers to do piece-work—ordinarily anathema to the labor movement—and work longer hours.

Though Tito was a dyed-in-the-wool communist and was leading the only viable guerrilla force in Yugoslavia, the Russians were uneasy about granting him material aid, for fear of offending a conservative government-in-exile. The British came through with help before the Russians did.

When hostilities ended, Stalin bailed the West out of one difficult situation after another. There is considerable evidence that he did not want revolution either in Europe or in China, for if he did he could have fanned existing flames into great conflagrations. In his own interests he planned, with American aid, to concentrate on rebuilding Russia. "Near the end of the war," writes D. F. Fleming, "Stalin scoffed at communism in Germany, urged the Italian Reds to make peace with the monarchy, did his best to induce Mao Tse-tung to come to terms with the Kuomintang and angrily demanded of Tito that he back the monarchy, thus fulfilling his [Stalin's] bargain with Churchill." [15]

The communists had played decisive roles in the European resistance. Of the five members of the Bureau of the National Council of Resistance in France (CNR), three were communists, and of the three members of CNR's Committee of Military Action (Comac), two were communists. In Italy the communists had formed a partisan movement known as *garibaldini,* and in March, 1944, were the organizers in Northern Italy of a general strike which Hugh Seton-Watson describes as "the most impressive action of its kind that took place at any time in Europe under Hitler's rule." [16] In both countries on the morrow of liberation—while de Gaulle was still in Algiers and Italy was in confusion—the resistance fighters seized control of the factories. With their following and their stockpile of armaments they might have marched full force towards political control. But General de Gaulle took a plane to Moscow, talked with Stalin, and French communists evacuated the factories and disarmed the partisans. Another word from Moscow and the revolutionary danger in Italy abated—the factories were relinquished, the combatants relieved of their weapons. So moderate was the communist policy that French communists refused to endorse nationalist movements in the colonies; the events in Madagascar, Tunisia, Algeria, and Morocco occurred despite them, not because of them.

Communists entered "bourgeois governments" in Europe willingly, even enthusiastically. For almost two years, Maurice Thorez, veteran communist, was vice-premier of France, and Palmiro Togliatti held similar status in Italy. Stalin's sights were set not on revolution but on Popular Fronts with de Gaulle and with the Italian Christian Democrats. Throughout Europe there were leftist communists, like Marty and Thillon of France, who felt they had been betrayed.

Here and there Stalin was unable to carry out a promise, but it was not because he did not try. He ordered Tito to bring King Peter's government-in-exile to Belgrade. Tito refused. According to Joseph and Stewart Alsop, Stalin directed him to "carry out the Stalin-Churchill bargain making Yugoslavia a joint Anglo-Soviet 'sphere of influence' on a 50-50 basis." Churchill, in his memoirs, mentions Stalin's concern. But Tito would not follow Stalin's directives.

In China, Mao Tse-tung rejected Soviet proddings to form a government with Chiang Kai-shek. The Alsops report: "Stalin actually did try, for a while, to keep the promises he gave Roosevelt at Yalta and T. V. Soong in Moscow. . . . Stalin ordered Mao Tse-tung and his fellow Chinese communists to enter a coalition government in China on the terms already laid down by [Patrick] Hurley as President Roosevelt's representative in Chungking. These coalition terms were calculated, or so Hurley then believed, to insure that the communist members of the proposed coalition would be controlled by Chiang and the Nationalists. It would seem the Hurley view was justified. At any rate, Mao Tse-tung shared it fully. He flatly refused to obey Stalin's command, declaring that his communists would win all China in the end and refusing to sacrifice this future victory to a subordinate place in any coalition." [17]

If there is any misconception in the mythology of the Cold War it is that the communists started it by stimulating revolution. On the contrary, they held it back. As late as 1947 Europe was distressingly vulnerable to internal revolt. After the great snowstorm that winter more than half of Britain's factories were out of production. No coal was being mined, millions were unemployed, tired, hungry. Germany was in far worse condition, its cities devastated, its currency virtually worthless, its people without homes or jobs. In Berlin a cigarette could buy as much on the black market as a worker could earn for a day's labor.

In that bleak winter two hundred people froze to death in Berlin alone. Manufacture was only a third what it had been a decade before. Conditions in France were somewhat better, but iron and steel production were merely half their prewar level. In the words of political scientist John W. Spanier of the University of Florida, Europe was "on the verge of collapse." [18] Not much was needed to fan the flames, yet the communists seized no factories, armed no guerrilla detachments, engineered no revolutions. As a matter of fact, they worked fulsomely to revive capitalism. Joseph Alsop, writing in the *New York Herald Tribune* in July, 1946, was struck by the co-operation Jean Monnet was getting from the communists in reconstructing France. "The key to the success of this plan to date, which has been considerable, is the enthusiastic collaboration of the French Communist Party. The communists control the most important unions of the C. G. T., the great French confederation of labor unions. Communist leadership has been responsible for such surprising steps as acceptance by the key French unions of a kind of modified piecework system. . . . Reconstruction comes first, is the Party line." [19]

III

The Cold War did not begin because the Soviets were exporting revolution. They were instead exporting restraint, joining coalition governments, prodding workers to produce more to speed economic revival, offering unity to socialist parties. There was neither altruism nor cynicism in their motives: before anything else they wanted to rebuild Russia, and moderation was necessary if the United States were to supply aid for that project. But in politics, as in physics, each action brings a reaction.

Britain, for instance, suppressed the EAM in Greece; twenty-two days later the Soviets responded by a purge of rightist "war criminals" in Bulgaria. Two thousand old-line generals and officials were executed, three thousand imprisoned.

Poland was another case of action-reaction.

The 1947 rigged elections in Poland must be studied together with Stalin's conviction, as he told Harry Hopkins in May, 1945, that "Great Britain wanted to revive the system of *cordon sani-*

taire on the Soviet borders." The arrests and executions in Poland were criminal acts, but in the light of obvious British goals for continued isolation of the Soviet Union during and after the war, there was at least some basis for Soviet suspicions that conservative Poles might act on behalf of Britain and threaten Russian security. Hopkins tried to reassure Stalin that the United States had no intention to isolate the Soviet Union. But attitudes were hardening. Perhaps the "Polish problem" was not resolvable under any circumstances, but it certainly could not be in the growing atmosphere of Anti-Communism.

Britain and the United States were hardly in a position to quarrel about the Polish elections, since Britain was denying a free and unfettered vote to the people of Greece, Iraq, Egypt, and Jordan. "Free elections" were obviously not a fundamental moral principle for the West. Poland had been assigned to the Russian sphere of influence at Yalta on the theory that twice in this century it had been used as a corridor for German invasion. The cry for "free elections" sounded to Stalin like an effort by Britain to penetrate into the designated Soviet sphere through the Polish exile groups.

A dozen items enlarged the suspicion that the Western nations were welding a bloc to dominate the world and leave the Soviets isolated and weak. Lend-lease had been curtailed without warning. The Allied promise to turn over certain German ships to the Soviet Union had not been kept. Argentina was admitted to the United Nations despite an agreement that only wartime Allies would be allowed to join. The talk of "democracy" seemed hypocritical to Stalin, since Poland and Eastern Europe, except for Czechoslovakia, had always been dictatorships, and had been part of a Little Entente dominated by France. If Britain were setting up puppet governments in Greece, the Middle East, and throughout Africa, why wasn't Russia free to form "friendly" —dominated—regimes in Poland and Eastern Europe? If Britain were intent on a *cordon sanitaire*, Russia determined to make Eastern Europe a buffer area between herself and the West. Judged as an isolated event, Russia's behavior in Poland was wrong. Judged morally it was wrong. But as a reaction to the power politics of Great Britain, France, and the United States, it was an act to defend what Russia considered "vital interests."

Wherever one turns in the jigsaw of the Cold War there are

missing pieces in the Western rationale. Conventional wisdom in America, for instance, claims that the Soviets obstructed every effort to unify Germany. But this is a myth; the conflict originated with France, not the Soviet Union. De Gaulle proposed to the Allies that the coal- and steel-producing areas of Germany, the Rhineland and the Saar, be directly annexed to France. The United States, Russia, and Britain rejected this piece of aggrandizement on the ground it would deprive Germany both of its industrial machine and its eastern breadbasket, making it impossible for it to survive. But France, smarting under its setback, thereupon vetoed every single act of the Allied Control Council aimed at forming a central German government. It reached the point where France refused even to permit uniform postage stamps for all four zones. Since all votes on the Council had to be unanimous, the French position prevailed. It was the Soviet Union in this period that pressed hardest for a unified Germany. But once it became impossible, she took the opposite road of constructing an East Germany in her own image. As James P. Warburg comments: "It was not at first Russian violation of the Potsdam agreement but French obstructionism that brought the breakdown of the four-power plan. Soviet exploitation of the breakdown came later." [20]

Once the paths of the two blocs diverged, wartime agreements became meaningless. Each side reversed previous pledges. At Yalta, for instance, the Allies had declared: "We are determined to disarm and disband all German armed forces; break up for all time the German General Staff that has repeatedly contrived the resurgence of German militarism; remove or destroy all German equipment; eliminate or control all German industry that could be used for German military production . . ." [21] The promise to permanently demilitarize Germany and Japan was so firm a matter of understanding that General Douglas MacArthur forced the Japanese to write a non-militarist plank into their constitution. But within four or five years, as the conflict with the East sharpened, all this was forgotten. The United States rearmed both defeated allies because it claimed that there was now a new menace from an "expansionist Russia." The West argued that Stalin began arming a "people's police" in East Germany first. Whether this was or was not the actual order of things, however, rearmament on either side of the line posed a threat to the security of both power blocs. For Russia it was particularly dire because she had lost millions of people as a result of Japanese intervention after World War I and two German invasions. Each action, therefore, could only bring forth reactions in kind and result in remilitarization, rather than demilitarization, of *both* Germanies. Specific behavior was less significant than the underlying philosophy of Cold War—that coexistence was not possible. Given that thesis, wartime agreements were doomed to the scrap heap.

For every Western argument there is an equally potent Soviet argument—if power politics are the criterion. Russia had agreed to evacuate Northern Iran by March 2, 1946. She refused. This was an oil-rich area, and Russia's oil production had fallen by five million tons a year as a result of wartime damage. In Czarist days, by agreement with Britain, Northern Iran had been a Russian sphere of influence. Now, the Soviet government sought to re-establish that status—despite her pledge.

When Iran placed this matter on the agenda of the United Nations Security Council, the Soviet Union countered by pointing to British behavior in Greece, Indonesia, Syria, and Lebanon. In all these areas British soldiers were trying to enforce the colonial past. If it were wrong for Russia to convert Northern Iran to its own ends, why, the Russians asked, was it right for Britain to use its troops for *its* purposes?

Under diplomatic pressure the Soviets *did* withdraw from Northern Iran. But it was inconsistent to condemn the one set of acts without condemning the other. If there were to be fulsome collaboration between the three great powers there was no need to be overly concerned with "security." But if security were to be the guiding motif, Russia was equally justified in joining to its sphere of influence whatever it could lay its hands on.

Consider another charge of the Cold War, that Russia milked its zones of occupation of mountains of machinery and foodstuffs. This is unquestionably true. But, as usual, it is one-sided. One of the first acts of the Truman administration was to terminate all Lend-Lease aid. Harry Hopkins, who visited Stalin at Truman's request, conceded that there should have been some notice given, but explained that American law had provided for help only until hostilities were concluded. Yet it was understandable that Russia expected aid to sew up its wounds. If Lend-Lease were not available there should have been, it felt, a substitute form of grants and loans. Russia's war losses were staggering— 32,000 factories, 15 large cities, 1,710 towns, six million buildings, 90,000 bridges, 70,000 villages destroyed, twelve to fifteen million casualties at the front, and many millions more dead behind the lines. The Germans had carried off two hundred million heads of cattle and poultry, had wrecked 1,135 coal mines, 3,000 oil wells, and 10,000 power stations. Twenty-five million people had lost their homes. To cut off aid at this critical moment was short-sighted. When the Soviets applied for a loan the application was "lost" for several months and then turned down. Very likely this was an American pressure to win a more liberal policy in Poland and elsewhere. But once aid was rejected the Soviet leaders had little alternative but to seize the wealth of conquered terri-tory. To do otherwise would have starved their own people and held off industrial recovery.

IV

To disentangle the Cold War into single incidents which assess blame to one side or the other is to lose overall perspective. The issue at root was how the world was to be organized. Roosevelt, whatever his motives, based his hopes on America's ability to steadily push Britain to relinquish its interests in the old order. He intended for the United States to mediate between Britain's concepts of balance of power and Russia's concern for its security. When Harry Truman became President—uninformed about his predecessor's plans, a novice in diplomacy, lacking patience—he was quickly seduced to a different policy. Prior to the first tripartite conference in which he participated, he sent Joseph E. Davies to persuade Churchill that it would be in every-one's best interest if the American President saw Stalin first so as to avoid the impression of "ganging up" on him. Churchill was outraged—and Truman retreated. "One cannot help wonder-ing," says James P. Warburg, "what might have occurred if Truman and Stalin had met privately at this time and established a personal contact." [22]

Frank Gervasi, writing for *Collier's,* claimed that immediately after Roosevelt's death Truman fell under the influence of Fleet Admiral William D. Leahy, Chairman of the Joint Chiefs of Staff. Leahy briefed the President daily and brought him up to date on previous meetings with the other allies. He was, says Gervasi, "one of the principle architects of the 'tough policy' towards Russia. . . . [He] did not singlehandedly bring the United States about in a full 180 degree turn on the course towards Russia. Other helmsmen had a hand on the wheel from time to time. But only Leahy was always near enough to make his influence felt constantly." 23

Truman was in office only eleven days when he gave Russia's Molotov a dressing down in what Drew Pearson described as "Missouri muledriver's language." Sumner Welles wrote in sorrow some months later that after incidents such as this "the Soviet authorities became persuaded that the United States was now far more under the influence of British policy than she had hitherto shown herself to be. . . . Since that time relations between the United States and the Soviet Union have consistently become more strained. Common understanding has all but vanished." 24

On March 5, 1946, Winston Churchill made an historic speech at Fulton, Missouri, which formulated in sharp terms what was to become—except for one point, British-American union—the American policy. Sitting on the platform with him was President Truman. The Soviet Union, said Churchill, is an expansionist state. "From Stettin in the Baltic to Trieste in the Adriatic, an iron curtain has descended across the continent. . . . The world is now divided into capitalist and communist blocs. To check the expansion of the Communist bloc, the English-speaking peoples—a sort of later-day 'master-race'—must sooner or later form a union. They should immediately contract a military alliance and coordinate their military establishments. They must lead 'Christian' civilization in an anti-Communist crusade." 25

Such intemperate remarks only a half-year after actual hostilities had ended must have shocked the Russians and reinforced their resolve to take extreme measures for "security." Many Americans, too, were taken aback; Churchill's phrases sounded like a war cry. Government officials hastened to deny that Truman's presence meant endorsement of Churchill's belligerency. Henry Wallace, still in Truman's cabinet, warned against the "tough" approach suggested by Churchill and other "reactionaries." "We must not let British balance-of-power manipulations determine whether and when the United States gets into a war. . . . 'Getting tough' never bought anything real and lasting —whether for schoolyard bullies or world powers. *The tougher we get, the tougher the Russians will get.*" [26] [Our italics.] His words were prophetic.

V

Anti-Communism was formalized as official policy on March 12, 1947. That day President Truman stood before a joint session of Congress and asked for $400 million in military and economic aid to save Greece and Turkey. After outlining the problems facing Greece, the man who succeeded Roosevelt drew a picture of a bi-polar world in which one section represented the virtues of freedom and the other the vices of totalitarianism. The United States, he said, can only survive if freedom predominates throughout the world. This objective cannot be achieved "unless we are willing to help free peoples to maintain their institutions and their national integrity against aggressive movements that seek to impose upon them totalitarian regimes. This is no more than a frank recognition that totalitarian regimes imposed on free peoples, by direct or indirect aggression, undermine the foundations of international peace and hence the security of the United States."

To make sure that no one misunderstood to whom he was referring, Truman noted that "the peoples of a number of countries of the world have recently had totalitarian regimes forced upon them against their will." Amongst these were "Poland, Rumania, and Bulgaria."

In less charged times, America might have realized how one-sided and out of focus was this Truman Doctrine. The communist countries were certainly dictatorships, but so were the majority of nations listed as part of the "free world." Most of Latin America was under rightist tyranny; most of Africa and Asia lived under foreign, imperialist rule; Portugal was a semi-fascist, and Spain an outright fascist, regime. It is significant that no effort has ever been made to overthrow the Spanish ally of

Hitler and Mussolini, Franco, even though the war had been fought to "destroy fascism" and only a few divisions, perhaps an economic quarantine, could have achieved the task. As Edgar Ansel Mowrer points out: "All the democracies desired the elimination of the Spanish dictatorship. Yet if destroying it would entail a serious risk of replacing it by the dictatorship of Moscow, then better leave the Spanish situation alone." [27] Franco has received from the United States as of the end of 1962, $1.7 billion of economic and military aid. The Truman Doctrine apparently was not aimed at rightist dictatorships. It was selective; it laid down the gauntlet only to the left.

More than that—the Truman Doctrine inevitably evolved into an instrument against revolution *per se*. Despite its idealistic phrases, it became a bulwark against social change. That this would be so was evident from the circumstances surrounding its promulgation.

In January, 1947, as already noted, a snow storm paralyzed Great Britain. The economy of the nation, already weighted down with foreign debts—$4 billion to India alone—was further weakened by the loss of $800 million in export production. Britain was in severe straits, and since she had already spent $760 million on Greece, to throw more money into this venture was impossible. Late in February the British government advised Washington that it would have to remove its army from Greece by the end of March.

Under the Truman Doctrine, the United States took over Britain's role of policing Greece. It inherited an unwholesome situation and a legacy of strife that required careful handling. The communists had enormous popular support. They had formed in September, 1941, the EAM (National Liberation Front) and ELAS (National Popular Liberation Army), which attracted not merely communists but thousands of non-communists, as well as other political parties. Their membership totaled at least a half million—out of a population of seven and a half million. War correspondent Leland Stowe wrote in the *New York Post* on February 20, 1945: "If there was any real resistance in Greece it centered chiefly in EAM and ELAS. I would stake my entire record of 19 years as foreign correspondent on this fact."

As the Germans relinquished their positions during the war, EAM and ELAS took over the functions of government. Except for three isolated areas, they controlled the country. For Britain this was a serious menace to previously formulated plans to install a conservative exile regime headed by George Papandreou. The communists, according to L. S. Stavrianos, never planned to make a revolution "because the current international communist 'line' called for national unity and Allied cooperation . . ."[28] But if they did not conspire to seize sole power, they also did not intend to permit pre-war conservatism to re-entrench itself. They were willing to become part of Papandreou's government and to disarm, but they had no intentions of doing this so long as outright fascist groups were permitted to retain weapons and harass liberal and leftist elements.

Almost immediately after liberation, therefore, Greece was plunged into civil war. In December, 1944, EAM tried to hold a demonstration in the center of Athens but were attacked by the police. Twenty were killed, 140 wounded. Next day EAM called a general strike that completely immobilized Athens and Piraeus. But the British reinforced their garrison in Athens and after weeks of fighting were able to seize the southern half of Athens and much of Piraeus. An armistice was signed one week later and a Varkiza Agreement, dealing with political issues, on February 12, 1945.

The Varkiza pact provided that ELAS would surrender its arms in return for recognition of the Communist party and EAM as legal political institutions. Elections were to be held within a year.

But almost immediately a reign of terror was instituted. *The London Times* reported that "EAM and its followers are being penalized in a variety of ways. Former ELAS men are beaten up, arrested, and tried on trumped-up charges. Hundreds of employees of public utility companies in Athens are being discharged for what is described as 'anti-national' activities, which simply means membership in EAM. Many of these men worked loyally for the British during the German occupation."[29]

John Sophianopoulos, foreign minister in the government of Plastiras, said: "If I had known that the honored ELAS arms by which our people resisted the invaders would have been turned over by the State to the X-ites (a rightist terrorist group) I would never have signed the Varkiza Agreement and would have preferred the hard fight to continue."[30]

It was not just the communists who were being alienated by British policy. In April, 1945, the moderate Plastiras government fell, to be replaced by the royalist-conservative regime of Vice-Admiral Petros Voulgaris. Three weeks later terror broke out in Larissa, reminiscent of Hitler's gangsterism prior to his ascent to power. The Minister of Justice admitted that thirteen thousand citizens were being kept in jail without trial or habeas corpus. This figure corresponded with that given out by the communists, who added that 258 men had been killed and forty-eight liberal and leftist printing presses destroyed.

"In this manner," according to Stavrianos, "an assortment of rightists, Royalists, and collaborators, unchecked either by their own government or the British, worked their way into control of the armed services and the administration." [31] The *New York Herald-Tribune* of September 17, 1946, reported "a pitiless war on scores of thousands of women and children in a desperate effort to halt a growing rebellion and wipe out not only communists but all democratic, liberal and republican elements."

The labor movement had been purged by the government, its elected leaders ousted; the economy was in chaos; the rightists and gendarmerie on rampage everywhere. In desperation the communists and other radicals retreated to the mountains and began guerrilla warfare once again. From September, 1946, to February, 1947, the number of guerrilla fighters grew from three thousand to thirteen thousand.

This was the "free" Greece President Truman inherited when he took the scepter from British hands.

Dwight Griswold, former governor of Nebraska, was sent to Athens in July, 1947, to guide the American Mission for Aid to Greece. At the head of the Greek government then was the former president of the National Bank, M. Maximos, a royalist and a rightist. But Griswold was intent on keeping hands off politics. He would do an honest job, so that American dollars would not be siphoned off by corrupt Greek politicians. He believed a line could be drawn between economics and politics.

Within two months, however, as the guerrillas grew stronger and the Maximos government collapsed, the United States was totally embroiled in the internal politics of Greece. Loy Henderson, chief of the State Department's Office of Near Eastern Affairs, was sent to Athens to force the Royalists to form a coalition with Liberals—upon the threat of withdrawal of United States aid. The new government that emerged—thirteen Royalists and eleven Liberals—was in fact an American product. It was less objectionable than the Maximos regime, but as with many other American-sponsored governments, it lacked the vitality to resolve pressing social problems. The rightists and moderates cancelled each other out. Though the Sophoulis coalition did offer an amnesty to guerrillas, this was the totality of its program to assuage a disoriented people. Perhaps, due to its makeup, it could have done no more. But what is so revealing is that the United States was willing to accept so meager a gesture.

Here was the point at which American policy needed razor-sharp definition. There were two opposite emphases in dealing with the "guerrilla problem." One was simply to destroy the rebels physically. The other was to weaken their popular support by granting overdue reforms, suppressing the rightists, and conducting a democratic election as promised. Had the United States used economic aid as bait to effectuate these changes, the guerrilla war would have collapsed. The communists, almost certainly, would have abandoned it; and if they had not, their efforts woud have been doomed without the village masses on their side. The United States certainly could have enforced such a policy. The Greek government and economy were on the brink of disaster without massive outside aid. But the American government failed to apply the total pressure needed for a *social* policy. It was far easier to supply guns, tanks, planes, and advisers to the Greek army than to prod a right-of-center government towards a reformist policy. The United States was to repeat this folly over and over again—with more dire results—in other parts of Europe, in Asia, Africa, and Latin America.

The overriding concern of the United States, like that of the British before it, was military. Boatloads of armaments were sent to Greece to help suppress the rebels. American military officers trained the Greek army. But the United States did not demand, as a *quid pro quo,* that the Greeks break the rightist control of the army or seriously liberalize the machinery of state. It was clear to everyone that America was engaged in an indirect intervention.

Despite such support, however, the Greek regime was remarkably ineffective. One hundred and thirty-two thousand government soldiers were unable to vanquish a guerrilla force of seventeen thousand to twenty-five thousand.[32] This was twice as many troops as the Germans had used against ELAS during the occupation.

Eventually the guerrilla effort did collapse, but not entirely as a result of either Greek or American power. Within the communist world by this time there were serious divisions not only over Greek strategy but other matters. Stalin told Yugoslav communist leader Milovan Djilas early in 1947 that "the uprising in Greece must be stopped, and as quickly as possible. . . . We should not hesitate, but let us put an end to the Greek uprising."[33] The Yugoslavs politely disagreed, but a year later Tito was expelled from the communist bloc and the repercussions of this split contributed heavily to the defeat of the Greek guerrillas. Not only did they lose a haven—Yugoslavia—to which they could retreat, but their own ranks splintered. Early in 1949, the leader of "Free Greece," Markos Vaphiades, resigned as premier of the "Provisional Democratic Government," and the Communist central committee denounced Titoist "opportunist deviations" as "the basic enemy and danger within the [Greek] Communist party." The communists were finally routed in September, 1949.

Anti-Communists in the United States were greatly encouraged by this victory, and perhaps this led them to the conclusion that the policy of containment would succeed elsewhere as well. But few stopped to consider either the circumstances—the split in the communist ranks—without which victory was far from assured, or the results. It had taken two years and hundreds of millions of dollars to defeat a guerrilla army. A total of more than $2 billion was contributed by the United States to the resuscitation of Greece over a period of a decade, but communism refused to be stilled. In 1952, the pro-communist EDA party, working under the handicap that the official Communist party was outlawed and innumerable of its followers were (and still are) in jail, received 10 per cent of the vote. In June, 1958, their share jumped to 24 per cent. They received either a majority or near majority in the big cities. Per capita income in Greece rose considerably, as it did throughout Europe under rightist regimes, but according to John P. Capsis, reporting from Athens to the *New Leader,* "most economists agree that about 400 families still control all the key positions in the Greek economy and a scandalously high proportion of the national income. In short the rich have gotten very much richer, while the poor have stood still." [34]

Few Americans were concerned that Greece remained—and remains—conservative and unstable. The important thing was to defeat communism, and this had been done. A pattern of indirect —and sometimes direct—intervention was being established, which seemed invincible. History, however, was to prove the fallacy of this thesis. Greece represented a tactical and episodic victory for Anti-Communism. It was to be followed by many more significant setbacks for America's balance of power.

IV

The Alliance of
Conservatives and Ex-Radicals

BEFORE we examine the effect of the Anti-Communist policy on Europe and Asia, we must dwell for a moment on postwar changes in America's power structure. An alteration in American strategy so wide-ranging and so enduring could not result simply from the wishes of a single man—no matter how great his authority—or a group of men. The factor of leadership is significant and sometimes decisive, but the area of choice for a public servant in a democratic society is circumscribed by the multiple pressures with which he must contend. The weakness or sincerity, ineptness or integrity of a President, despite his considerable power, is not alone enough to set a democratic nation on a new course.

Ours is a pluralistic society. Thousands of pressure groups, ranging from labor unions, liberal organizations, civil rights and peace movements on one side, to business lobbies and rightist groups on the other, make an impact on the sensitive antennae of government to create a consensus. Policy reflects this cacophony of demands. In this pluralism lies a center of gravity which moves left or right, depending on the weight applied from either direction. In the 1930's, the center of gravity was drawn leftwards by a combination of union, radical, and liberal pressures. Political students were often surprised at the "radicalism" of Franklin Roosevelt, who as Governor of New York had been essentially moderate. The pressures of a depression era, however, steered him toward militant liberalism. Since 1945, the center of gravity has moved to the right, as those elements which have a stake in Anti-Communism have enlarged in numbers and influence, while those which normally stand against it have contracted or have been immobilized. All these forces existed during World War II, but the Roosevelt leadership and the group of strong liberals around him were able to hold them in check. With the end of the war, the death of Roosevelt, and the schism of liberalism, the pendulum shifted right of center. The persistence of Anti-Communism was not the whim of this or that President, but a coefficient of its wider base in the power structure. It was not merely a failure of ideas, but a rearrangement of social forces.

Three decisive changes in the base of power mark the postwar period. First and foremost has been the manifold increase in the prerogative of the military, in its metamorphosis into a semi-independent force. The armed services, and its allies in the intelligence and police agencies—the CIA and FBI—are no longer merely organs of state subservient to the state, but molders of public opinion, generators of policy, and reservoirs of political power on their own. Secondly, the great corporations which today receive vastly greater rewards from military procurement than ever before have, as a consequence, developed a firmer relationship both with the military itself and the rightist groups that echo its dogma. Thirdly, there has been a shattering decline of radicalism and utopian liberalism, and a concomitant emergence of a segment of ex-radicals as the savants of Anti-Communism. The combination of these three developments has drawn America steadily to the right and mired its policy in the status quo. Our statesmen reflect what has been happening at the grass roots of power.

I

Probably nothing in America today is as foreboding as the pyramiding role of the military in everyday civilian life. This is a total reversal of tradition. As defined by William Henry Chamberlin: "Americans have never taken kindly to a large standing army, to peacetime conscription, and to a domineering military caste. All these things were associated with the Old Europe, against which the American Revolution was a testimonial of protest." [1] When the Revolutionary War ended, Washington disbanded his army and left the defense of the nation to haphazard local militia. After subsequent wars a standing army survived, but in skeleton form, its officers downgraded in rank and its budget severely reduced. Opposition to militarism has been a firm characteristic of American life—until the present epoch.

During World War II, the armed services fashioned an empire

of imposing proportions. They commanded 12,300,000 men and dispensed hundreds of billions of dollars. Their demand for civilian prerogative was already visible and growing stronger. Donald Nelson, head of the War Production Board, records that "from 1942 onward the army people, in order to get control of our national economy, did their best to make an errand boy of WPB." He warned that "the question of military control will confront us not only in war but in peace." [2] A Bureau of the Budget report in 1946 asserted that the army sought "total control of the nation, its manpower, its facilities, its economy." Whenever the military leaders were checkmated, they "took another approach to secure the same result; they never abandoned the sincere conviction that they could run things better and more expeditiously than civilians." [3]

When the war ended, the services should have been contracted, by past precedent, to prewar levels of 265,000 men and assigned prewar budgets that ranged between $500 and $900 millions. But this time the spectre of communism offered a convenient lever for badgering America to reverse tradition.

Even before the war ended, prominent businessmen, whose interest in military procurement was far from negligible, were urging a permanent preparedness program. Charles E. Wilson of General Electric proposed that every major corporation designate a liaison man with the armed forces, with the rank of colonel in the Reserve, and that America proceed to a "permanent war economy." [4] In mid-1945, before the war had ended, the Pentagon assigned General J. Lawton Collins to draft plans for a peacetime armed force. He suggested that the services maintain 1,732,000 men in regular status. For the next two years military propaganda toward this end was unremitting. The Harness Committee of Congress in 1947 "found that, in some cases, the propaganda and material prepared by civilians at the War Department followed a pattern unworthy of any Department of Government." [5]

Colonel William H. Neblett, national president of the Reserve Officers Association, noted in 1947 that "the Pentagon line was that we were living in a state of undeclared emergency; that war with Russia was just around the corner; and that the safety of the nation was dependent upon the speedy rebuilding of the lower ranks of the Army, Navy and Air with the Pentagon form of UMT [Universal Military Training]." [6] General Omar Bradley, Army Chief of Staff who replaced Eisenhower, proclaimed in 1948 that war prospects had risen, which prompted *United States News & World Report* to observe that "war scares, encouraged by high officials only a few weeks ago, so alarmed the 144 million U.S. public that top planners now are having to struggle hard to keep Congress from pouring more money into national defense than the Joint Chiefs of Staff regard as wise or necessary. It is proving more difficult to turn off than to turn on war psychology." [7] Countless generals were warning the nation of "emergency." Lieutenant General Leslie R. Groves stated that in the first five hours of an atomic attack forty million would be killed. General Carl Spaatz explained that it would be too late for defense after atomic bombs started falling. We would be devastated by attacks from the air, across the North Pole. This was all before the Soviets had developed the atomic bomb, or even tested one, but by focusing on potential danger and elevating the possibility of war with the former ally to immediacy, the American military was able to secure $12 billion in 1947 for the Army and Navy—almost one-third of the total U.S. budget.

Military men assumed key posts in government—Leahy as White House advisor, General George C. Marshall as Secretary of State, General Walter B. Smith as Ambassador to Moscow, General Lucius Clay as High Commissioner of the American zone in Germany. "Military control of American foreign policy, as a wide variety of critical observers pointed out," wrote Arthur A. Ekirch, Jr., professor of history at The American University, "involved not only a sharp break with the American past but also posed a strong threat to peace and democracy. The military's lifelong identification with the use of force and contempt for the workings of diplomacy was viewed in the long run as likely to lead the United States into war. Even if such a contingency were avoided there was the danger that the almost exclusive reliance on armed power in the conduct of American foreign relations would go far to stifle the workings of democracy." [8]

The military, with an immense propaganda apparatus at its disposal, was able to turn the "communist danger" to its own advantage—and though it violated law and tradition no one was able to stop it. According to Fred Cook, "by 1948 General Douglas MacArthur had 135 military and forty civilian personnel assigned to public relations; the Commanding General, European Theatre, had 107 military and thirty civilians taking care of his image." When the army proposed a peacetime draft in 1948— for the first time in our history—it enlisted the support of 370 national organizations "including the U.S. Chamber of Commerce and the American Legion; it . . . contacted 351 mayors in the principal cities of the land; it . . . promoted at least 591 articles and editorials in the press." The Boy Scouts were prevailed on to distribute fact sheets and the American Legion was induced to print 600,000 copies of a brochure titled "You and the Army Reserve." [9] Today the armed forces have nine thousand men, worldwide, in their public affairs sections, spreading propaganda that suits military interests, "educating" troops in its version of the present conflict, feeding reams of material to the press and magazines.

It is inherent in the nature of every institution that it try to perpetuate itself, and the American armed forces are no exception. Colonel Neblett says: "There was never any reason for an armaments race. Its real purpose here was to keep our professional military forces at a level high enough to give Regular officers continual employment until retirement at the high temporary ranks they held during and right after World War II. . . . Some ninety percent of the officers in the regular services hold ranks from two to three grades above their permanent ranks, with the emoluments and pay that go with their inflated grades." [10] This is a harsh estimate. It implies that professional officers have been more interested in their own status than in the needs of the nation. Yet, whatever the subjective demands of the officer caste, there is little question that militarism has an *objective* logic of its own. Like all bureaucracies, the military strikes for a greater role, and like all bureaucracies it must point to a dire need for its services. The menace of communist Russia —alleged or real—has suited that purpose admirably.

In due course the military establishment grew to proportions unknown in American life before—or anywhere else, for that matter. Today it owns $200 billion in property, three times the combined wealth of U.S. Steel, General Motors, Metropolitan Life, American Telephone and Telegraph, and Standard Oil of New Jersey. The Defense Department's payroll for 4.5 million soldiers and civilians is twice that of the entire auto industry. In 1931, the military held 3.1 million acres of land for its use; by 1959 the figure was 31.3 million—larger in area than the seven smallest states together. It spends approximately $25 billion a year on procurement; it grants more than $6 billion to business for research and development and a billion to universities and colleges. As of 1960, it operated 3,553 military installations in the United States and more outside our borders.

The impact of so vast an institution can hardly be exaggerated —on industry, science, education, and government. It leaves its imprint on youth, on labor, on local and state administrations, on Congress, on the mass media. Thousands of businessmen regularly beseech their Congressmen to secure for them more military orders. In 1962, Mayor Richard J. Daley of Chicago journeyed to Washington to arrest, if possible, the decline in Chicago's share of defense contracts. With him were other community leaders from groups adversely affected by the drop in armament procurement—the president of the Association of Commerce and Industry, the president of the central labor body, and representatives of several universities. One can only visualize—since there are no statistics on the subject—the frenzied pressure of all such forces on Congressmen, Senators, defense department officials, and the newspapers.

It is small wonder that President Eisenhower warned in his farewell address on January 17, 1961, that "this conjunction of an immense military establishment and a large armaments industry is new in the American experience. The total influence—economic, political, even spiritual—is felt in every city, every state house, every office of the Federal Government. . . . We must not fail to comprehend its grave implications. Our toil, resources and livelihood are all involved; so is the very structure of our society. In the councils of government we must guard against the acquisition of unwarranted influence, whether sought or unsought, by the military-industrial complex. The potential for the disastrous rise of misplaced power exists and will persist."

Secretary of Defense Charles E. Wilson (not to be confused with the Wilson of General Electric) said in 1957: "One of the most serious things about this defense business is that so many Americans are getting a vested interest in it: properties, business, jobs, employment, votes, opportunities for promotion and advancement, bigger salaries for scientists, and all that. It is a troublesome business." [11]

Senator William Proxmire charged in April, 1962, that the Pentagon had one lobbyist for every Senator and Congressman. This figure may be high: the Pentagon claims only one-third that number, and it denies, of course, that they are lobbyists. They are keeping the legislators "informed." On the other hand, the figure may be an understatement, for many military men who are not specifically assigned to lobbying actually do so when the occasion demands. The interplay between Congressmen, Senators, and an organization with tens of billions of dollars at its disposal is worrisome, to say the least. Legislators are given free junkets on military planes—sometimes to football games or home for a holiday—and lavished with minor favors for their constituents.

Nor is this all, for there is a wholesale intertwining of the military with both government and big business. There are, by one estimate, 1,300 military men, retired or on leave, working at key jobs in federal departments. A Congressional Reserve unit, headed by Air Force Major General Barry Goldwater and Army Brigadier General J. Strom Thurmond, numbers 175 members— just about one-third of the 535 Congressmen and Senators. According to a House subcommittee, in 1961 there were 1,400 retired officers of the rank of major or higher, 261 of them generals or admirals, employed in top executive capacities by the one hundred biggest defense corporations. General Dynamics alone had 186 such men on its payroll, including seven generals and twenty admirals. Lockheed Aircraft had 171, North American Aviation 92.[12] General Douglas MacArthur, after retirement, became chairman of Sperry-Rand; General Lucius Clay became chairman of Continental Can; Admiral Ben Moreel became president of Jones and Laughlin Steel. Former officers on the staff of corporations negotiate armaments orders with associates still in the Pentagon. Since more than 80 per cent of procurement is done without competitive bidding, through direct negotiations, the retired military men are invaluable.

For this military-industrial complex, Anti-Communism is a vital necessity. A crisis in Korea or Viet Nam is always helpful in securing from Congress additional billions in defense allocations. The "communist menace" must be kept in the forefront of American consciousness if the nation is to continue spending mountains of money for armaments. It is no accident, therefore, that there has been such a pyramiding of rightist groups in America, or that they are financed by corporate interests, many of whom benefit from Cold War tensions.

"The role of Big Business in its sponsorship of the Radical Right," says Fred Cook, "has become evident in many sections of the country. In California, the 1961-62 wave of seminars, alerts and schools established sponsorship links not just to Schick and Technicolor and Richfield Oil and Dr. Ross Dog Food, but to such massive corporations as Southern California Edison Co., Tidewater Oil, Carnation Milk, Papermate Pen—and to others less well-known. . . ." [13] Among the first leaders of the John Birch Society were three former presidents of the National Association of Manufacturers and the heads of many prominent manufacturing companies. The American Security Council, which keeps 3,200 corporations informed as to who is and who is not a "security risk," has an advisory council that includes some of the most respectable men in American business. Men like H. L. Hunt, Texan oil magnate, finance in part or in whole all kinds of propaganda and organizational efforts of the ultra-right. Not all these businessmen have a direct involvement in defense production, but all understand how pivotal is the $50 or $60 billion arms budget for the present economic health of the country. The frenzied charges by such movements as the John Birch Society, which labels men like Eisenhower and Supreme Court Chief Justice Earl Warren as communists or communist-dupes, fit closely the needs of those pressure groups which seek more military spending and less social change. A decade ago, scores of big businessmen were aligned with the China Lobby in an effort to plunge America into war with Red China, so that the irrepressible Chiang Kai-shek could be returned to his haven on the mainland. More recently, others have joined the "crusade" to save Moise Tshombe's Katanga, dominated by Western mining interests.

Allied with the rightists, big business, and the military is another social strata—what Irving L. Horowitz has called the "new civilian militarists." These writers and men of science, such as Edward Teller and Herman Kahn, lend an intellectual aura to military contentions. Many are employed directly or indirectly by the Pentagon, many more by corporations. Their role, wittingly or unwittingly, is to minimize the dangers of nuclear war, to undermine efforts at securing disarmament, and to justify defense spending. Aided by a pliant press, the words of the new civilian militarists become gospel. The nation listens intently to a Dr. Teller, who is "tough," in preference to a Dr. Leo Szilard, who has an equal if not more impressive scientific background, but who advocates planned disarmament. A Herman Kahn makes frequent headlines while a Charles Osgood, president of the American Psychological Association, who favors initiatives by the United States to de-escalate the arms race, labors in relative obscurity. Power begets more power; predominance of the military-industrial complex assures a more receptive press for the civilian militarists who serve it.

II

Perhaps the most interesting development in the United States since World War II, in terms of power alignment, has been the simultaneous decline of the Left and the conversion of some of its adherents into an Anti-Communist phalanx. The Communist party, as already indicated, has declined from 100,000 to less than ten thousand adherents. The Socialist party suffered, relatively, even worse losses, with some of its members eventually becoming the nucleus of the Americans for Democratic Action. Other leftist groups numbered a few hundred each at best. But many ex-radicals, whose impact was negligible when they were associated with the Left, have gained a new and impressive status by becoming the most fervid proponents of Anti-Communism.

After the Bolshevik Revolution of 1917, all sections of the Socialist party in the United States rose to Russia's defense. The left wing socialists, soon to become the core of the Communist party, hailed the Revolution as a major step forward in world history. But even right wing socialists, such as Louis Waldman, called it an "awakening to freedom and to self-government." [14] Radicals and liberals were inexorably drawn to the left, to some form of identification with Lenin's Russia. By a vote of two and a half to one, the Socialist party in January, 1920, applied for membership in the Communist International. Liberal muckrakers like Lincoln Steffens became enamored of the Soviets. When asked by Bernard Baruch about his 1919 trip to the Soviet Union, Steffens replied: "I have been over into the future, and it works." [15] Such writers and artists as Max Eastman, John Reed, Robert Minor, and Isadora Duncan were quick converts to the Soviet experiment. Many of them deserted the cause in a short time. But while the West was sending soldiers into Russia and A. Mitchell Palmer was organizing his raids against the Left, the major liberal and radical community was strongly unified in resisting such measures.

After World War II, however, a considerable segment of the radical and liberal forces were drawn in the opposite direction, increasingly hostile to communism and Russia. Old friends of the Soviet Union with socialist, communist, Trotskyist, or liberal backgrounds, such as Max Eastman, J. B. Mathews, Eugene Lyons, James Burnham, Sidney Hook, and Jay Lovestone, became the intellectual leavening for Anti-Communism and, in some cases, for ultra-right organizations.

Many of these men reflected the factional struggles within the Soviet Union, between Stalin and Trotsky, for the most part, but also between Stalin and Bukharin. The ideology and practices of communist Russia had altered considerably in the late 1920's and 1930's, causing schism in leftist circles everywhere in the world. The left was torn by dispute over "socialism in one country" versus world revolution, as well as by internal practices within the Soviet Union. The criticisms of the dissidents against increased terror, labor camps, purges, and decline of dissent were justified. But in recoiling from such transgressions, many American leftists went far in the opposite direction, centering their new dogma in the primacy of communism as the enemy of mankind, and joining with certain rightists, on occasion, whom they would have eschewed in the past.

The establishment, instead of finding resistance to its negative, Anti-Communist policy, was thus reinforced. Where in the first postwar period the establishment's hysteria was counteracted by liberals and radicals, in the second postwar period it was aided and abetted by many radical defectors. The ex-radical, like the civilian militarist, found a new and exciting place in the sun. The phenomenon was so widespread it prompted the witticism from

Ignazio Silone that the next war would be fought between communists and ex-communists. Max Ascoli, publisher of *The
Reporter* magazine, wrote in 1952: "There are men possessed by
a craving to detect conspiracies, hunt down suspects, and then
wring confessions from those they have suspected. Almost in-
variably, those self-appointed vigilantes are those ex-Communists
whose Anti-Communism has become an obsession and a pro-
fession. . . . They can't help suspecting everybody, planning
purges, demanding confessions. *They* have confessed." [16]

The ex-leftist, when he was still a radical, considered capitalism a permanent enemy to be uprooted by revolution. Now, in
his about-face, he sees communism as the permanent enemy.
Once he detected little or no good in capitalism; now he detects
none whatsoever in the communist world.

Early in 1963, forty-four Americans formed the Citizens Committee for a Free Cuba. Included in this group were such military
men as Admiral Arleigh A. Burke, former Chief of Naval Operations; such ex-communists as Jay Lovestone; a few labor leaders
of the Anti-Communist blend; and some ex-socialists. Executive
secretary of the Committee was Daniel James, former editor of
the *New Leader*, once a mildly socialist journal but now a literary
haven for many Anti-Communists. Each issue of James's bulletin,
Free Cuba News, is negative from first to last. Thus the June 1,
1963, number asks whether the Soviets are "reaching for Caribbean control?" Peasants, we are told, have turned against Castro,
cab drivers are "fractious," Russian troops are fighting Cubans,
Russians are "digging in to stay," an "estimated 100,000" political
prisoners "are rotting away in 57 prisons and 18 concentration
camps," Cuba is officially "promoting subversion" and is conspiring against Bolivia, Chile and Peru.[17] Nowhere can one find
either a saving grace in the Castro regime or a positive proposal
of what should be done about it. Nowhere is there a hope, muted
or otherwise, for accommodation or reconciliation. The only
solution is permanent conflict with Cuban communism.

Such ex-radicals have been invaluable to the Anti-Communist
cause, for they know their way around the communist maze.
They turn up frequently as the intellectual spirits behind Congressional committees investigating communism, the CIA, or
the AFL-CIO, and other powerful forces. J. B. Mathews, who
was forced out of the religious-pacifist Fellowship of Reconcilia-

tion many years ago for having too close an affinity with the communists, turns up as research director for the House Committee on Un-American Activities to charge that "the largest single group supporting the communist apparatus in the United States today is composed of Protestant clergymen." [18] Jay Lovestone, former general secretary of the Communist party, has become top advisor to AFL-CIO President George Meany on international affairs. One of Lovestone's followers, Irving Brown, who had never been abroad before, was sent to Europe after the war as an AFL representative; he is credited with having slipped hundreds of thousands of dollars to Anti-Communist union leaders in Europe. In a laudatory article about Brown in the *Readers Digest* of September, 1952, Donald Robinson describes how "at the risk of his life, he has organized a whole army of vigilantes to battle the Red fifth columns in Western Europe and has helped establish underground groups behind the iron curtain." In reacting to Stalin's crimes, these ex-radicals have not only forsaken past allegiances, but have traveled the full circle to become leading Anti-Communist philosophers and strategists.

The views of this ex-radical stratum show a mechanistic and schematic strain that is reminiscent of that held by the communist movement during the early 1930's, when socialists were labelled the twins of fascism—"social fascists." Thus, neutralists are rigidly considered as allies of communism. A report by the executive council of the AFL to its 71st convention in September, 1952 (almost certainly written by Lovestone), speaks of neutralists as "aides de camp" of communism. Neutralism, it says, "is embraced by those honestly mistaken, or advocated and pushed by the dishonest and concealed enemies of world democratic unity against Soviety aggression." As such, neutralism is "a conscious or unwitting ally of Soviet imperialism . . . [and] plays right into the hands of the Russian warlords." [19]

The ex-radical like Lovestone or Irving Brown sees the communists both as the dominant enemy and as a permanent one. "We should beware," Brown told an AFL convention, "of any movement which doesn't denounce the system of totalitarianism and slave labor in the U.S.S.R. and Eastern Europe as the main and primary danger to peace in the world." [20] Each diplomatic act is a *battle,* at the end of which one either records a new victory or concedes a new defeat. There is little room for compromise or accommodation. In the January, 1963, issue of the AFL-CIO *Free Trade Union News,* Lovestone's paper, there is an interesting critique of U Thant which illustrates the point. The Secretary General of the United Nations had noted the month before that there were some changes for the better in Khrushchev's Russia, and that these changes should be explored to help improve East-West relations. Thant observed mildly that the Cold War began from 1946 to 1950 over such issues as the "presence of Soviet troops in Iran" and the Korean War. He was willing to leave to "future historians" the task of "allocating responsibility" for this period. But Lovestone, consonant with his position that the Soviets are a "permanent" enemy, would not yield a point. "In our opinion," says the rebuttal to Thant, "the world does not have to wait for 'future historians' to learn who is responsible and who is to blame for the emergence of the cold war." Thant is advised to look at the United Nations records concerning "for instance . . . the Soviet-instigated Civil War in Greece, the Communist coup of February 1948 in Czechoslovakia, the Berlin blockade, etc."

The Secretary General of the United Nations, charged with the task of protecting the peace, searches for hopeful signs. "In my view," he writes, "the system created and maintained by Stalin was manifestly ruthless and obsolescent even before his departure. . . . [Khrushchev,] who is now in control of the reins of government, belongs to a different category of leaders, with a coherent philosophy of the world based on the thesis, not of the inevitability of war, but of the imperative of competitive coexistence."

But Lovestone will not accept such evaluations. "The record does not support U Thant's affirmation about Khrushchev. In the first place, Khrushchev has never included in his condemnation of Stalin his predecessor's foreign policy. The present Kremlin ruler has branded neither Stalin's alliance with Hitler . . . nor his annexation of the Baltic States nor his enslavement of the satellite nations." The article repeats charges against the communists for "suppression of the East German uprising of 1953, the aggression against the Hungarian people in October 1956, the Berlin ultimatum, the erection of the Wall of Shame, and, finally, the establishment of rocket bases in Cuba." [21] One can agree with all these criticisms, yet note that they are blindly one-sided. (For instance, to counterbalance the communist suppression of 1953 there were the French suppressions in Indo-china, the British in Malaya and Kenya, the American intervention, through the CIA, in Guatemala. At the time of the Hungarian revolution of 1956 there was the invasion by Britain and France of the Suez.)

U Thant, to his credit, seeks to reduce tensions by relegating the past to tired history and looking for the silver lining in the present. Anti-Communism, however, cannot tolerate such beneficence, for it is a doctrine of permanent conflict and cold war—and in war the enemy is all-black, "our" side is all-white.

Unlike the ordinary ultra-rightists, Lovestone endorses the legitimate aims of the underprivileged peoples, but his arrows are aimed primarily in one direction. Thus in November, 1955, his paper offered a five-point program for: "gradual disarmament" as proposed by the United States; unification of Germany through "free elections under the United Nations"; UN-conducted elections in "all areas of dispute and division, in Asia as well as Europe, in the Baltic and Balkan captive lands, with a view of restoring their national freedom and human rights"; complete dismantlement of "the world-wide subversive Communist machinery"; and "positive steps to enable the Russian people to be free."

No one can quarrel with "gradual disarmament" or "free elections." But they are cleverly put so as to adversely affect the Soviets without any *quid pro quo* by the United States. The disarmament is to be in line with American proposals—which the Russians, of course, consider harmful. Honest elections are to be in Russian-controlled areas, such as Poland or Latvia, but not in the "free world" area where dictatorships exist, such as Iran, Thailand, Pakistan, Nicaragua, or Guatemala. The communists are asked to dismantle their world-wide "subversive" organization, but there is no similar request for the dissolution of the Central Intelligence Agency.

Such proposals are part of a one-sided gambit, known to be unacceptable beforehand and put forward only to expose the other side. They are part of a concept of "permanent war" between two systems, rather than serious planks for accommodation.

The influence of ex-radicals who have turned Anti-Communist is not to be taken lightly. These are not men of wealth, nor do they usually hold high positions either in corporations or in labor unions. But behind the scenes they are editors of rightist journals, writers, professors, educational directors, union functionaries, investigators for Congressional committees, assistants to prominent Senators. Their effect on the history of our times is not negligible.

Self-interest drove the military-industrial complex, after the war, to upgrade the menace of communism and communist Russia. The points of conflict between East and West were enlarged to give the impression of an immediate war danger. To its surprise, this power complex found an ally among certain ex-radicals and, as noted in Chapter 2, among certain liberals who came to Anti-Communism from other motivations. Together with the ultra-Right, which had been relatively dormant, this conjunction of forces pushed the center of gravity in American political life to the right, to a barren defense of the status quo. The men who held government positions and made policy reflected this remorseless pull. Even when they sought to buck the Anti-Communist tide, on one issue or another, they could find few allies in the liberal or radical Left to help create a favorable public mood.

The Anti-Communist crusade is linked indissolubly with this major shift in American power relationships. It is not the product of any single man's mistakes or venality, but of the tipping of the power scales inexorably to the right. Positive leadership might have checked this development and averted the Cold War. But without such leadership the pressures for "toughness," for a military rather than a social stance, became too strong for government officials to resist.

V

Pax Americana in Europe

IF THE Cold War is judged by its short-run results, Americans can console themselves that "it could have been worse." In addition to China—large and important though it may be—only North Viet Nam and Cuba have broken out of "containment" since the Truman Doctrine was promulgated in 1947. Western Europe was saved by the Marshall Plan, and most of Asia and Africa have gone neutralist rather than communist.

But if the Cold War is viewed by its long term implications, the results are far less promising. We are, as it were, in the middle of a chess game. Each side has six or eight pieces remaining on the board. Superficially, each still appears to have an even chance of victory. But the chances are already heavily weighted against the prospective loser. His position is so poor, his men so badly placed, that—though many moves will still be made—the chances of his reversing the tide are rapidly declining.

The United States today is in such a position. It is strong and powerful, but its strategy is out of tune with reality. In a world that is in revolution, it is the main prop for the status quo. In an era when military power no longer achieves major political purposes, it is wedded to a militarist policy. Even more, it is the victim of a basic shift in its own power structure—the decline of liberalism and radicalism, and the concomitant escalation of military-industrial influence—that leads it toward continuation of a futile course. If America's catastrophe is not yet fully apparent, it is merely because the world revolution, which we find ourselves incapable of joining, is only in its incipiency.

There are still many more moves in the chess game. India, Indonesia, Egypt, Burma, Ghana, Guinea, Tanganyika, and Algeria have achieved national liberation, but they are only *beginning* the social phase of their revolutions. So far their efforts have been slow, halting, often ineffective, but the pace is bound to accelerate, just as the American Revolution accelerated after the middle of the nineteenth century. There are still thirty or forty countries, many in Latin America, which are on the threshold of major upheaval. To round out the panorama, the advanced industrial powers themselves are affected by a growing malaise internally, as their rate of economic growth slackens, unemployment slowly inches forward, and necessity demands more state planning, more welfare reforms. The drift in our world, despite zigs and zags in its course, is unmistakeably to a continued transformation of present social structures. But the mainsprings of American power impel the United States to align itself with the conservatives, and frequently the rightists, who stand opposed to real change.

Each move in our chess game strategy has reflected our desire for conservatism, for a world as close to the old status quo as possible. Under the flag of Anti-Communism, we have placed ourselves as a barrier to social change. We have shown a predilection for a Christian Democratic Europe over a Social Democratic one, for a mild welfare state over a fulsome one. Where the status quo could not be held, we have cast our lot with the least radical alternative. Some of our chessmen, it is true, are more strongly emplaced than others. We seem to have fared better, for instance, in Europe than in Asia. But that is only because our overall strategy has not yet been put to the full test in Europe, not because it is inherently valid. History may yet prove—in the not too distant future—that a Christian Democratic and Tory Europe is a tenuous ally, not only incapable of warding off reformist pressures, but unwilling to be further guided by our leadership. History may still prove that a Social Democratic Europe would have been much more favorable to America's long-term interests.

I

Americans in the late 1940's and early 1950's talked of a "Line"—a Line beyond which we would not permit Russia to "expand." John Fischer, editor of *Harper's* magazine, recorded in 1951 that "the Line of Containment has held, under great pressure, in Korea, Greece, Indochina, Turkey, Berlin and Yugoslavia. We have suffered one major defeat—China—but that may yet be recovered . . ." [1] Debate in certain circles hinged on where the Line should be drawn. The Russians were to be told that if they invaded or subverted any country on "our" side of the Line, it would mean war. Bases were built around the Soviet periphery, and alliances forged with dictatorial regimes in Pakistan, Turkey, Thailand, Iraq, and others to hold the Line.

The Line, as might be expected, was more than a geographical phenomenon; it had far-reaching political ramifications. The two-dimensional world prior to World War I had been held together by Pax Britannica. Britain played one nation against another and thereby sustained capitalist and feudal social systems. In this manner she dominated the planet. Now, in a three- or four-dimensional world, President Truman hoped to imitate the British method by forming an alliance of the whole non-communist world, under the American shield, strong enough to prevent expansion by anyone else. It was to be, in a sense, a Pax Americana, and it was to usher in the American Century. Such a peace, however, could be maintained only so long as the countries behind the Line were dependable and permanent allies. It made no sense, for instance, to establish military bases in Iraq if Iraq were to be seized by nationalists hostile to the American cause. It made no sense to re-arm France or Italy if local communists were on the verge of winning national elections. The search for "safe" allies meant that American policymakers, fashioning the world in our own image, must rely on elements in Europe and Asia who were least likely to collaborate or compromise with the communists.

A Christian Democrat was safer than a socialist, and a military dictator safer than a non-communist nationalist bent on revamping the old power structure. A socialist or a true nationalist might, under some circumstances, join united fronts with the communists; but conservatives and dictators were much less prone to such tactics. The hardening of attitudes, symbolized by the concept of a Line, dictated a social stance as well as a military one.

This was already obvious even before the Cold War was formalized by the Truman Doctrine. It is significant that while Britain, and later the United States, were engaged in a battle to prevent a radical alliance from seizing Greece, no effort was made to undermine the semi-fascist dictatorship in Portugal, or the outright fascist regime in Spain. Former Secretary of State

James F. Byrnes, whose publishers called him "the chief architect of our postwar foreign policy," does not even mention these nations in his book *Speaking Frankly*. Neither does Robert E. Sherwood in *Roosevelt and Hopkins*. Though the war had been fought to "defeat fascism" and to "extend democracy," no plans were at hand to deal with two obvious rightist cancers. Tens of thousands of Spanish Republicans were in exile, ready and eager to return to a democratic homeland, hopeful that the Allies would help them bring it about. But the Allies refused to intervene against Franco Spain or to force change through something as mild as a commercial blockade.

The end of the war saw a surge of leftist sentiment all over Europe. The British Labor Party defeated the Tories in England. New governments in France, Italy, Holland, and Belgium were coalitions of Catholics, socialists, and communists. Germany was under four-power rule, but most observers are agreed that had elections been held early after the war the Social Democratic Party would have won handily. Four years later, after the Allies had taken many steps which weakened the socialists, such as the reintroduction of private enterprise in the Ruhr, they lost the elections in West Germany by only 400,000 votes and received but eight seats less than Konrad Adenauer's Christian Democratic Union. Adenauer became Chancellor of his country by the margin of a single Bundestag vote. If the Social Democrats could have done so well under these circumstances in the West, they were certain of victory in a unified election, for they were proportionately stronger in East Germany.

Throughout Europe, American aid and American pressure could have tipped the scales in whichever direction Washington pleased. Europe was prostrate, dependent on UNRRA and, later, Marshall Plan aid to survive. Governments could be made and broken by American desires. The rule of occupation armies, particularly in Germany, and later the effects of aid and trade, gave the United States a decisive voice in the character of Europe.

But American preference for a conservative Europe was made apparent early in the game by a shift in policy toward Germany. At a meeting of the Cabinet in the summer of 1944, Secretary of the Treasury Henry Morgenthau, Jr., had proposed that Germany be reduced to an agrarian nation. According to James Forrestal, it was agreed "that the Germans should have simply a subsistence

level of food—as he [Morgenthau] put it, soup kitchens would
be ample to sustain life—that otherwise they should be stripped
clean and should not have a level of subsistence above the lowest
level of the people they had conquered." [2] This plan was not
only harsh, but impractical, since the iron and steel of the Rhur
were vitally needed to rebuild the rest of Europe. But if German
heavy industry were to be reactivated, who would operate it?
The Allies had pledged to "eliminate or control all German industry that could be used for German military production . . ."

In the opinion of Great Britain, this meant that the Ruhr factories should be nationalized. Labor's Foreign Minister, Ernest
Bevin, argued in October, 1946, that Germany's heavy industries
"were previously in the hands of magnates who were closely
allied to the German military machine, who financed Hitler, and
who in two wars were part and parcel of Germany's aggressive
policy. We have no desire to see those gentlemen or their like
return to a position which they have abused with such tragic
results." [3] The London *Economist* counseled that conditions in
the Ruhr "make far-reaching socialist experiments a necessity . . .
Let the British administration openly and deliberately evolve a
plan for public ownership of the essential industries and services
in North-West Germany. No amount of backing of Dr. Schu-
macher, the leading socialist in the western zone, in his fight
against fusion with the communists, will be effective so long as
the communists can compare the 'social backwardness' of the
British zone [in which the Ruhr was situated] with socialization
and land reform in the eastern zone." [4] In Germany, not only the
Social Democrats and communists favored nationalization, but
many Christian Democrats, as well as the Parliament of North
Rhine Westphalia. Under American pressure, however, the core
of West Germany's economy went back to private enterprise and
to the very men who used it in support of the Nazis. A conservative power elite in America, expanding its influence, was bent on
preserving similar power elites elsewhere.

Secretary of the Navy James Forrestal recorded in his diary
May 7, 1947: "We do not propose to endorse socialization in
Germany under any circumstances and this should be com-
municated at the highest level . . . It is clear that the British
policy is determined by their desire to impose a socialized
economy and government in their zone. I said [to Assistant Secre-

tary of State Major General John H. Hilldring] that this was distinctly contrary to American policy and belief and that we would not win support for the British in Congress or of the American public; that at some point it would have to be made clear to the British at the highest levels that they were operating their economy on three and a quarter billion capital obtained from this country, and that they would probably need additional working capital, and that we did not propose to have our money used to implement a German system contrary to our own ideas . . ." [5]

Forrestal's position, it should be emphasized, reflected that of the President. Truman had made a similar reference to "free enterprise" only two months before. "There is one thing that Americans value more than power," he noted. "It is freedom. Freedom of worship, freedom of speech and freedom of enterprise." International trade, based on "private buyers and sellers, under conditions of active competition," leads, he said, to freedom, while government control drives a nation towards dictatorship.[6] The New York *Herald Tribune* headlined Truman's speech: PRESIDENT SAYS AMERICANS LOVE FREE ENTERPRISE MORE THAN PEACE. Thus, while much of Europe sought to curb the industrial oligarchs who had opened the door to Hitler, the United States, seeking to rebuild the world in its own image and for its own trade and investment benefits, forced the British to retreat from their plans for nationalization. In 1948, when the German government of the Ruhr voted a socialization law by parliamentary majority, the British vetoed it.

The West had an excellent opportunity to establish a different kind of Germany. In Munich and elsewhere there had been small uprisings against the Nazis. In the Ruhr and in Bavaria, workers had set up works committees, taken over factories, and had immediately offered their co-operation to the Allied armies. But the victors disbanded such committees and prohibited unions and labor parties from functioning during vital months when they might have set the tone for the future.

The bias toward the German industrial barons was obvious from the outset. President Roosevelt had once sent a memorandum to his Secretary of State, Cordell Hull, denoting his attitude toward German Big Business: "The history of the use of the I. G. Farben trust by the Nazis reads like a detective story.

Defeat of the Nazi armies will have to be followed by eradication of these weapons of economic warfare." [7] Federal orders existed prohibiting renewed production by the major German industrial firms. But the American military government, under General Lucius Clay and General William H. Draper, whose business training was with Forrestal's investment firm of Dillon, Read & Company, refused to dismantle such factories. American companies, at the last count in 1943, had owned a controlling share of 316 German firms, worth more than a billion dollars. Draper's own firm, Dillon, Read & Company, held an investment of $105 million. "It would be easier," writes Howard K. Smith, "to imagine Stalin embracing the Pope and Catholicism than General Draper forsaking his German business colleagues of a lifetime's collaboration in favor of the German workers." [8] In due course, most of the businessmen who had collaborated with Hitler regained their largesse. Their political influence was also restored. According to John Gunther in 1961, "The great Rhineland-Ruhr industrialists . . . support the CDU [Christian Democratic Union] heavily, and have a massive lobby in the Bundestag; roughly seventy deputies are supposed to be direct representatives of big industry." [9] The first postwar Chancellor, Adenauer, who retired in 1963, was "on terms of intimate personal friendship with the Ruhr magnates and their bankers." Yet he was, as James P. Warburg points out, "the hand-picked candidate of the American Government" to lead Germany in the postwar period.[10]

The Germany that evolved as a result of American policies was democratic (though not a few former Nazis played important roles in its development), but it was—and is—conservative, revanchist, and militarist. To speak of the Adenauer and Ludwig Erhard regimes as "allies" of the United States is premature, for Germany's efforts so far have been directed toward forging a strong economy and a military machine, independent of Western controls. Once these goals have been achieved, there is no telling in which direction the industrial oligarchs will push it. Admiral Donitz, who before his suicide was appointed by Hitler to lead the nation, once said: "We must go along with the Western powers [in the] hope of retrieving our land from the Russians." [11] This was more than one man's view; it was a repetition of German strategy after World War I. America may yet find that a conservative Germany, far from being a dependable ally, will become one of its worst enemies; and that a Social Democratic Germany might have been a much more reliable friend in buttressing world democracy.

As in Germany, American aid throughout Europe became a force pushing the political center of gravity to the right. "There is as yet," wrote Stuart Gelder, New York correspondent of the London *News Chronicle,* "no clearly drawn scheme for help to France, but I am informed on high authority that the State Department policy is that 'it is in the interests of America to see the establishment of an independent democratic moderate Government in France.' It was expected that very substantial aid would have to be given during the next two years." [12] That very month, May, 1947, the Ramadier government suddenly dismissed the communists, who had been part of a coalition since the end of the war, from the cabinet.

Joseph and Stewart Alsop, writing in the *Saturday Evening Post* nine months later, related that Italian Prime Minister Alcide de Gasperi pleaded with the American Ambassador in Rome that "without your help we have only a few weeks to last, only a few weeks. The Government will be finished on the day we have to cut the bread ration. Then will come an impotent government of national unity and after that the Communists in full control." The United States responded to this appeal, but American officials warned they "*would find it hard to do so as long as the Italian Government included Togliatti and his Communists.*" [13] There was no outright deal, said the Alsops. "But there was at least a shadow of a hint of an outline of a tacit understanding." De Gasperi went home, another government crisis ensued, and a new cabinet emerged with the communists, second largest party in Italy, expelled. In Germany, the Communist party was eventually illegalized. We need not shed any tears for the Stalinist movement of the 1950's. Yet it is undeniable that it had forced the European regimes to make important reforms. Once it was removed from a share of power, the governments of Europe could return to traditional rule by the conservative upper classes.

II

Despite the good intentions of many American leaders, Anti-Communism pulled American policy toward a militarist path, and militarism toward "safe" conservative allies. Large scale American aid was necessary, but it could have been used as a lever to uproot old oligarchies, rather than entrench them. The results would have been far-reaching, not only in Europe itself but in far-off Asia where European power elites were fighting nationalist revolutions in the Dutch East Indies, Indochina, Malaya, and elsewhere. Future setbacks might have been avoided, in Vietnam for instance, if the two hundred leading families of France had been reduced in power and a leadership fashioned more sympathetic to social change and the Asian revolution. The threat of nuclear war might have been mitigated if the revanchist big businessmen of the Ruhr had been subdued, thereby decreasing world militarist pressures. American aid "stabilized" Europe, but it added fuel to the fires of other continents, and it gave wing to a useless and self-defeating arms race.

In early 1947, Europe's sickness became painfully apparent. The great snowstorm of that winter hit Britain like a sledge hammer. By February, more than half its factories were out of production. The coal pits were shut, and electricity was cut off to industrial consumers for several days and to the population at large for three hours daily. The drive to increase exports and close the "dollar gap" had collapsed. In the words of the financial editor of Reuter's, "the biggest crash since the fall of Constantinople—the collapse of the heart of an Empire—impends." The cause, he said, was not a few snowstorms but an "awful debility in which a couple of snowstorms could have such effects." [14] Millions were out of work, demoralized, and disillusioned.

Before the war Britain had imported more than half its meat, three-quarters of its wheat, 85 per cent of its butter, three-quarters of its sugar, and most of the items for its industry— cotton, rubber, iron ore, wool, oil, and timber. She had paid for these with revenue from three sources: exports, shipping, and earnings from foreign investment. By the end of the war, however, Britain had sold $3 billion of her overseas holdings and had mortgaged most of the rest, about $9 billion, against her debts. War damage and shipping losses had depleted her capital assets by $9 billion. If British citizens were to enjoy 1939 living standards, the country's exports would have to rise by 75 per cent; but in fact they had fallen by two-thirds. Each day Britain was losing precious dollars to the United States, and this dollar gap threatened her with bankruptcy.

Conditions elsewhere were even worse. France was producing only half as much iron and steel as before the war. Germany lay in rubble; its major cities—Cologne, Essen, Berlin, Frankfurt, Hamburg, Munich, Mannheim—immobilized. Food was scarce, money almost worthless. There were no apartments to be had, and few jobs.

Unless something were done and done quickly, disaster was imminent. The very communists from whom America was protecting the world would absorb a disoriented Europe—and with it Asia and Africa as well. It would not be a matter of Soviet "expansionism," but an unavoidable coefficient of social decay. To meet this challenge the United States formulated the Marshall Plan for massive economic aid to Europe. Originally it was to include the Soviet Union and East Europe, but the Russians refused to accept some of its provisions and thereafter denounced it as a "program for interference in the internal affairs of other states." Parenthetically, it should be recorded that this was one of Stalin's crudest mistakes, for most observers are agreed that if Russia had included herself in the Plan, the measure could not have passed Congress; certainly it would have been seriously delayed.

Secretary of State George Marshall, in outlining his plan at Harvard University on June 5, 1947, dwelt on Europe's inability to supply goods to farmers or receive sufficient food in return. The Plan was "not directed against any country or doctrine but against hunger, poverty, desperation and chaos. Its purpose should be the revival of a working economy in the world so as to permit the emergence of political and social conditions in which free institutions can exist." From 1948 to 1952, the United States spent $12 billion for this purpose, more than half of it going to Britain, France, and Germany. There is little doubt that the

Marshall Plan saved Europe. By 1950, the western nations had exceeded prewar production by 25 per cent and the dollar gap had been steadily reduced.

The Plan, however, was not an undiluted success. One of its purposes was to raise living standards so as to render the workers, particularly those of France and Italy, immune to communist attraction. American labor attachés tried to convince French and Italian businessmen to accept this thesis, but in vain. Real wages in France, for instance, remained lower than in the prewar period. Until February, 1950, the government forbade any strikes, despite a steady and severe inflation. "It was pointless to explain to the workers," writes Theodore White, "that without the Marshall Plan they would have been entirely unemployed, that they might have starved or died, that the Plan had saved them. The workers could see only that what had been saved was the status quo, that the recovery had preserved their discomfort and given its fruits to the privileged. In the slums the communists held on to their votes even through the happiest days of the Plan." [15]

Americans prodded European businessmen to share increases in productivity with their employees, but the conservative classes were able to squirm out of such commitments. In 1950, an ECA labor team, headed by teamster Harold Gibbons, pointed to a French factory which had increased productivity by 500 per cent as a result of Marshall Plan equipment, but still paid the same wages as companies with antiquated equipment in the same neighborhood. Lee Dayton, chief of the ECA mission in Italy, charged in October, 1950, that business and industrial leaders paid "lip service to the need for raising the standard of living and to the basic principles of low cost and high production. But of all the firms in Italy, you can count those who practice these precepts on the fingers of your two hands." [16]

What had been saved was an old order, with ancient patterns of inequity. Postwar Europe was not a carbon copy of prewar Europe, for there were inevitable changes. There were new welfare measures in France and Italy. There was a considerable amount of planning and state pressure. Ludwig Erhard, in charge of the Germany economy, imposed severe strictures on capital formation. The state gave incentives to those who would invest in essential industries, and checked to some extent those who put their money in non-essential ones. Under this form of indirect planning, progress was sensational. But most important is that the prewar power elites remained in control. What this meant for Asia and Africa is already known; what it will eventually mean for Europe itself (and the United States) is not yet recorded by a lackadaisical history. For, in the course of saving Europe, we also strengthened the moribund hand of militarism and buttressed a policy of intervention against revolution in Asia and Africa.

The Marshall Plan, though conceived in humanistic terms, was inevitably molded to the necessities of the Cold War. The same conservative classes in France who could not see their way to share productivity increases with their workers at home, also were unable to grant legitimate independence to the people of Indochina and Algeria. Holland continued to fight the people of Indonesia; Belgium, the people of the Congo; and Britain, the people of Malaya and Kenya.

The British, it is true, did grant independence to India, Ceylon, and Burma. The Labor Party, then in government, must be given credit for this belated execution of a promise made as far back as World War I. But Britain could not have held on to these areas even if it wanted to. It was much too impoverished by war to spend billions subduing a hostile India. Almost immediately after Japan surrendered in 1945, there was a wave of strikes and large demonstrations in India. A few months later, early in 1946, five thousand naval workers walked off their jobs and hauled down the British flag. Revolts hit the Indian Army and Air Force. Large meetings organized by Mahatma Gandhi and his non-violent resistance movement were held everywhere. *Time* magazine bleakly predicted "a historic blow-up." Britain yielded not only because it had a new Labor government more friendly to India, but because it could not afford to control the situation. The British policy in India, however, was counterbalanced by standard imperialism in Malaya, East Africa, the Rhodesias, Nyasaland, Nigeria, and elsewhere. It took many revolutionary storms to complete the liquidation of that ancient British policy.

With Europe entangled in crisis, the Marshall Pan might have been used to force the colonialist powers to withdraw from their colonies. But it was not. Instead it was used as a means to involve them in the sterile course of Anti-Communism.

As the United States saw it, Western Europe could be an effective counterfoil to Russia only if it were united. The Marshall Plan, with its machinery for joint planning, was a start toward economic integration. The inevitable handmaiden on the road to political unity was a military alliance. In March, 1948, Britain, France, and the Low Countries, prodded by the State Department, signed a pact of collective defense. Each signatory agreed to come to the aid of the other in case of attack. In the words of John W. Spanier, professor of political science at the University of Florida, this was "a military counterpart of OEEC [Organization of European Economic Cooperation]. Just as OEEC represented an organization dedicated to economic cooperation, the Brussels Pact represented one dedicated to military cooperation. And just as the vitality of OEEC had depended upon American capital for its success, the Brussels Pact members expected their alliance to attract American military support." [17]

President Truman quickly gave the Pact his blessings, and a year later, in April, 1949, twelve nations, including the United States and Canada, signed the North Atlantic Treaty. For the first time in American history the United States had entered a military alliance in peacetime. And just as the U. S. had underwritten Marshall Plan aid and OEEC, so it now poured billions of dollars in military equipment into the North Atlantic Treaty Organization (NATO). From 1946 to 1962, Europe was to receive the staggering sum of $16 billion in military gifts, and the world as a whole twice that much. He who pays the piper calls the tune; Western Europe became a military fortress tied to the purposes of America's Anti-Communism, and the tensions of the world multiplied by geometric progression.

It is impossible to believe that the Marshall Plan and NATO were not viewed by American policy makers as two fingers of the same hand. One may even concede that they were arrived at independently and that Secretary Marshall was motivated purely by idealism. But once the Truman Doctrine had become policy and the conflict with communism viewed as permanent, until one or the other side collapsed, it was only natural that all facets of policy be co-ordinated. Thomas K. Finletter, an official in the Truman regime, records this connection: "The first postwar step toward a union of the North Atlantic . . . was economic . . . NATO came soon afterwards; NATO might never have been born if the Marshall Plan had not come first." Finletter notes "that foreign policy and military policy cannot be thought of separately." [18]

The United States plan for containment needed military bases around Russia; the NATO nations supplied many of them. It needed ground forces in Europe itself, to prevent Russia from breaking through to the English Channel, for once communist troops were in Bonn, Paris, Amsterdam, and Rome, the nuclear superiority of the United States would be rendered useless. The United States could hardly bomb the cities of its allies, and Russia would acquire economic largesse of such proportions that it could hold out for a very long time, perhaps even win. The role of NATO, therefore, was to contain the Russians militarily at the Elbe or the Rhine, while United States nuclear power checkmated the Soviet Union itself.

But an Atlantic alliance was of little value unless its members were stable enough to ward off revolt from within. The Marshall Plan served this purpose. By strengthening the old classes and the old order, by re-investing the men who made Hitler and the conservatives who could be depended on to resist leftist blandishments, it made the alliance secure. Measured in a vacuum, the Plan was a humanitarian gesture. Measured in the context of the Truman Doctrine and NATO, it was support for a worldwide Anti-Communism, leading toward a bitter clash in Asia, Africa, and Latin America, and to the mushrooming of militarism.

The limited success American policy gained in Europe was won at the expense of a more viable policy in the underdeveloped areas. The United States could not prop up the past in Europe and at the same time hope to join the revolution of rising expectations elsewhere. It could not do this because—if for no other reason—the old order in Europe was the beneficiary of an old order in Asia and Africa.

Sumner Welles had foreseen with fearful pessimism this frittering away of opportunity. A few months after the war ended, he wrote: "We stand at the threshold of a new era . . . Man now has within his hands the means of destroying all life upon the planet. He also holds the means whereby humanity can be assured that the new day which is dawning will be a day of peace, of security, of human progress and of liberty." The prospect, however, "is obscured . . . Greed and the lust for power are still omnipresent. The insane delusion that democracy and Communism cannot simultaneously exist in the world is rampant. Stupidity, reaction and timidity dominate the councils of the nations." [19]

VI

Nationalism and Communism in Asia

WHEN Dr. Frank P. Graham, former President of the University of North Carolina, arrived in Indonesia in 1947 to mediate the dispute between the Netherlands and the nationalists, college students everywhere pleaded with him to lecture on the American Revolution of 1775. In the streets of Saigon, Indochina, at about the same time, young men were plastering the walls with slogans from the American Declaration of Independence. There was a spontaneous feeling among Asian intellectuals that the revolutions they were about to make were related to the one made by Americans 170 years before. Thousands of leaders who hated British, Dutch, and French imperialism believed that "the United States is different." A decade later this goodwill was gone. Disillusionment with America was as severe as it once was with Britain or France. American influence receded; communist influence advanced.

Speaking before the United States Senate a few years ago, Premier Achmed Sukarno of Indonesia hinted at an explanation for this reversal. "Nationalism," he said, "may be an out-of-date doctrine for many in this world, but for us it is the mainspring of our efforts. Understand that, and you have the key to much of postwar history. Fail to understand it, and no amount of thinking, no torrent of words, and no Niagara of dollars will produce anything but bitterness and disillusion." [1]

The vast majority of people outside Western Europe and America lived at war's end in geographic units that were sometimes called "nations," but were nothing of the sort. They were neither free, independent, united, nor economically viable. For centuries the people of these areas had tolerated their lot in hopeless stupor; now they were in a state of excited desperation, ready to give their lives for nationalist goals. A small minority of them spoke of Marxism and proletarian revolution, but the overwhelming number were motivated by simple nationalism, the same nationalism that had sparked the *bourgeois* revolutions

94

in the sixteenth, seventeenth, and eighteenth centuries. Their hopes envisioned independence, land reform, industrialization, and twentieth-century living standards; and if they were sometimes vague about the last two objectives, they were crystal-clear on the first two. Anyone who would raise the banner of independence and land reform would win their allegiance.

Herein lies the strength of communism—it attached itself to the objectives of simple nationalism; it formed united fronts with the non-communist nationalists. And therein lies the weakness of the United States—it was either indifferent to nationalism, bewildered by it, or hostile to it when there was a danger that the communists might become its leaders. In Asia, as in Europe, America edged close to the power elite; and when the colonialist power elite had fallen, it allied itself with native power elites.

For both the Chinese and Russian communists, nationalism in Asia, Africa, and Latin America is considered a close relative to their own "socialism." "The national democratic revolutionary movement in these areas," writes the central committee of the Chinese Communist party, "and the international socialist revolutionary movement are the two great historical currents of our time. The national democratic revolutionary struggle of the people in these areas is an important component of the contemporary proletarian world revolution." [2] The Russians express it somewhat differently, but note the same inherent kinship: "The international revolutionary working class movement represented today by the world system of socialism and the Communist Parties of the capitalist countries, and the national liberation movement of the peoples of Asia, Africa, and Latin America—these are the great forces of our epoch. The correct coordination among them constitutes one of the main requisites for victory over imperialism." [3]

Nowhere in the Western world does one hear the same emphasis on nationalism as the motor force of present international development. The free world does not look on nationalism as the defense of its own historic goals, but a thing apart, disengaged from its own objectives. In the well-known discussion of "national purpose" conducted by *Life* magazine in May, 1960, Adlai Stevenson noted that "at a time of universal social upheaval and challenge, our vision of our own society seems to be of limited social significance. An air of disengagement and disinterest hangs over the most powerful and affluent society the world has even known. Neither the turbulence of the world abroad nor the fatness and flatness of the world at home is moving us to more vital effort. We seem becalmed in a season of storm, drifting through a century of mighty dreams and great achievements." [4] The communists think of nationalism in "passionate" terms, vital to their own interests; we look on it as a peripheral phenomenon with which we must somehow reckon, but which is not the touchstone of our existence. We manifest a spirit of "disengagement," and if we give aid to nationalistic countries we consider that we are helping "them," not ourselves— except in the derivative sense that we are keeping communism from their doors. We do not consider nationalist revolution to be "our" revolution, despite the fact that in the eighteenth century we were one of its prime movers. The communists embrace nationalism with fervor and seek to lead it; we, on the other hand, have no central strategy relative to it, except the negative one that we must prevent it from falling into communist hands, and so we deal with it on a stand-offish basis.

This difference in approach is clear in developing nations. In some of the countries, communism has become the core of revolutionary nationalism—in China and North Viet Nam, for instance. In other areas, even where communism has been inept and made serious errors—as in Algeria, Indonesia, India, Burma, and Cuba—it has been able to cement a new alliance with nationalism. In such countries it has often been too sectarian to join the nationalists at once (Cuba is an excellent example), or it has broken with nationalist allies too quickly and tried to make a second revolution on its own (as in Burma or Indonesia). But in almost all cases it has been intelligent enough to catch its breath and try again to unite with this dynamic force. Though they have made innumerable mistakes in tactics, the communists, in their overall strategy, refuse to be divorced from nationalism for any long period.

The United States, on the other hand, has never drawn close to radical nationalism. So far as we know, there is not a single instance of the United States actively supporting nationalists *before* they came to power. Our Central Intelligence Agency has fed hundreds of millions of dollars to various political movements, but almost always to rightists. In a few instances, when the old order was crumbling—as in Trujillo's Dominican Republic—the CIA switched allegiance to moderate nationalists. Usually, however, it clung to the coattails of reaction—as in Cuba or South Viet Nam—to the very end. Once certain revolutions succeeded, the United States policymakers *did* give succor in the form of grants and technical know-how. But it was done out of negative motivations—to contain communism—and in the hopes finally of wooing the revolutionaries into America's military alliances, rather than from the positive desire to enhance revolutionary nationalism.

A cursory examination of American foreign aid illustrates this point. On a per capita basis, far more was made available to nations who joined our military pacts and granted us military bases than to those who were truly nationalist but neutral. During the three years, 1954-1956, by way of example, the U. S. granted $199.5 million in economic aid to India, or an average of 17¢ for each of its 387 million people. But Pakistan, with less than a quarter of India's population, received $221.7 million, or an average of $2.69 per capita. South Korea was given $595.2 million, and Formosa $216.4 million, though both together have only one-twelfth India's numbers. These figures do not include military aid, which India at that time refused to accept. Pakistan, Formosa, and South Korea were military allies of the United States; India, though it was by far the most important non-communist new nation, and therefore merited much more concern, was not.

Looking back on the history of Asia since 1945, the opposing attitudes of the Soviet Union and the United States toward nationalism are evident again and again. The results of nationalist efforts have been different in India than in China, in Indonesia than in Indochina, in Burma than in Laos. But in all there has been a nationalist center to which communism has tried to attach itself, and from which Anti-Communism has remained totally or partially aloof. Communism has been an "insider," even though it has sometimes quarreled with the nationalists, because it has engaged in many struggles against imperialism prior to nationalist victory. The West, on the other hand, has been considered an "outsider"—even though it has aided the nationalist cause either at the moment it was coming to power or thereafter—because it has been equivocal. Neutralist Asia has had the feeling that the U. S. was *forced* to support it, had no other alternatives, not because it was America's real desire to do so.

Thus the communists remain important factors in the lives of nations such as Indonesia, India, Burma, and many others, where they have blundered shamefully; while the United States has lost its original attractiveness, and is today lumped with Britain and France as part of "imperialism."

Let us consider two opposite examples—Indonesia, where the communists were hasty and tried to overthrow a nationalist government, and China, where the extreme patience of Mao Tse-tung gave him dominance over a nationalist movement and brought the communists victory after three decades of effort. In the former instance, the United States played a moderately progressive role, helping Indonesia to enforce independence. But because it was an "outsider" and it lacked central purpose, it was unable to benefit from that revolution, while the communists, with all their mistakes, are again a rising force in that country.

I

For almost 350 years the complex of islands known as the Dutch East Indies had been a colony, supplying 15 to 25 per cent of the national income of the Netherlands. A quarter of a million Dutchmen lived here in a luxury they could not have enjoyed elsewhere, tending to an investment of $1.5 billion in tin, rubber, oil, quinine, and copra. On the other side of the social spectrum, 93 per cent of the Indies' inhabitants were illiterate. There was one doctor for every sixty thousand people. Seventy-two million people lived in disease and economic slumber.

Early in World War II, Japan seized the Dutch East Indies— as it did the rest of Southeast Asia—and ruled it until August, 1945. On five occasions a dogged resistance movement organized small, but abortive, revolts. To appease the nationalists, Japan in 1944 promised independence. Whether they would have honored this promise is open to question, but two days after the Japanese surrender, Achmed Sukarno and Mohammed Hatta issued a ringing declaration of independence, reminiscent of the American document 169 years before: "We, the Indonesian people, hereby declare our independence. Independence is the right of every nation. . . . With the blessing of God Almighty and led by the highest ideals of a free national life the Indonesian people do hereby and for ever declare their lasting freedom. . . . The Republic is for righteous and moral humanity, for the unity of Indonesia, and for democracy." [5] The new regime began immediately to disarm the Japanese and release the few thousand Dutch soldiers who had surrendered in 1942.

If the Atlantic Charter had been taken literally, this is where the matter should have rested. The United States and its allies had an obligation, by the terms of the Charter, to speak out immediately and unequivocally for "self-determination." But six weeks later British troops arrived from India and the Dutch sent back Dr. Hubertus J. van Mook to act as governor general. Major Frederick E. Crockett, head of the United States Military Mission in Java, reported in *Harper's* magazine that the British mission "smelled suspiciously of a return to the old order." [6] The Indonesians "accepted it with equanimity and awaited results," but their worst fears were soon confirmed. The Dutch poured in men and material as quickly as they could mobilize them. Japanese soldiers—yesterday's enemies—and the *Kempeitai*—Japan's Gestapo—were enlisted to keep order.

Despite this disheartening beginning, the United States continued material aid to the Netherlands, while much of it was being used to shoot down Indonesia's rebels. Indonesians lodged a protest that military vehicles operated by the Dutch carried American markings, but the U. S. merely asked the Dutch to remove the labels. America, it must be said, was not sympathetic to Dutch colonialism, but neither was it ready to take decisive measures in something as remote as a nationalist struggle for independence.

As it turned out, the Dutch were merely stalling for time. Their own economy was too enervated to mount an all-out campaign, and Britain, in its own weakness, had to curtail support. In these circumstances Holland effected a momentary compromise settlement in November, 1946. The Linggadjati Agreement recognized the "*de facto* authority [of the Republic of Indonesia] over Java, Madura and Sumatra," and pledged that the "areas occupied by Allied or Netherland forces shall be included gradually" under Indonesian rule not later than January 1,

1949. In return, the nationalists promised to form a Netherland-Indonesian Union, under a common Queen, and to restore Dutch property. In case of dispute the matter was to be arbitrated. This was not yet independence, but it represented a significant step forward and was approved by the Indonesian Federation of Labor, the Socialists, and the Communists.

The Dutch, however, had no intention of yielding their lucrative colony. According to acting governor van Mook, their plan was to prepare the nation for sovereignty in fifteen or twenty years, not earlier. Meanwhile the build-up of the Dutch army continued, and a few puppet states were established with the help of the feudal lords, beholden to Holland. Lieutenant General S. H. Spoor, in an interview with the *New York Times*, betrayed his country's real objectives: "The policy I will follow is that of the late President Theodore Roosevelt: namely, soft words backed up by a big stick." [7] By May, 1947, the "big stick" was ready. With 110,000 soldiers at their command, the Dutch took quick "police action." Their goal was to destroy all Indonesian armed forces and confine the Republic to a small area in Central Java, but though they achieved many of these military objectives, the struggle was far from over.

An aroused United Nations, responding to world opinion, sent in a commission headed by Dr. Graham to find a *modus vivendi* between the parties. The resulting Renville Agreement resolved very little, for it stripped the Republic of much of its economic holdings. The Dutch now controlled half the sugar mills of Java, three-quarters of its rubber, two-thirds of its coffee, and almost all of its tea plantations. The oil fields of Sumatra were similarly in the hands of the colonial power. For Indonesia to maintain its independence without control over its economy was impossible. Friction multiplied until December, 1948, when Dutch parachutists descended on the capital city of Jarkarta, arrested Sukarno, Hatta, and other leaders, and virtually restored Indonesia to colonial status.

To this point the United States had pursued a lethargic course. Nationalists had expected far more support from those whose own revolution in 1775 they sought to emulate. (A group of Indonesian women wanted to send a delegation to the United States to enlist the aid of the Daughters of the American Revoluion.) Public opinion in the United States was favorable to the nationalists, but the government was marking time. The United States failed to heed an appeal by Sukarno for mediation, and it provided arms for the Dutch with little concern as to how they were being used. The 1948 outrage, however, provoked the United States to action. It was too blatant to be disregarded. Furthermore, there was now a "communist angle," to the travail of Indonesia. In September, a few months before, the impatient communists had triggered an uprising against the Republic in the Madiun area. The Republican government, they had said, was compromising with the imperialists. The revolt had been set down in short order, but it was something for Washington to think about. A combination of motives, then, stirred the American government to throw its weight behind the nationalists.

With the United States now leading the way, the United Nations Security Council unanimously ordered Holland to release the Republican leaders and come to terms. Holland might not have surrendered even then, but in surveying the situation it found itself in an impossible position. The major cities were in its hands, but the villages, where most of the people lived, were solidly behind the nationalists. Indonesians, determined to die for *merdeka*—independence—were ready to wage guerrilla war indefinitely. Had Holland continued its "police action," it would not only have isolated itself from the world community, but perhaps bankrupted itself in a long, drawn-out guerrilla war. It decided to cut its losses and submit to the inevitable. In August, 1950, after four and a half years of useless slaughter in which 100,000 men had died and tens of millions in property had been destroyed, Indonesia became independent.

American pressure on behalf of the nationalists was not an insignificant factor in their victory. But it had been a hesitant support, and open to the communist charge that Americans were easing out the Dutch only to take over their investments. In the leftist view there was no idealism attached to American efforts, just hard cash. The United States could have mitigated—or erased entirely—such attacks by limiting its investments to joint companies together with the Indonesian government. But in far-off Washington, President Truman was defining freedom—in part —as "free enterprise," and the American state was not about to curb the investment proclivities of such major corporations as Standard Oil, U. S. Rubber, and B. F. Goodrich. The communists, though they fought the Indonesian government with arms, did it in the name of attacking imperialism. They appeared to be pulling a revolution to the left—and in a revolutionary country this is far from unpopular.

Neither the United States nor its friends in Indonesia were willing to match that radicalism. The result was that the U. S. gained no great mass support, while Moscow's adherents exploited nationalism and rebuilt a sizeable mass movement favorable to them.

In reflecting on this success, it is important to focus on the composition of Indonesian nationalism, for it was to be duplicated almost everywhere else. It stretched from the Muslin Masjoemi Party on the right, to the communists and Trotskyists on the left. In the center were Sukarno's nationalist party, Soetan Sjahrir's Socialist party, the Labor party, and a few others. Though they differed sharply on ideology and tactics, they were firmly united in opposition to foreign rule. This may appear to be a recitation of the obvious, but it is important in evaluating the role of communism in Asia. The communist may be anathema to Washington, but to the freedom fighters of the colonies he is a brother "fighting imperialism." In November, 1926, the Indonesian Communist party had led an uprising against the Dutch. It was an ineffective rebellion, isolated to Bantam and the west coast of Sumatra, and it was put down within two months. But it enhanced the communist image in nationalist eyes; communists had given their lives for *merdeka.*

In Asia, Latin America, North Africa, and to a limited extent in Black Africa, nationalism is made up of a similar spectrum of political doctrine—ranging from religious and conservative nationalism to various branches of socialism, communism, and, in some cases, Trotskyism. Which force dominates the nationalist alliance depends both on circumstances and the capacity of each group to gauge the mood of the people. The Indonesian communists seem to have been inept both in their 1926 uprising and again in 1948. They were unable, in 1948, to carry others with them, especially the socialists, and in their isolation they became momentarily discredited. In India, where Gandhi and his non-violent resistance movement prevailed, the communists supported the British war effort (against Gandhi's wishes) and also isolated themselves temporarily from the nationalist mainstream. Their influence declined. But it is interesting to note that both in India and Indonesia they showed great resiliency. They are today the second largest party in India, and the biggest, best disciplined, and financially best supplied party in Indonesia. By endorsing both nationalist revolutions, though trying to draw them toward a more radical course, they have been able to consolidate a great following. By contrast, the United States, though it has spent billions aiding these two nations, has but meager influence. It has not found the formula for fulsome alliance with a nationalist revolution. More properly, it *cannot* find it so long as it relies on the world-wide strategy of Anti-Communism.

II

That communism did not become the leader of nationalist alliances in Burma, India, Indonesia, Ceylon, and elsewhere is the result both of its own blunders and the talents of Gandhi, Nehru, U Nu, Ba Swe, Sjahrir, and similar men. But in China and Indochina it achieved dramatic ascendancy. Here, too, the rainbow of nationalism was a blur of many colors, from tepid nationalism to communism and Trotskyism. Social democrats, of the Second International variety, radical nationalists, intellectuals, students— many forces were involved in the revolutions. Yet communism emerged predominant because those who sincerely believed in nationalism had no other place to go.

The worst defeat for America's policy of Anti-Communism was China. No single victory of the West—in Iran, Greece, Guatemala—or all of them put together, can outweigh the setback in China. Mao Tse-tung's ascent to power in 1949 was an event which, in historical retrospect, may loom more significant than even the Bolshevik Revolution of 1917. That the most populous nation on earth, with almost one-fourth its inhabitants, should have fallen into communist hands punctured any hopes the United States may have had of sustaining the favorable "balance of power" it enjoyed in 1945. As its economy becomes more viable in the next few decades, China's impact on world affairs will be even stronger.

Communism's victory in China in 1949 is viewed by most

Americans as an aggressive and treacherous thrust against the established government of Chiang Kai-shek and the Kuomintang. This is, however, an oversimplified estimate, for it leaves the main actors—the Western powers—out of the drama. It dates history from the moment that is most convenient for the present Anti-Communist argument, rather than placing the issue in full perspective. The fact is that the West, including the United States, had fought and harried Chinese nationalism for more than a century. It seized China's land, operated its ports, imposed extra-territorial rights, financed war lords, and did everything necessary to keep China disunited and impotent. When the Chinese people sought to rectify their plight, the West unleashed its armies against them, or underwrote reactionary war lords. It is impossible to read the China Story without noting the culpability of the West in driving this great nation to the final desperation.

When a British emissary, seeking trade relations with China in 1792, met Emperor Ch'ien Lung, he was politely told, "The Celestial Empire possesses all things in prolific abundance; there is therefore no need to import the manufactures of outside barbarians." [8] Nonetheless, the "barbarians" did pry open the doors of trade. In the Opium War of 1839-1842, Britain forced China not only to accept opium imports—which averaged twelve tons a day until 1911—but to cede Hongkong and open five other ports for trade and residence. The then Chinese Emperor expressed the bitterness of his nation when he said: "I cannot prevent the introduction of the flaming poison; keen-seeking and corrupt men will, for profit and sensuality, defeat my wishes; but nothing will induce me to derive a revenue from the vice and misery of my people." [9] By 1900, Britain controlled 60 per cent of China's foreign trade.

From 1850 to 1864, the T'aiping Rebellion against the Manchu Dynasty swept sixteen of the eighteen provinces of China proper. Influenced by Christian missionaries, the rebels called their leader the "younger brother of Jesus Christ" and preached a Christianity of "peace." They promised land to landless and burned landlord title deeds and the promissory notes of usurious money-lenders as a demonstration of their identification with the peasants. In the initial stages of the revolt Britain aided the rebels, but after a few years it took advantage of the Manchu preoccupation to declare war and exact new concessions. Then, after making peace with the ancient dynasty, Britain and France turned their military power against the nationalists and helped to suppress them. Literally millions died in battle.

Decade by decade thereafter, China lost control of its ports, its trade, its land, its judicial rights. Russia annexed the area north of the Amur River; France seized Indochina; Britain took Burma. Twenty-eight nations in all were stationed in China, each with its extra-territorial privileges, its military contingent, even its own laws and the right to try its own citizens.

In a lightning war in 1894-1895, Japan detached Korea from China, took Formosa, and imposed an indemnity of $170 million. Five years later the Boxer Rebellion broke out—a peasant revolt aimed not only at alleviating the lot of the village poor but at ousting the foreigners. Britain, Germany, Russia, Japan, and the United States joined hands to put down the rebellion—and impose another indemnity of $325 million.

China was not a colony in the traditional sense, occupied by a single power. But it was a colony in the sense that *many* powers divided it and dominated its economy. By 1925, the foreign powers held six thousand miles of railroads, most large banks, shipping companies, tobacco firms, mining industries, and cotton producers. Britain alone could count an investment of $1.2 billion. Reports a decade later noted that half of China's coal mines and two-thirds of its shipping tonnage belonged to foreigners. On the other side of the dreary picture, 80 per cent of the Chinese people lived under a backward feudalism, few owning their own land, and per capita income was perhaps $25 a year—50¢ a week per person. If there were any country poorer or more miserable than China, it was difficult to find.

The Chinese Revolution was directed against these twin evils: foreign domination, internal feudalism. It began in 1911, six years before the Bolshevik Revolution. Led by a physician named Sun Yat-sen, it quickly disposed of the decadent Manchu Dynasty, but—like the Mexican Revolution which had begun a year before—it was unable immediately to unify the country, evict the foreigners, or convert the feudal land system. For fifteen years the Chinese Revolution not only had to contend with the many war lords who contained it in the southern part of the country, but the world powers who very often subsidized these war lords. In 1915, during the first war, Japan issued a twenty-one point ultimatum to hapless China demanding all previous German rights, a monopoly of transport, natural resources, and capital investment in South Manchuria and Inner Mongolia, and ninety-nine year leases at Port Arthur. Two years later the United States quietly and without a pang of conscience recognized Japan's "special interests" in China, and at the Peace Conference of 1919 Japan was permitted to lavish on her gains.

The Versailles Peace Treaty legalizing this seizure was greeted with bitter resentment in China. Demonstrations were organized by students, farmers, merchants, and workers. A boycott was instituted against Japanese goods. To appease this and similar storms, the United States called a conference of the nine powers that had a major stake in China, and made certain concessions. Japan was forced to relinquish her rights in Shantung. The nine powers agreed to eliminate special "spheres of influence" and recognize the "Open Door Policy." It was, however, a long way from independence and social change.

But if the West would not heed the cry of nationalism, Moscow was more than willing—and the Chinese had no other place to go. Sun Yat-sen's Kuomintang made an agreement with the Communist International and invited Bolshevik technicians and political advisors to build a revolutionary army that would unify the nation. The membership of the Communist party of China, founded only in 1921, joined the Kuomintang as individuals, eager to help it spread nationalist rule throughout the country. Communists organized unions, peasant movements, student groups, and military units. If it were not for their skill and effort, it is fairly certain that the Kuomintang would have failed in its mission. Whatever the motives of the communists—and they were no doubt thinking of nationalism only as a stepping stone to communism—the fact is they made common cause with Sun, while the West either stayed aloof or impeded his way.

Sun Yat-sen died in 1925. On his death bed, March 12, 1925, he wrote a letter to the Central Executive Committee of the Soviet Union expressing the kinship between nationalism and communism. "I am suffering," he said, "from an incurable disease of the body, but my heart turns towards you, towards my Party, and the future of my country. You are the leaders of a free union of republics. This free union of republics is the world inheritance bequeathed to the oppressed peoples by the immortal Lenin. Peoples suffering from imperialism will safeguard their freedom by it, and will emancipate themselves from an international system based upon ancient orders of enslavement, war and injustices by it. What I leave behind me is the Kuomintang. I hope the Kuomintang will, in the process of completing the historical work of emancipating China and other oppressed nations from the imperialistic system, co-operate with you." [10]

Had Sun lived it is possible that the nationalist-communist coalition would have survived under nationalist leadership. But the Kuomintang, like all nationalist movements, had its left, its center, and its right. The right, under Sun's brother-in-law, Chiang Kai-shek, turned on its allies and thereafter leaned on the feudal elements and the Western powers. It aborted the revolution, paving the way eventually for those who would manage its rebirth.

The rapprochement of the Kuomintang and the communists lasted from 1923 to 1927. The Soviet Union trained officers for the nationalist army at Whampoa Military Academy. Communists sent political workers into the countryside to organize the peasants. They organized students, workers, and merchants behind the Kuomintang effort to unify China. In the short period of a few months a coalition of friendly militarists, Kuomintang members, and communists marched northward in one triumph after another until it reached the Yangtse River. In a few months, however, the coalition was sundered and Chiang's right-wing drowned the communist allies in a terrible bloodbath. Thousands of leftists and their union followers were slaughtered in Shanghai alone. "Though many men who had been double-crossed and massacred were communists," writes Graham Peck, "the men who did it became cheats and murderers . . . The way they came to power determined the personnel, techniques, direction, and final destination of their government." [11] The alliance with Russia was broken in favor of an understanding with Britain, France, and the United States.

The West had an opportunity even then to pressure Chiang for major reforms, to make nationalism meaningful instead of stagnant and reactionary. But it did none of these things. Nor did it interfere, after 1931, when Japan moved deeper into Manchuria. The United States, to its credit, condemned the conquest, but the world stood by while China continued to be carved up and Chiang Kai-shek plunged severely to the right.

In these circumstances many nationalists turned to the communists. The non-communist Fourth Army deserted to Mao Tse-tung and became the nucleus of the communist army. Tens of thousands of Kuomintang members, literati, professors, members of the middle class, and socialists, joined the communists to complete Sun Yat-sen's dream of nationalism. While Chiang and his friends were enriching themselves, seizing hundreds of thousands of acres of land for their private use, the communists and their allies were dividing the land amongst common peasants. This was their bridge to power. As D. F. Fleming writes: "The peasant revolution was in the womb of history. In refusing to midwife its birth the Kuomintang left the opportunity by default to the communists. . . . When the time came that the unfinished revolution could no longer be stopped, the Kuomintang had to be swept away and, logically, the communists had to win." [12]

III

This is the prelude to the communist victory of 1946-1949 in China. It followed decades of Western indifference to the plight of the Chinese people, decades of imperialist occupation and profit-taking. In China, as in Russia in 1917 and in Cuba in 1960, the communists were the benefactors of a revolution which they did not start. They were the benefactors by default because no other force was able (or willing) to do anything for the landless peasant. They won because they completed a revolution which others were trying to obstruct.

It is idle to estimate the success of this, or any other revolution, in terms of guns, tanks, or planes. Revolutionaries are always *inferior* in military weapons, and that was just as true of China's communists as of the American revolutionaries of 1775-1783. They prevail because they have won the people to their side or at least neutralized them. Foster Hailey, a former *New York Times* correspondent, says, "The reason the Communists finally won China was because they based their campaign on the people, the great, inert mass of 500,000,000 from whom Chiang and his inner circle had held themselves as remote since 1928 as does the Dai Lama from Western civilization. The Communists put their hopes in the political activation of the illiterate peasant and the underprivileged worker by promising him a change. Chiang put his hopes in a military campaign, financed by the United States, that would maintain the status quo. It was inevitable that in the long run the Communists would win." [13]

Many responsible officials in the United States understood the fatal flaws of Chiang's policy. General Joseph Stillwell, in 1944, wrote in his diary: "We were fighting Germany to tear down the Nazi system—one-party government, supported by the Gestapo and headed by an unbalanced man with little education. . . . China, our ally, was being run by a one-party government [the Kuomintang], supported by a Gestapo [Tai Li's organization]. . . . To reform such a system it must be torn to pieces . . . Because it was expedient to back this government, it was not necessarily advisable to endorse its methods and policies. We could have required some return for our help." [14] Prices in China were now two hundred times higher than prewar. The poorly-fed and often-robbed soldiers showed little desire to fight. They frequently used their arms, instead, to plunder the peasants.

President Roosevelt demanded that Chiang reform, but in vain. After the war General Marshall, as Truman's emissary, tried for thirteen months to edge Chiang and the communists into a democratic coalition that would assure important changes. United States advice was never heeded. By the time Marshall's mission had failed, America was embarked on its policy of Anti-Communism. Though it was concerned with the corruption and ineffectiveness of Chiang, it feared the communists even more. It could not break with Chiang; it gave him billions of military aid in a useless cause.

The myth has evolved in recent years that the communists could have been vanquished if only we had given more weapons to Chiang Kai-shek, or if we had sent American troops into the fray. Neither of these claims has the least merit. Chiang Kai-shek controlled the major cities of China and at least three-quarters of the population when his regime began to totter. His government received $3 billion in aid from the United States, plus weapons from a million disarmed Japanese soldiers.

The Kuomintang, according to Mao, had four million men under arms at this time, but in seventeen months of combat, from

July, 1946, to November, 1947, it lost 1,690,000, two-thirds of them made prisoners. Mountains of American weapons fell into rebel hands. Communist General Chu Teh told Foster Hailey: "During the last few months of fighting we have annihilated thirty-five Nationalist brigades. In these operations we have seized much United States equipment. It is very good. We hope to get more of it." [15] After the Communists came to power, Western observers were amazed by the quantity of American weapons displayed. One can make a good case, it seems, that American supplies to Chiang helped the Communists as much as or more than Chiang.

It is true that after Russia entered Manchuria she gave some weapons to the Mao-ists. But Soviet help for the Chinese communists was minuscle compared to what the United States did for Chiang. As Hailey put it: "The USSR did not garrison any troops in Manchuria or North China to hold cities for the Chinese Communists: The United States did (for Chiang). The USSR did not fly any Chinese Communist armies to strategic cities; the United States Air Force did. The USSR, so far as it can be ascertained, did not send military missions to Chinese Communist territory to train their officers and men; the United States has had large military missions in China since the end of the war, advising Chiang and his military leaders." [16]

Former Secretary of State Dean Acheson made this appraisal of Chiang's defeat: "Nobody, I think, says that the Nationalist Government fell because it was confronted by overwhelming military force which it could not resist. Certainly no one in his right mind suggests that. . . . The broad picture is that after the war, Chiang Kai-shek emerged as the undisputed leader of the Chinese people. Only one faction, the Communists, up in the hills, ill-equipped, ragged, a very small military force, was determinedly opposed to his position. He had overwhelming military power, greater military power than any ruler had ever had in the entire history of China. He had tremendous economic and military support and backing from the United States. . . . No one says that vast armies moved out of the hills and defeated him. . . . What has happened in my judgment is that the almost inexhaustible patience of the Chinese people in their misery ended. They did not bother to overthrow this government. There was really nothing to overthrow. They simply ignored it throughout the country. . . . Added to the grossest incompetence ever experienced by any military command was this total lack of support both in the armies and in the country, and so the whole matter just simply disintegrated. The communists did not create this. The communists did not create this condition. They did not create this revolutionary spirit. . . . But they were shrewd and cunning enough to mount it, to ride this thing into victory and into power." [17]

Nor was Mao's victory the result of a "Moscow Plot." There is ample evidence that Stalin was unhappy with the course of events. Theodore H. White, in *The Reporter*, notes that "in conversations with foreigners, Stalin wrote the Chinese Communists off as 'guerrillas.' . . . During the war between China and Japan, Stalin sent all his military aid to Chiang, and nothing to Mao's forces, which were at one point given four Russian artillery pieces by Chiang as their share of Russian largesse." [18]

Stalin actually tried to drive Mao into a coalition government. In a conversation with Yugoslav communists in 1948, he told them: "It is true, we have also made mistakes. For instance, after the war we invited the Chinese comrades to come to Moscow and we discussed the situation in China. We told them bluntly that we considered the development of the uprising in China had no prospect, and that the Chinese comrades should seek a *modus vivendi* with Chiang Kai-shek, that they should join the Chiang Kai-shek government and dissolve their army. The Chinese comrades agreed here with the views of the Soviet comrades, but went back to China and acted quite otherwise." [19]

Robert Guillain, a French journalist with long experience in the Far East, comments: "The Russians have shown, particularly by their accommodating attitude towards Chiang Kai-shek till the spring of 1949, that they are not over-keen on having a nation of 450 million united on their Asian flank. The victories of the Chinese Communists are useful for propaganda purposes: but policy might well have preferred the victories slower and harder won. The Nationalist blockade of Shanghai is a case in point. The Russians did not lift a finger to help Mao rid himself of a disastrous nuisance when it would have been easy to lend only a few planes to dispose of it." [20]

The British Royal Institute of International Affairs reported that a delegation from Moscow warned the Mao-ists in 1948 against an "all-out offensive to crush the Kuomintang and seize power. Russia preferred that the civil war should continue on a guerrilla basis, because this weakened America by inducing that country to continue to pour arms into China in aid of Chiang Kai-shek. . . . Contrary to popular belief, China is not a land where secrets can be kept. News of this debate, though not of the outcome, reached Peking in a few weeks." [21]

The claim that the Chinese Communist Revolution was a Soviet-hatched conspiracy is a misreading of history. Mao Tse-tung was far more realistic when he told Foster Hailey in 1946: "It's not only a question of the USSR. In the latter part of the nineteenth century, before the USSR was formed, the Western powers supported undemocratic elements in China. Two instances of this were in 1850 and 1863. The T'aiping Rebellion was ninety years ago. There was no USSR at that time. You also supported reaction from 1900 to 1917. All the Western powers were against Sun Yat-sen's democratic movement. It was not a question of the USSR then. The USSR now is only an excuse." [22]

This, briefly, is the story of communism's greatest postwar victory—the greatest setback the West has suffered in many decades. The communists clung to nationalism while the West was trying to subvert it. They clung to nationalist objectives with singleminded determination even after the right-wing nationalists killed their followers and outlawed their movement. They understood, as the West did not, that nationalism is—in the words of Sukarno—"the mainspring of our efforts." And they proved once again, as did the Russians in 1918-1920, that military intervention, direct or indirect, is not the answer to revolutionary striving.

Yet the lessons of China have failed to penetrate the consciousness of American administrations. Individuals have understood what was wrong, individuals as highly placed as Dean Acheson. But they have never been able to elevate this knowledge into a thoroughgoing strategy. The myopia of Anti-Communism has caused them to travel a double course, usually ending in support for conservatives and reactionaries, if not in colonialism itself. The same mistakes were to be repeated over and over again. Defeat actually hardened American Anti-Communist policy. Today, after two decades of this barren approach, it is still impossible to challenge it without laying one's self open to the charge of "soft on communism."

VII

Their Side and Ours: People Versus Arms

PERHAPS the most puzzling question of the Cold War is why "our" allies fight so poorly, while the "other" side performs miracles. Chiang Kai-shek, with an army of four million, with three-quarters of the population under his rule and $3 billion in American aid, is unable to defeat an adversary with less than a fourth as many forces. France must bring *outside* soldiers into Indochina and Algeria, while the nationalists can recruit tens of thousands at home. The North Koreans can put their *own* army into the field in the first stage of the Korean War and inflict severe setbacks on Syngman Rhee's government, while the South Koreans must call for American and United Nations troops to rescue them. South Viet Nam, with 200,000 soldiers and 100,000 auxiliary men, plus 14,000 to 16,000 United States "advisors" and $450 million annually in American aid, is incapable of erasing a Viet Cong guerrilla army of only 20,000. Batista, with 43,000 soldiers, American-trained and to a large extent American-supplied, cannot demolish a *fidelista* "army" that never exceeded 1,200.

The argument is sometimes made that "their" side is secretly outfitted with more and better equipment than "ours"—presumably from nearby communist countries. But a moment's reflection indicates how unlikely that is. From 1946 to 1962, the United States furnished $8.4 billion in military aid to the Far East alone. The Soviet figure is unknown but it certainly can be nowhere near this sum. If the contest for world power were to be decided solely by each side's ability to supply the most weaponry, the free world would win easily. In 1951, when the revolutionary wave in Asia was at its peak, the Soviet bloc was producing only 28 million tons of steel, 14 per cent of the world total, while the United States and Western Europe milled 160 million tons, more than 80 per cent of the total. The Western capacity to supply arms was, and is, far greater than that of the East.

The effectiveness of "their" side is due not to superior military power, but to superior political methods. In reviewing his victory against France, General Vo Nguyen Giap, leader of the Viet Minh army, noted that "political activities were more important than military activities, and fighting less important than propaganda." [1] The guerrilla, whether under communist or other leadership, is a military expression of the political fervor of nationalism. He fights for an ideal and is willing to die for it. He is potent because he has the virtually unanimous support of the masses on his side. "I have never talked or corresponded with a person knowledgeable in Indochinese affairs," writes former President Dwight Eisenhower, "who did not agree that had elections been held as of the time of the fighting, possibly 80 per cent of the population would have voted for Ho Chi-minh." [2] The communists and nationalists were certainly inferior to France in military materiel, but they more than made up for it by their determination and by the overwhelming support they enjoyed from the populace.

The ineffectiveness of "our" side, in China, South Korea, Indochina, and Cuba, is a coefficient of unpopularity. Chiang, Rhee, the French, Bao Dai, Ngo Dinh Diem, and Batista failed to win the people; and without the people their military advantage was useless. A hundred years ago, fifty years ago, people were "unimportant"—dictators and colonial powers could ride roughshod over them. Today they are decisive, unbeatable so long as they can maintain mass allegiance. In today's underdeveloped areas, a contest between people and arms will end, in the majority of instances, in a victory for the people. The "big stick" has become a broken reed.

The guerrilla is effective because he combines rudimentary military tactics with revolutionary nationalism. With the support of the rural masses, the guerrilla can do many things that the regulars cannot. He is almost invincible, for though he may lose a battle here and there, he can be reinforced and rise up again somewhere else. An Italian partisan of World War II has described guerrilla warfare in most lucid terms. Auro Roselli points out that "you never 'advance' against guerrilla formations, because the true guerrilla does not occupy any definite position." [3] Nor can you "expect" a guerrilla attack, because the partisan will not attack if you expect him. He attacks only at the unexpected moment and in the unexpected place. He can do so because he can disappear and reappear without being apprehended—the villagers will shelter and hide him. The army regular wears a uniform and moves in formation with supply packs on his back. The irregular fighter has no uniform (until his forces are large enough so that he can flaunt his strength) and he has no supply pack. He accomplishes his mission, usually during the night, and in the morning he is back at work on his farm or in the baker's mill. To wipe out a guerrilla force, the regular army must win the people to its side (that happened, for instance, in the Philippines, but in few other places). Contrariwise, the guerrilla remains effective so long as he has the support of the citizenry. Once he loses that support he is finished, but so long as he has it he can "hide into yesterday or tomorrow."

The regular army cannot find the "enemy," for the guerrillas are everywhere and yet nowhere. The baker who is being questioned about where the rebels are, is himself a rebel. He may not yet have put a gun on his shoulder, but he hid a guerrilla gunman the night before and gave him bread that very morning. Later, when enough regular soldiers are disarmed, he too will take a gun. Even the elderly woman or the eight-year old child playing marbles are "enemies" of the established regime; they filch information about the regular armies and carry messages back and forth across the lines. Soon the regular army is demoralized; at darkness it becomes jittery. The regular soldier shoots at every noise, imagines movement where there is no movement. He is like a blind man surrounded by enemies on all sides, incapable of estimating the enemy's strength or learning when it will attack.

In the beginning, the guerrilla is a part-time soldier. At night he blows up bridges and disarms regulars. By day he works in his normal occupation. But when the first guerrillas have captured enough materiel and money (which they expropriate from the regular army), the movement becomes a regular guerrilla force of full-time soldiers, as well as the part-time "saboteurs and diversionists." At this stage the guerrillas are much more formidable. They are still mobile, still able to "hide into yesterday," but when they stop the regular soldiers on a road or gain control of a section of the railway, they break the unity of the official command. Once the roads and railways become useless, the modern army becomes easy prey for guerrillas. The regular army cannot function without heavy and constant supplies; the guerrillas can live off the people and need no lines of communication. The regular army needs a *front* to do battle; the guerrillas offer no front. One of the constant hopes of the French in Indochina was that the Viet Minh would "stand up and fight." But the very nature of guerrilla warfare is that it offers no front where it can be destroyed. It will not "stand up and fight" until its forces are superior.

That nationalism can make lions out of seeming kittens should come as no surprise to Americans versed in their own history. At the time of the American Revolution, Great Britain was the undisputed master of the seas and had an army far better trained and supplied than the tattered legions who made up Washington's forces. There were times in the Revolutionary War when Washington had no more than four thousand troops under his command, many without shoes or adequate winter clothing. There were times, particularly in the South, when it seemed that Cornwallis's and Clinton's armies could march unimpeded wherever they pleased. But as if from nowhere "minutemen" sprang up to harass the Redcoats and eventually to defeat them. It was not Washington's military prowess, though he was adept and competent, that brought victory to the American forces, but the fires of nationalism, fanned by Samuel Adams's fiery propaganda, Thomas Paine's *Common Sense,* and Thomas Jefferson's Declaration of Independence.

Today, almost two centuries later, half or more of humanity is imbued with the same spirit, activated by the same nationalism for which they are willing to offer their lives. Where communism has won—outside of Eastern Europe—it is because it has capitalized on that fact of life, because it has joined in the quest for independence and land reform, because it has identified with the peasant revolution in "the womb of history." Even where it has failed—in Iran, for instance—it is like the boy on the merry-go-round who has missed the gold ring first time around. It will try and try again, with the odds growing in its favor if the Western world refuses to compete in the same game.

I

Consider a few incidents in the Cold War which bear out this thesis.

The background of the Indochinese revolution is monotonously similar to that of other colonies. Murder of a French missionary in 1857 gave France the pretext to progressively occupy Indochina. Once installed, she reaped the usual profits from tin, tungsten, zinc, iron ore, rubber and coal. By contrast, 80 per cent of the people remained illiterate—after three-quarters of a century of French rule—and living standards were as low as those of China. The inevitable peasant revolt broke out in 1930, led by the communists and the Viet Nam Nationalist party (VNQDD).

History, however, was not yet ready for successful peasant revolts; it was to wait another two decades. Two nationalist groups, formed in 1941-1942—the Viet Minh League (Viet Minh means "national front") and the Dong Minh Hoi—collaborated throughout the war period. The former contained a large communist contingent; the latter was friendly to the Kuomintang in China. When Japan seized Indochina toward the end of World War II, she was met by a guerrilla band of ten thousand men determined to smash both "French Imperialism and Japanese Fascism." Of the two nationalist forces, the Viet Minh emerged the most forceful. Led by Ho Chi-minh, it liberated six northern provinces and established a broad national government which commanded the support even of Chiang Kai-shek in China. On March 6, 1946, France itself recognized the regime as "a free state with its own government, parliament, army and finances, forming part of the Indochinese Federation of the French Union." [4] The honeymoon between colonialism and the colonial people, however, did not last. France sought to fragment the country, hoping to find allies in other sectors. It insisted that the southern part of Viet Nam have its own separate administration. In four months of negotiations with Ho, France refused to relinquish control over the army, diplomatic functions, currency, and the economy. The formula of a "free state within the French

Union" was in reality, as with the Dutch in Indonesia, a figleaf for continued domination.

The usual incidents flared up. At Haiphong on November 23, 1946, the French cruiser Suffern fired on the Vietnamese section of town, killing six thousand people. France seized all of Indochina, just as Holland had done in Indonesia, and guerrilla warfare again erupted in full fury. In World War I, France needed only two thousand troops to keep order in Indochina. After World War II, seventy thousand guerrillas under General Giap tied down 166,000 French soldiers.

It is noteworthy that far from driving wedges between the communists and other nationalists, French repression welded them together. Though they opposed Ho's ideology, democrats, socialists, and others continued to collaborate with him. The Democratic party (Vietnam Nam Dan Chu Dang), which emerged from a nonpolitical student movement at Hanoi University, held forty-five seats in the National Assembly as against eighty for Ho's Viet Minh. The Socialist party (Vietnam Nam Xa Hoi Dang) was formed only in 1946, with a philosophy closer to the Second International than to the communists, but its twenty-four assembly members also joined hands with Ho against the common enemy. In some Western eyes the events in Indochina may have appeared as another "communist aggression," but to Indochinese nationalists and to Asians generally it was, as Nehru put it, a "war for national liberation." [5]

In typical colonialist style, France dredged up a discredited former emperor, Bao Dai, who had collaborated with the Japanese, to head the government. According to the *New York Times* of November 8, 1953, Bao Dai was supported by no more than 20 per cent of the population, and probably less. He was known throughout the world as a playboy who had spent most of his time in France. His administration, as might be expected, was composed of men of wealth and presided over by a financier, Tran Van Huu. Tran was succeeded by Nguyen Van Tam, a chief of the secret police.

Meanwhile, Ho Chi-minh conducted his forces with impressive moderation. "We do not advocate the class struggle," wrote Ho in 1947, "for an obvious reason. All the classes in Vietnam have been bled white beyond recovery by French imperialists, and as a result the Vietnam economy has been destroyed. What we do advocate is to develop private capital in Vietnam. We welcome all French and foreign investments on the basis of a sincere cooperation." [6] To foreign writers he insisted that his was not a communist but a coalition nationalist government. According to Virginia Thompson and Richard Adloff, who wrote for the Institute of Pacific Relations: "Ho's nationalist noncommunist supporters tend to ridicule the idea that the communists will actually control the government." [7] A representative of the Socialist party, Ly Vinh Khuon, told me in 1950 that until the 1949 victory of Mao in China the socialists and democrats represented 60 per cent of the coalition and could have taken over the government, had they wanted. By 1950, however, it was too late. The war had lasted too long; the example of China was too compelling. The factions closed ranks behind Ho.[8]

By the end of 1953, the war had already cost France $7 billion, 71,500 dead, and another 106,000 wounded. This was a mammoth effort, draining off more dollars from a weak French economy than all she had received from the United States since 1945. The loss in manpower was greater than that suffered by the United States in Korea. Under such conditions the inevitable cry for help went out to Washington, and Washington responded favorably. No one asked why France was unable to recruit an army of native Indochinese to fight Ho Chi-minh. No one tried to make contact with the non-communists in Ho's alliance, or to mediate with Ho himself. We were "containing" communism, and the only friends we sought under this negative formula were the power elite—French colonialism. As of 1952, the United States had shipped 100,000 tons of supplies to the French forces, and as of 1954 it was paying 78 per cent of the cost of battle.[9]

The American establishment, totally out of touch with nationalism, remained hopeful to the end. Periodically there were glowing reports of imminent French victory. A month and a half before the final catastrophe, Admiral Arthur Radford, Chairman of the U.S. Joint Chiefs of Staff, emphatically predicted that "the French are going to win this war." In May, 1954, the flower of the French army was surrounded and humiliated into surrender at Dienbienphu. Undaunted, the United States continued to urge France to fight on. Secretary of State Dulles proposed sending two hundred American planes into the maelstrom; and Vice President Richard Nixon suggested troops as well. "If Indochina goes," President Eisenhower had said, "the tin and tungsten that we so greatly value from that area would cease coming." [10]

The dilemma of the United States was a painful one, but given its policy of Anti-Communism, it had few viable choices. Its travail is aptly described by D. A. Graber in his book, *Crisis Diplomacy*: "The United States was not sympathetic with French ambitions to re-establish control over French Indochina. But its traditional ardor for colonial people who were trying to shed foreign ties was cooled by the knowledge that the fires of Indochinese nationalism were stoked with communist coals." If the United States were to pursue a policy of neutrality "it would be interpreted as hostility by both camps. Siding with France and its protégés for the sake of anti-communism might jeopardize the friendship of anti-colonial nations who proudly hailed the Indochina war as a colonial conflict in which Asians at last were proving a military match to Europeans. Siding with the Indochinese nationalists in their fight against colonialism would, on the other hand, antagonize the European friends of the United States and aid the cause of communism. Since the colonial problem, like most of the issues of postwar United States foreign policy, was so inextricably intertwined with the overall East-West struggle, the ultimate decision to intervene on the side of France was made in terms of that struggle. If the communists triumphed, all of Southeast Asia might collapse, as Eisenhower had pictured it, like 'a row of dominoes' before the might of Moscow." [11]

Here again is the "first . . . and then" thesis developed so clearly by Senator Goldwater: first, we will unhinge the communist military force, then we can deal with colonial and social problems.

It did not work here, any more than in China.

France was tired of a war she could not win, A new government, headed by Pierre Mendès-France, came to office on the promise that it would end hostilities by July 20, 1954. Mendès-France negotiated a settlement with Red China's foreign minister, Chou En-lai, providing for a truce, the division of Viet Nam into two segments, and elections two years later to form a single administration for the whole country. Laos, which had not been involved in the guerrilla fighting, was to be neutralized. France was now rid of the problem, but the United States became the legatee of its headache, just as it became legatee of Britain's headache in Greece.

Again there was an opportunity to make amends with nationalism, but the United States was thinking in military rather than social terms. With China and North Viet Nam lost, Secretary of State Dulles's strategy was to build a semi-circle of military bases around Asian communism. Though there was little material to work with, the Secretary went through with his plans. Of the nations who signed the Southeast Asian Treaty Organization, only three were Asian—Pakistan, the Philippines, and Thailand —and none were particularly redoubtable.

Inside Viet Nam, meanwhile, the United States placed its reliance on a "safe" leader. Bao Dai voluntarily left for exile, to be replaced by a Catholic nationalist of uninspiring mien, Ngo Dinh Diem. Both Diem and the United States had no intention of permitting the promised elections of 1956 to take place, since "our" side could not win. "It is no secret . . .," wrote C. L. Sulzberger, "the elections really will never be held." [12] Instead Uncle Sam concentrated on training 140,000 native troops.

Such a hard course was an open invitation to toughness on the other side. With the election avenue closed, the communist-nationalist coalition—still paramount where it counted, in the villages—rose once more. Guerrilla warfare began at a slow tempo in 1955 and increased from year to year. "Our" side had an endless supply of money—$300 to $450 million a year from the United States—and, on paper, a ten to one superiority in military manpower; the "other" side had only tattered guerrillas—and the people. Jerry A. Rose, a former *Time* correspondent, wrote in 1961: "In one degree or another, seventy to ninety percent of the entire peasant population now leans toward the Viet Cong." [13] Max Clos, a correspondent for the conservative French newspaper *Le Figaro*, described the relationship of forces thus: "The South Viet Nam rice granary is politically controlled by the Viet Minh. . . . The national army is in exactly the same situation as the French expeditionary corps in 1950, and for exactly the same reasons. It holds the main roadways and the important towns, but the very substance of the country—the men and the rice—have escaped it.' [14]

United States officials applied benevolent pressure on Diem to institute reforms and woo the people; instead he and his coterie became more corrupt and dictatorial. Not only did he reject all-Viet Nam elections, but those held in his zone were rigged and dishonest. Professor Hans J. Morgenthau, of the University of Chicago, reported in 1956 that "of the eleven parties opposing Diem, only two splinter groups, the Socialist and the Republican parties, dare operate in the open. The others, of which the Communist Party, called Viet Cong, is the most important, work underground or else are engaged in open rebellion. Freedom of the press does not exist . . . Whenever one tries to engage private persons in political conversations, one meets a furtive glance and silence." [15] General Thomas R. Phillips (Retired) wrote in the *St. Louis Post-Dispatch*: "Diem operates a police state, with secret police harassment, arbitrary arrest, police brutality, political prisons, and economic favoritism. He trusts no one except his family." [16] There were twenty to thirty thousand political prisoners in South Vietnamese jails.

The difference between "our" side and "their" side is poignantly illustrated in Viet Nam. Ho Chi-minh may have lost support since 1954. It is possible that many who were with him in the struggle aaginst colonialism have been alienated by one or another facet of communist rule. But Ho's nationalist-communist alliance has solid roots. It began with overwhelming popular endorsement. If that following has fallen from an original 70 or 80 per cent, it still provides the nationalists and communists with a core of highly dedicated men ready to die for a "cause." These men joined not from motives of personal aggrandizement but in idealist identification with nationalism. If their government does not fulfill their dreams, they write it off as a temporary aberration, or blame it on "American imperialism." Ho—like Mao, Castro, Tito—is sure of a leadership cadre that can hold the state together.

The conservative and rightist governments on "our" side, however, live in quicksand. They have no base on which to establish a firm footing. Since they have little following among the people, they must rely on a class of opportunists. Not an ardent cause, but the prospect for bribes and profit motivates them. Once corruption corrodes the state establishment, the only thing that can keep it together is more corruption and severe repression. When the people begin to fight back, there is no nucleus around which the state can be solidified; the opportunists desert the burning ship to enjoy largesse stored in Swiss banks. The dictator has no power to rule; he collapses.

This mechanism of decay was obvious in South Viet Nam. Not only communists harassed the Diem government. It was falling apart from within as well. In November, 1960, young army rebels seized Saigon but were unable to hold it. *Time* magazine wrote that "with the revolt safely crushed Diem last week turned more dictatorial than ever. He reneged on mid-revolt promises of reform, declared himself in favor of 'personalism' (i.e. rule by Diem alone). Pro-Diem vigilantes sacked five newspapers that dared print news of the rebellion, helped secret police round up 75 intellectuals and politicians on flimsy charges of complicity in the uprising." [17] Three years later, a sharp conflict ensued between Catholic Diem and the Buddhist majority which constitutes one half to three-quarters the population of the country. Demonstrations broke out and Buddhist monks set fire to themselves to protest Diem's discriminatory measures.

Threatened by this steady disintegration, the dictator resorted to more and more distasteful measures. One of them was to uproot peasants from their homes and place them in large, fenced-in "agrovilles." These compounds, like those Britain established during the twelve-year guerrilla war in Malaya and during the Mau Mau war in Kenya, presumably can be policed more easily and guarded against "infiltration." Simultaneously, American planes, with Diem's assent, rained toxic materials on the foliage of Viet Nam in the hopes of uncovering guerrilla hiding places. The defoliants, used on a wide scale, were poisonous and killed— according to the *New Republic*—"not only the vegetation, but also the animals and humans who are within its reach." [18] For American Anti-Communists these were acceptable measures. The right-wing *National Review* argued that we should have told Moscow: "'Yes, indeed, we're using poison gas to defoliate the jungle and track down the hit-and-run Communist bandits. And we promise you we've got other trumps to play. Out in the forest, up in the hills, far from dense population, we could quite easily—and mercifully, for that matter—use some of our stock of nerve gas, and so paralyze a whole area, or strip of country, bringing peace once more, and saving Vietnam from Communist tyranny.'" [19] In the name of democracy and humanism the Anti-

Communist—and not just the *National Review* editors, by the way, but the leaders of American government—are willing to use undemocratic and inhumane methods, without grasping the fact that even as expedients they can only backfire.

In late 1963, the situation in South Viet Nam became so intolerable that the military officers, encouraged by the United States, overthrew Diem, killed him and his brother, Ngo Dinh Nhu, and installed a new regime. The basic problem, however, remains—and will remain—unanswered: how to deal with the social aspirations of the large number of people who support Viet Cong? For the Pentagon, as *Time* reported on October 27, 1961, American military participation gives the United States the "invaluable experience of guerrilla war." But what the military fails to understand is that anti-guerrilla tactics are not primarily a military but a social question. A coup by Viet Nam's military elite does not change this. Without basic social reform the Viet Cong will continue to hold mass support and continue to fight indefinitely, until America's allies are forced to give in. "The war in South Vietnam," writes Jerry A. Rose, "cannot be won. This is now the on-the-spot opinion of numerous Vietnamese, American and other foreign experts. After four years of closely observing the situation, I concur." [20] The chief of state of Cambodia, neutralist Prince Norodom Sihanouk, comments philosophically in a French-language publication: "The fate of Vietnam appears to me to be sealed. That of my own country will be also some time later. At least we shall have the slim consolation of having frequently warned the Western world. . . . Our American friends are remarkable organizers and excellent soldiers. But their incontestable realism stops short of the realm of politics, where the attitude of the ostrich seems to them to conform best to their interests." [21]

It is sometimes difficult to see the point made by Prince Sihanouk, because almost without exception, the new nationalist and communist nations travel a troubled course. Their economy remains dislocated for a time, their rate of growth inadequate to need, their democratic structure seriously marred by dictatorial measures. This leaves the impression that their revolutions were useless efforts. But a moment's reflection on America's own travail at the end of the eighteenth century should dispel this reservation. The United States, though favored by a literate population, protected by two oceans, and blessed with hundreds of millions of acres of unsettled land at its disposal, suffered through five "critical years" in the 1780's. During that time there were a number of "leftist" rebellions against the government, such as those of Daniel Shays in Massachusetts. Finances were in a shambles, the currency "not worth a continental." For a period, during the presidency of John Adams, the Alien and Sedition laws threatened to sunder the democratic structure. The violence of Hamiltonians against Jeffersonians similarly created an aura of instability. But who would say, in retrospect, that without the American Revolution the United States could possibly have achieved its present state of economic and political sophistication? All revolutionary nations must undergo a period of adjustment, long or short, depending on leadership, resources, and other factors. The important achievement of nationalism is that it *begins* the process of removing social obstacles of the past. Without that, progress is impossible. With it, it may be halting, confused, and sometimes too moderate. But the first prerequisite is to clear away the social debris which hinders advance.

This is being done, for the most part, both in communist and most neutralist nations. They are thus able to give their people a sense of belonging, even though they usually do not practice political democracy.

Whatever the shortcomings of the Ho Chi-minh government in North Viet Nam—and they are doubtless weighty—they evidently have not alienated the people of South Viet Nam, for the Viet Cong which accepts Ho as its model enjoys massive support. Nor have they alienated men like Prince Sihanouk. He feels he will have to travel part or all of the road that Ho has traveled, and he evidently believes this will not cost him popular backing. On the contrary, he expects it will enhance his public acceptability.

Communism to us in the United States is an unsavory system. We dislike its lack of elementary democracy. But in areas which have never known elementary democracy, the communists exercise attractive power because they emasculate feudalism and they strive to improve economies. Their methods may be harsh, but Asia, Africa, and Latin America have known nothing but harshness for centuries. They are choosing between harshness-with-stagnation and harshness-with-economic-development. If the United States and the West were to join in making their revolutions or prospective revolutions more viable, that harshness would be mitigated. But unless and until the U. S. does, their choices are more limited.

II

Wherever one turns in the Cold War, the inability and unwillingness of the West to find accommodation with revolutionary nationalism has been its undoing. The Korean War cost the United States 144,173 casualties, and the United Nations as a whole, including South Korea, 1,474,269. Communist North Korea committed the first aggression in this unhappy interlude, but it was a war that would not have happened if a more sensible policy had been adopted by General John R. Hodge five years before.

Experts, who knew something of the magnetic appeal of nationalism, could and did foresee the debacle. A year before hostilities, Owen Lattimore stated flatly: "The [South Korean] army cannot be trusted to fight; the people do not trust the government; the government cannot be depended on, and does not depend on itself; it appeals for continued American occupation and protection. If there is to be a civil war, South Korea would not be able to subdue North Korea without a great deal more American help than is now available. North Korea would be able to overrun South Korea without Russian help, unless stopped by American combat troops."

Lattimore's explanation for this prediction, soon to come true, is worth serious study: "In South Korea the Americans organized not a national army, but a constabulary, the backbone of which consists of men who served in the police under the Japanese—the most hated of all who collaborated with the Japanese. There has already been one serious mutiny in this force, and there will be more. Syngman Rhee, a returned exile, is at the head of the political structure. He has completely tainted himself by his wholehearted association with the relatively prosperous, crooked, and pliable Koreans who collaborated with the Japanese. Various enterprises have been 'nationalized,' but have been staffed with personnel in political favor, whose outlook is not one of serving the state but one of building individual power for themselves and eventually converting public property into private property. Land reform has resulted in a large increase in the number of owners of land, but control of the land, through the political, administrative, and tax machinery, is in the hands of politicians whose idea of farming is to be a landlord, not a working proprietor. Peasant dissatisfaction has already been shown in a number of risings; there will be more." [22]

When the war came to an end, there already existed in Korea a resistance movement against Japan, which had ruled the country since 1910 and owned 80 per cent of the wealth. Many of the resistance leaders were communists, but there were not a few non-communists as well. In the province of Cholla Nam Do, the revolutionary committee was headed by a pro-American Christian pastor, and the executive council was fairly conservative. Two days before General Hodge landed to assume command of the Korean occupation, Committees of Preparation for National Independence held an assembly and formed a national government for all Korea. This was exactly what had happened in Indonesia and Indochina. Hodge, however, refused to recognize the Peoples Republic Government; he insisted instead on military rule. The popular force was certainly leftist-inclined, but as E. Grant Meade wrote in his book *American Military Government in Korea,* "If the Peoples Republic exhibited radical tendencies, it only reflected with reasonable accuracy the views of the Korean majority." [23]

But for General Hodge, radicalism was a menace. He settled instead for a government headed by an aged exile, Syngman Rhee, and an assortment of landlords and other conservatives. Since Russia would not accept Rhee and Hodge would not accept the northern radicals, there were soon two Koreas. In the North the Soviets used the revolutionary committees as the kernel of their regime; in the South the sceptre fell to Rhee's band of profiteers.

No one can be sure what might have happened if the United States had collaborated with the original nationalist committees and recognized the Peoples Republic Government. Chances are, however, that the country would have been unified and that the non-communists would have played a far greater, perhaps decisive, role. There are many instances, as we have pointed out, in which communism was relegated to secondary status in the nationalist coalition—Algeria, Ghana, Guinea, India, Ceylon, Burma, and Egypt, to name only a few. A similar result was possible in Korea if there had been an intelligent effort to work with the best nationalists, rather than with the former landlords and collaborators with Japan.

Hodge, it appears, was fearful that war with Russia was imminent. He was determined therefore to have a "reliable" regime in the American zone of occupation. The "reliable" regime, however, turned out to be "unreliable"; it lacked the inner vitality to resist the communists. Though South Korea held more than twice the population of North Korea, twenty-one million against nine million, it could not fight without outside help. It would unquestionably have fallen if the United Nations and the United States had not come to its aid.

Since the war, South Korea has remained weak, chaotic, and undemocratic. Rhee is gone, but a military leader, General Chung Hee Park, rules in his place. After spending $6 billion of American money, and after nearly two decades of "independence," South Korea, in the words of a United Press International dispatch, "appears no nearer stability than it did when it was freed from Japanese domination in 1945, and became an independent nation in May, 1948." [24]

III

The weakness of "our" side seems to be endemic.

Consider Laos, a mountain-segmented country with only two and a half million people, and virtually no exports except smuggled opium. The French ruled it as part of Indochina, Japan seized it during the war as she did most of Southeast Asia, and in due course a nationalist resistance movement, the Pathet Lao, threw guerrillas into the field to harass the Japanese. As in Viet Nam, the nationalists—Laotian Independence Movement—formed their own government after Japan surrendered, and as in Viet Nam the French smashed it. Guerrilla warfare broke out again, this time against France, and by 1953 the Pathet Lao, led by Prince Souphanouvong, had overrun a large part of the country.

At the Geneva Conference of 1954, Laos was granted its sovereignty, with the United Nations assigned the task of supervising elections. Pending the formation of a coalition government to include the communist-oriented Pathet Lao, the neutralists under Souvanna Phouma, and a rightist group, each of these forces was to administer one section of the country. The United States, though it did not sign the Geneva compact, announced that it would do nothing to hinder its execution.

There is serious question as to whether Secretary of State Dulles ever planned to live up to this pledge. In the next six years, the United States pumped $300 million into this primitive land, two-thirds of it in the form of military supplies. "American representatives in Laos," writes Maurice Goldbloom, a strong non-communist who served for several years in the U. S. Foreign Service, "repeatedly succeeded in blocking the creation of the coalition government envisaged in the Geneva agreements. One of the important instruments they used was a threat to terminate American aid. Another may be guessed from the blossoming of Cadillacs and Mercedes—despite the limitation imposed on their utility by the absence of roads." [25] Living standards for the mass of Laotians failed to rise, but that of the favored few evidently pyramided appreciably.

In 1957, neutralist Souvanna Phouma was finally able to form a coalition regime and hold elections. Of the twenty-one seats contested in May, 1958, the Pathet Lao and its ally, the Santiphab (Neutrality) party, won thirteen. This victory, says Goldbloom, "apparently scared both the Americans in Laos and a good many Laotian politicians." Thereupon the United States cut off its aid to the established government, and a military faction headed by Phoumi Nosavan raised the banner of revolt. Secretary Dulles's intense desire to construct a ring around Communist China induced him to abandon the Geneva principles. The rebels were paid from American coffers and given new arms. Fighting from bases in Thailand, the rightists won a momentary victory and established a government under Boun Oum and his "strongman," Phoumi Nosavan. This "pro-American" regime was made up of men whom Keyes Beech of the *Chicago Daily News* labelled "bare-faced crooks." In the spring of 1959, it arrested the leftist leaders, including Prince Souphanouvong, but was unable to hold them. The prisoners escaped to resume guerrilla fighting, this time against the puppet regime of the United States. As usual, the leftists advanced, the government forces retreated steadily.

By the time President Kennedy was inaugurated in 1961, the situation was dire. All the money and guns pumped into rightist hands had proved useless. "Our" side did not seem capable of fighting; had the war continued it would doubtless have been smashed. Kennedy was wise enough to cut his losses. He appealed to the Soviets to re-establish the neutralist government of Souvanna Phouma, and that is what happened. The situation in Laos, as this is written, remains unstable and tenuous. Sporadic fighting between the rival groups continues. What will happen when the Viet Cong wins in Viet Nam is anyone's guess. One thing is certain, however: the conservative "allies," bought and paid for by Washington, were worse than useless. And in their defeat they discredited American policy further.

IV

It would be wrong to say that the United States does not want reform in Asia, or that it has not pressured for it. It tried to induce Chiang Kai-shek to make serious changes. It sought to have Syngman Rhee mend his ways. Time and again American diplomats have applied a combination of threat and cajolery to dictatorial allies in an effort to get them to alter their practices. Nor can it be said that the United States favors colonialism as a policy. It freed the Philippines after the war and gave Puerto Rico a far more favorable status.

But America's best intentions are subverted by its primary allegiance to Anti-Communism. Where it must choose between reform and a dictator who is "Anti-Communist," it chooses the latter, agrees to postpone the former. Where it must choose between the interests of a great ally, as France or Britain, it usually casts its lot with the European power—as in Indochina—as an expedient in "fighting communism."

Thus, with the United States posing no obstacle, Western policy since World War II has been one of military intervention, direct or indirect; support of rightist power elites; frequent defense of landlordism; and thwarting of nationalism. In Malaya, the result was a long, twelve-year guerrilla war. To defeat a nationalist and communist force varying from 1,800 to 12,000 men, Britain had to employ 40,000 of its own troops, 100,000 police and 200,000 home guards. It grouped 500,000 villagers into compounds and spent $120 million a year for "police action." If it were not for the racial division of the country—44 per cent Malay Moslems, 44 per cent Chinese, and 10 per cent Indians—the guerrillas might have won. Dissension between the groups, however, led to the decimation of the communists, and Britain was intelligent enough to grant freedom at the strategic moment. By doing so it cut the ground from under the Red Chinese elements.

In Kenya, Britain had to deploy 50,000 soldiers, police, and home guards against a ragged group of 14,000 Mau Mau. There were no communists here. The Mau Mau were eventually defeated, but the *political* victory went to the rebels. After five years of battle and an expenditure of $150 million, Britain and the white settlers were forced to grant independence to Tanganyika and Uganda, the other two East African states, and Kenya, too, is now free.

In Algeria, the French commanded 500,000 outside troops against only 45,000 Algerian guerrillas, spent $3 million a day, $1 billion a year, but were unable to subdue an infinitely weaker force which, it should be noted, had no common border with any communist country and received only minute outside aid. After seven and a half years, Algeria became independent in 1962, political victor in the contest with colonialism.

A century ago, Britain was able to impose its will on all of India with a mere fifty thousand troops, and six decades ago it pacified China with only twenty thousand men. But since World War II the situation has been reversed. Revolutionary nationalism—with or without the communists—has been able to defeat Western contingents far larger than its own, in one instance after another. There is no power, someone has said, like the power of an idea whose time has come!

Anti-Communism has refused to heed this maxim. It flails blindly with both hands, seldom landing a punch. It has reached a stage where it is unable to recognize even its own friends. It leans so much on conservative forces that when a genuine noncommunist nationalist comes to power it shies away from him, too.

A case in point is Iran, under Mohammed Mossadegh. Mossadegh fell from office because in the critical moment he refused to lean on the communists. Had he done so he might have remained in power. Yet the Central Intelligence Agency overthrew him anyway. It is an interesting story.

The Russian Revolution (Russia and Iran have a common frontier of 1,200 miles) stirred Iran just as it stirred Turkey, China, and other underdeveloped countries. The first unions were formed, a big strike broke out in the oil fields, other strikes and demonstrations shook Iranian society to its foundations. Faced with a threat to its oil production, the British imposed Reza Shah, a military leader and the father of the present Shah, as ruler of the country.

Reza Shah quickly broke the strikes, killed many nationalists, imprisoned others and ruled as an absolute dictator until 1943. He expropriated many feudal lords and appropriated to himself six thousand villages as his own barony. The Shah, however, came to an inglorious end when he misread the signposts of World War II. After France fell, he was sure Germany would win and he made overtures to the Nazis. When the British and Soviets learned of this, they jointly occupied the country in 1941, the north going to the Kremlin, the south to Britain, and Teheran jointly administered.

The British initiated few reforms in their zone, but the Soviets organized the Masses Party, Tudeh, to press for change. Tudeh's agitation among the peasants to withhold rents and insist on land reform fell on willing ears. For a year a communist government in the north, headed by a man named Pishevari, reduced rents, divided estates of absentee owners, and built schools, two colleges, and a health clinic. None of this was startling in itself, but it was in such sharp contrast with what was happening in the British zone that Tudeh gained national support. By the time the British withdrew, and the Russians—under sharp American pressure—removed their troops, the fires of nationalism were burning fiercely throughout Iran.

Despite the revenues from oil, the nation remained backward beyond belief. Eighty per cent of its population was agrarian, almost 25 per cent tribal. According to a United States Point Four official, nine-tenths of the peasants lived at a mere subsistence level, with no buying capacity whatsoever. In Teheran, water ran in open *jubes* along the streets and was used not only for washing and toilet purposes, but for drinking. Of every thousand births, three hundred children died. Fifty per cent of the population suffered from trachoma. Neither the Shah nor Britain had done anything to remedy such conditions; the people were ready for someone who would.

Mohammed Mossadegh, leader of the National Front, appointed by the Iranian Parliament as prime minister in 1951, and clearly non-communist, was entrusted with the task. After he ousted the British, closed their embassy, and took over their oil refineries, Mossadegh was confronted with a momentous problem. The immediate need was to uproot the landlord system and evolve a non-feudal agriculture. Mossadegh decreed a reduction in rents of 20 per cent and the formation of democratic village councils to govern in place of the feudal classes. But these remained dead letters because the state had no power to enforce them. The army and the police (as subsequent events proved) were strongly infiltrated by rightist elements. There were too few roads or other forms of communication. And, unless Mossadegh could sell his oil abroad, he did not have the money to implement his program.

Mossadegh could have appealed to the peasants to seize the land themselves—he informed me during an interview in 1953 that he had contemplated it. But since Tudeh was strong in the villages this would have virtually placed the country in communist hands. He preferred to wait, meanwhile balancing himself between the communist and non-communist forces, always hoping he could work out a *modus vivendi* with the West relative to the oil fields. If he were able to sell eight million tons of oil abroad he would find it possible to build roads, reclaim thousands of acres of land, electrify the country, erect dams, make credits available to the peasants, and continue with the seven-year plan promulgated in 1949.

The British, however, with American support, throttled this design. They successfully instituted a world boycott of Iranian oil. No Western country was willing either to buy it or provide tankers to ship it. Mossedegh was mercilessly squeezed.

When he decided finally on resolute action to smash the conspiring feudal elements who clustered around the new Shah, he confronted a dilemma. On the one side was the Shah, who had made the gesture of distributing to peasants some of the lands taken by his father, but was withal a creature of the feudal aristocracy. On the other side was Tudeh. In the middle were a host of little parties, such as Maleki's third force, the Iranian Party, the religious socialists—but all of them together were inadequate for Mossadegh to lean on. When he expelled the Shah from the country, Tudeh organized large demonstrations in his favor. Yet for him this represented an equal danger, for Tudeh might seize power or become strong enough to make him its vassal. He therefore called on the army to put down his own "supporters." In the turmoil, the army switched sides and not only broke Tudeh but Mossadegh himself.

There is no question today that the U. S. Central Intelligence Agency manipulated the return of the Shah and the ouster of Mossadegh. Andrew Tully, a semi-official chronicler of CIA history, records that "the CIA stage-managed the overthrow of Premier Mohammed Mossadegh, that celebrated compulsive weeper, who had seized Britain's monopolistic oil company and was threatening to do business with the Kremlin." [26] H. Norman Schwartzkopf, a CIA agent who had helped solve the Lindbergh kidnapping case many years before, and was close to Major General Fazlollah Zahedi, "supervised the careful spending of more than ten million of CIA dollars. Mossadegh suddenly lost a great many supporters." [27] Some Iranians, says Tully, got rich in those few days.

The Shah was returned to his throne, and with him General Zahedi as premier. The epilogue to this story, in Tully's words, was that "the American-approved regime stole everything it could lay its hands on, despite the well-meaning but perfunctory efforts of the Shah. The Shah . . . has felt constrained to spend most of the national budget on his 200,000-man army and 50,000-man police force, and although land reform laws have been in operation for more than a decade, by June 1961, the Shah still was the personal proprietor of nearly half his seven hundred crown villages totalling 600,000 acres." [28]

Since 1953, the United States has spent between $1 and $1.5 billion on this country of eighteen million people. Iran, however, is still a long way from being a showcase of democracy. The elections held in September, 1963, received a favorable press in the United States, but they were rigged and undemocratic.

They were held while martial law was in effect, and with candidates hand-picked by the Shah and the secret police (SAVAK).[29] Only 11 per cent of the electorate participated. Tudeh and Mossadegh, each or both of whom would unquestionably have polled large votes, probably majorities, were excluded from the ballot. Few new nations in underdeveloped countries hold democratic elections. In their unstable circumstances they fear the propaganda impact of the middle and upper classes. But the lack of democracy in Iran, as in other rightist countries, stems from an opposite fear—fear of the lower classes.

The Shah claims to have instituted a widescale land reform, but if the example in his own villages is a barometer, it is a highly exaggerated phenomenon. The villages which he inherited from his father were supposed to have been distributed *free* to its lowly inhabitants. Instead, a quarter of them have been sold to the peasants payable in fifteen installments, and about two-thirds, according to the United States Overseas Mission, will eventually "become an endowment to the Crown Prince." [30] The backbone of feudalism, it is fair to say, has not been broken.

The United States can record Iran as a victory for Anti-Communism—the communists were certainly defeated. But as with Greece or Guatemala, the other two "successes" for this policy, one may question whether it is a permanent one. Temporary victories against nationalism in Indonesia, Indochina, Kenya, Madagascar, Tunisia, Morocco, Algeria, Ghana, and Malaya all proved illusory. Nationalism rallied for second and third tries, to carry the day. The same fate may await Iran, for it is still at the mercy of oligarchs—allied with the United States—who command little or no popular support. Next time a sincere nationalist movement rises to power in Iran—and there very likely will be a next time—another non-communist nationalist will have learned from Mossadegh's experience. He will not be so chary about aid from the communist-oriented Tudeh, or leaning on the Soviet Union.

On balance the policy of containment, which has driven the United States into alliance with unwholesome political leaders in Viet Nam, Laos, Korea, and Iran (and in Jordan, Saudi Arabia, Guatemala, Nicaragua, and elsewhere), cannot long be sustained. It runs counter to a demanding history.

VIII

Burma: Case History of a Positive Policy

AFTER TWO decades of Cold War, Americans feel that a military shield is indispensable for security. They are ordinarily unaware of, or unconcerned with, the political corollaries of a militarist policy—the proclivity to lean on conservative and dictatorial allies, the tendency to postpone social reform, the predisposition to the status quo, and the isolation of America from radical nationalism. For ever so long, armaments and intervention have guaranteed Western power. How else—so the question goes—can the communists be held in check or set back? The three "victories" recorded for the Anti-Communist crusade—Greece, Guatemala, Iran—and the stalemates enforced in Berlin and Korea, lend a degree of credibility to this thesis. Despite the far more serious setbacks in China, Indochina, and Cuba, and the fact that *as a policy* Anti-Communism has failed to defend the favorable balance of power for America and the West, there is a glimmer of hope that it might still work. The average citizen believes that a non-militarist policy never has worked anywhere—and cannot.

It is fruitful, therefore, to compare what happened in Indochina, where the policy of Anti-Communism has prevailed since the war, with what happened in Burma, where an opposite route was charted.[1]

Both Indochina and Burma are bounded by China on the north. Both are approximately the same size, though Indochina (when united) had five or six million more people. Both countries have a common heritage of imperialist domination, and both, at the end of the war, had sizeable nationalist movements able momentarily to declare independence. The communists in both countries were influential and represented important leadership segments in the ranks of nationalism. According to the World Almanac of 1948, the Indochinese Communist party had two thousand members, the Burmese Communist Party, four thousand. In all likelihood these are underestimates, but the figures indicate that the Burmese communists were at least as formidable as their counterparts in Indochina.

Yet in Indochina, the combined efforts of France, the United States, hundreds of thousands of local troops, and many billions of dollars of outside help have resulted in a pitful of defeat for Anti-Communism and a glowing victory for Ho Chi-minh's communists; while in Burma a socialist-Buddhist government, which received not one penny or one gun from outside sources, and which commanded an army of no more than fifty thousand men, entirely routed the communist movement.

If anything, the situation in Burma was more propitious for the communists than in Indochina, because Burma suffered far more wartime damage. Half to two-thirds of its productive facilities were destroyed, two and a half million acres of rich riceland were converted into useless jungle, and one-sixth of its thirty thousand villages were reduced to scorched earth. The shipping flotilla, the oil wells, lead mines, port installations, and electrical equipment were wrecked. Under such circumstances, radical solutions should have been more attractive in Burma than in Indochina, but the communists could not capitalize on the situation. They confronted a different *kind* of enemy than did Ho Chi-minh in Indochina.

The early nationalists in Burma were members of the land-owning class, willing to remain under British rule if assured more privileges for their own select group.[2] Beginning in 1935, however, a number of students who called themselves Thakins became the fulcrum of a radical nationalism. Imprisoned by the British, many of the Thakins studied Marxism; a few converted to socialism, others to communism, but all collaborated against the common foe, British imperialism.

Tired of waiting for Britain to implement promises of independence, the Thakins decided to enlist the aid of Japan. At Tokyo they were well received and offered 200 million rupees to form a Burma Independence Army—under Japanese command—to foment insurrection. Japan agreed that after the nationalists had wrested Burma from the Europeans, they would immediately be recognized as a sovereign government. The Thakins promised in return only that Nippon would receive commercial preference and control of the Burma Road. The response to this understanding, according to observers, was enthusiastic and widespread.[3] Men joined the BIA right under the noses of the British administration. But the pledges of Japan, as might have been expected, were worthless. Neither arms nor money was forthcoming; nor did Japan recognize Burmese independence in the areas controlled by BIA. We must wait, she said, for "total victory." Disillusioned, the Thakins turned on their ally and helped Britain reconquer Burma.

The British, let it be said, were intelligent enough to bend with the wind. They did not attack the nationalists or seek to smash them as the French did in Indochina or the Dutch in Indonesia. If they had, they would undoubtedly have driven the socialists, Buddhists, and communists together into an unshakeable unity, probably under the aegis of communist leaders Thakin Soe, Thakin Than Tun, and Thakin Thein Pe. The communist members of the Anti-Fascist People's Freedom League (AFPFL), here as in Indochina were—according to experts—"the best organized and aggressive unit."[4]

Instead, Britain relaxed its colonial yoke. It signed a pact with the Burmese in January, 1947, agreeing to "a free and independent Burma, whether within or without the British Empire." Elections for a constituent assembly were scheduled for the following April. As a quid pro quo for independence, Britain was to be given certain military rights and was promised fair compensation for its properties if nationalized.

To the communists, these two concessions seemed too high a price. They urged the socialists to fight rather than yield, and when the socialists refused, the communists boycotted the April, 1947, elections. AFPFL, nonetheless, won 172 of the 182 seats. It might have consolidated Burma with little further violence, but three months later seven cabinet members, including the nation's undisputed leader, Aung San, head of both the Socialist party and the All-Burma Peasants Association, were assassinated by conservatives.

The process of disintegration, as we shall see, now accelerated to the point where the socialist coalition was soon fighting on five different fronts and ruled only the capitol effectively.

Shortly after the war, a minority group of the Communist party—still affiliated with the AFPFL—had insisted that the only way to achieve independence was through arms. There was no sense, according to these Red Flag Communists, led by Thakin

Soe, in negotiating with London; the only way to gain true independence was to take to the hills for guerrilla action. The Red Flags were outlawed and finally took the violent course—against the AFPFL—they had counseled against Britain.

This defection would have been of little significance if the majority of the communists had not followed suit some time later. This faction, the White Flag Communists, was directed by Thakin Than Tun, who had been the first Secretary-General of the AFPFL and was a powerful influence in the country. Than Tun charged that the government, in its talks with Britain, was "acting as a weapon in the hands of imperialism against the people." He too resorted to guerrilla action against the government. Soon the communists were followed by a majority of the People's Volunteer Organization (White-Band PVO's), the former military arm of the resistance movement. As the state continued to fragment, the powerful Karen and Shan tribesmen, spurred on by more than a hundred secret British agents, joined the avalanche. They demanded full autonomy, and when they were turned down they became the fourth group in the civil war. Finally, as a backwash of the events in China, twelve thousand Kuomintang soldiers pushed across the border into Burma to avoid arrest by Mao Tse-tung. On entering Burma they should have submitted to being disarmed, but they insisted on remaining an intact military force using Burmese soil as a future jumping-off base to re-enter China. The Burmese government obviously could not tolerate such a state of affairs, but it lacked the military power to expel the Chinese while fighting four native enemies.

In the face of this array of difficulties—economic, political, and military—the Burmese socialist-nationalist coalition, under U Nu, Kyaw Nyein, and Ba Swe, worked themselves out of a seemingly impossible situation.

The British withdrawal and the grant of some economic aid from London, it must be conceded, helped the non-communist cause. The communists—both in Burma and Moscow—were unable to wave the flag of anti-imperialism as potently as in Indochina. They continued to declaim that "the real lords of the country's seventeen million depressed and downtrodden inhabitants" were five British firms who "beat all records even in colonial piracy." They argued that Britain would not yield real independence for "loss of control of this country would be a terrible blow to the City." [5] But such propaganda could not be as effective as that of Ho Chi-minh in Indochina, where the French were still emplaced militarily. Yet, the Burmese communists were favored with a near-monopoly of mass support. The trade unions, the large peasant organizations, the youth, and a major portion of the military were under their leadership. On the eve of the civil war, they were able to summon 75,000 peasants to a conference at Pyinmana.

Early in 1948, the socialists were isolated to the capital city, Rangoon, while the rest of the country was in the hands of one or another group of insurgents. The government caught its breath, however, threw up a stopgap military defense, and placed its main reliance on a political-social offensive. The issue was fought with guns to be sure, but primarily it was decided by winning away the people from communist authority.

The communists, slavishly following Mao Tse-tung's practices in China, seized the land of rich and poor alike, divided the acreage by the number of people in the area, and bureaucratically split it into "equal" shares. Some of it was fertile, some poor or wooded, but the insistence on "equal shares" created inequities and discontent which were to lead to serious desertions from the communist cause. "Rich" landowners, many of them peasants who merely had a little more than their neighbors, were some-times harried and murdered. In the Prome area, the communists killed the members of the Land Committees. A decree was issued that no man might own more than one suit and five kyats (one dollar). Even cattle was taken from the peasants and divided on an artificial basis.

The AFPFL government charged that communist methods were a "direct transplantation of other countries' practices without examining whether they are suitable in the peculiar conditions of Burma. If power is seized by armed struggle in Russia and China so must it be seized in Burma; if land is distributed per head in China so must it be distributed in Burma; if People's Courts are established in China so must they be established in Burma. But the result is confusion and disillusion." [6]

Communist tactics made many enemies. Their reforms were unrealistic and bureaucratically administered. The socialist land reform, on the other hand, was based on realities. With civil war raging and with little industry to sustain big scale farming, the socialist-Buddhist alliance contented itself with more modest measures. The debts owed to the chettiyars (money lenders)— far and away the worst peasant grievance—were cancelled outright. Rentals were reduced to only twice the tax, about $1.60 an acre. Hitherto the peasant had had no occupancy rights; he could be moved from one piece of land to another at the will of the landlord. Now a tenancy disposal board was elected by the peasants in each village to guarantee land tenure and assure that no one was shifted to a tract that would not provide him a living. The state loaned millions of dollars to the peasantry for seed, cattle, and other needs. Thirteen million dollars of such loans were abrogated when the regime realized that recovery was difficult.

Revocation of debts, reduction of rents, and land tenure had the same effect on the peasant as formal land-ownership. He was now beholden neither to landlord nor money-lender. He had his own organizations and his own elected land committees. The early socialist palliatives made more sense to him than the mechanical methods of the communists. Furthermore, no peasants had to be killed in implementing the program. It was administered by the villagers themselves rather than by a party.

The peasant, first attracted by the communists, now veered toward the more solid reforms of the socialists. He no longer welcomed communists to his village, no longer fed them, no longer hid them from the advancing government army. Without mass support, the communist effort was hopeless. The rebels could harry the regime, hit and run from shelter in the woods, but they could not take the offensive nor undermine the government.

The Burmese socialists and nationalists soon broke out of encirclement, gained hegemony of the unions and peasant organizations, and reconquered their lost territory. By 1951, there was sufficient stability in Burma to hold an election for parliament. AFPFL won 135 out of 233 seats. It was strong enough so that it could permit the Workers and Peasant party to participate in the voting though everyone knew it was little more than a communist front. A year later Burma promulgated its eight-year Pyidawtha Plan for moderate industrialization and large scale irrigation. To give the peasants an incentive, the state offered free land, loans for seed and cattle, plus tractors and other machinery, when available, to any group that would form a "mutual aid team." These teams of four or five families were granted a few hundred acres of land which they were to work in common but own separately.

Burma today is a long way from having solved its problems. Political democracy has been hindered twice when General Ne Win seized the reins of government. But these are the normal problems of most underdeveloped countries. The significant fact is that the communists were set back *without* intervention, and without major reliance on guns. In this instance, "social deterrence" was infinitely more effective than "military deterrence."

This lesson, though unique in postwar developments, ought not to be lost. The Burmese saga was a setback not only for communism but a repudiation as well of the axioms on which Anti-Communism rests. It proved again that political philosophies and ideas cannot be contained today by military force. They can only be challenged by a superior social program. The reliance on a military shield as the primary instrument of American policy not only is unavailing, but as Indochina proves one way and Burma the other, actually helps communism. It achieves the opposite of what it intends.

IX

Anti-Democracy at Home

THE FAILURE of Anti-Communism on the domestic scene is a corollary of its failure as a strategy in foreign affairs. Theoretically, our purpose overseas is to win "freedom for the people and independence for the Government." [1] But in practice, an emphasis on negative Anti-Communism shifts policy toward defense of the status quo and postponement of measures for social change. Similarly, though our overall goal is to preserve the democratic values associated with our heritage, the military posture and the inevitable reliance on what the late John Foster Dulles called "brinkmanship," subvert the individualist élan which is the mainspring of democracy.

Once the decision was made that we could not co-exist with Russia, that no matter how long the conflict endures, we had to "win," it became necessary to impose on America a sense of national discipline. "To fight," wrote Woodrow Wilson, "you must be brutal and ruthless, and the spirit of ruthless brutality will enter into every fibre of our national life, infecting Congress, the courts, the policeman on the beat, the man on the street. Conformity would be the only virtue and every man who refused to conform would have to pay the penalty." [2]

We are not yet, and we can only hope we shall never be, fighting a hot war. The full measure of conformity that Wilson predicted has therefore not overtaken us. But we veer in that direction. We are at the halfway house. In actual war we would be living in a garrison state, with the government dominating every aspect of our behavior far more stringently than even in World War II. But since we are only in a "half-war," a Cold War, we stand midpoint between the values of individualism and those of the garrison state, continuing to manifest characteristics of the former, but yielding to the demands of the latter.

In this Cold War the central government inevitably gains more power over its citizens. Countervailing checks and balances by the people are reduced, and "participative" democracy is

143

subtly transformed into "manipulative" democracy. Citizens are remade in the image of foreign policy—in the image, that is, of militarism. "From a mania to make ourselves internally secure and safe from the probing of foreign espionage agents," says former Senator Harry Cain, "we have wound up refusing and afraid to exchange information and views among ourselves. As the web of internal security is drawn tighter and closer, a tendency develops for the government and the people to move further and further apart. Each becomes more skeptical about the other's motives." [3]

"An army," writes Brigadier General C. T. Lanham, "by its very structure is the antithesis of everything held dear by a democratic community. It is authoritarian." [4] And that authoritarian spirit inevitably permeates an anxious society. Just as the army private must unhesitatingly heed the command of his lieutenant, so the citizen is expected in the present security-conscious society to rally behind his government with little or no question. The civilian in the "rear," like the soldier at the "front," must be ready to obey—to conform.

The curbing of dissent and individualism is therefore neither an accidental nor an incidental feature of modern America, but a *sina qua non* of Anti-Communist strategy. When the late Senator Joseph McCarthy was censured by the Senate on December 2, 1954, liberal Americans sighed in relief, expecting a return to the normalcy of democratic tradition. But it did not happen. The improvement was only partial, because McCarthyism, inept and excessive though it was, nevertheless was meat and marrow of the same need to suppress dissent that the Anti-Communist course dictates. Senator McCarthy was censured not because of his basic purpose, but because of the clumsy and divisive manner he used to implement it. In the decade since, the various suppressive methods and institutions—investigating committees of Congress, loyalty oaths, security checks, limitations of dissent—have not only survived (though in less virulent form), but have gradually been accepted as part of the "American way of life."

Never in American history has there been so long a period of suppression. It is more sophisticated, less violent than in other eras, but also more wide-ranging and insistent. There has been nothing like it, says Harvard professor Zechariah Chafee, "since the hysteria over the Popish Plot in England around

1680." [5] The number of people who have been jailed for communist views has been small; the number who have lost jobs because of blacklisting practices is no more than a few thousand. America has no concentration camps and its FBI is far from a Gestapo, as some leftists have insisted. So many basic traditions are being eroded, however, that the groundwork is laid for far more serious repressions. Not a few basic precepts are today widely breached. Anti-Communism, though it pays ceaseless obeisance to the virtues of freedom, has made us less, rather than more, free.

I

It is axiomatic that any state must have the power to defend itself from internal revolt. In a democratic and affluent society, this problem seldom arises since society is stable and feels secure. But in moments of anxiety, government balances delicately between the merits of freedom and the need for discipline. During World War II, for instance, workers lost the freedom to change jobs; they were subject to manpower controls. Employers lost the freedom to invest where they pleased; they were subject to allocation of materials and other checks. Where there are "clear and present dangers"—as in war—the state tends to curb individual prerogative. All this is to be expected. But there are periods in the life of a nation when the peril is small but fear exaggerates it out of all proportion. It multiplies it many times over. What is so remarkable about the present period is the extent of that fear and the extent of that exaggeration. Never has the United States been so rich, so exempt from the danger of revolution or militant strikes, yet so morbidly apprehensive for its future.

It is interesting to compare the present era with other moments of national anxiety, to see how we are repeating—and increasing—past errors.

The first wave of suppression in American history occurred during the Napoleonic wars at the end of the eighteenth century. French ships roamed the Atlantic and the Caribbean, seizing American vessels as they traveled to and from British ports. Americans were concerned. Was this a prelude to invasion of the United States by its former ally, France? Did Napoleon's ambitions stretch so far that he intended to recapture old French colonies in the Western Hemisphere? Federalists in Congress urged a declaration of war against France to forestall this possibility. Washington was called back to command the army. President John Adams, though he resisted the pressure for military action, approved two measures for suppressing freedom—the Alien and Sedition Acts. Under the former he was authorized to expel or imprison not only outright French agents, but Irishmen who in their hatred of Britain sympathized with France. Under the latter—the Sedition Act—courts could impose fines and imprisonment on those who combined to oppose a government measure, who intimidated a United States officer, or who published anything that might bring "disrepute" on the government. The Alien Act was never enforced, but the Sedition Act resulted in innumerable injustices. Newspapers were closed down, Republican editors jailed, and those who attended meetings where speakers dissented from government policy were brought to trial. Alexander Hamilton pleaded with his countrymen: "Let us not establish a tyranny." [6] Jefferson urged defiance of both laws. The legislatures of Kentucky and Virginia passed resolutions condemning the bills. The Acts, which had a two-year limitation period, were not renewed when Jefferson became President.

In his inaugural address, the third President and author of the Declaration of Independence stated what most people have since accepted as the American credo: "If there be any among us who wish to dissolve this union, or change its republican form, let them stand undisturbed, as monuments of the safety with which error of opinion may be tolerated where reason is left free to combat it." [7] Dissent should be untrammeled in a democracy, since reason is "free to combat it."

During the Civil War, suppression took the form of a Conspiracy Act, which provided six-year terms for any two or more people who conspired to forcefully "overthrow, put down, or to destroy" the government. During World War I, in 1917, an Espionage Act was passed which punished not only spies, but those who by speech or writing "interfered" with the recruitment of soldiers. Under its strictures, socialist leader Eugene V. Debs and others were sent to jail for preaching against the war. It is worth noting that opposition to hostilities was much greater in

1917 than during World War II. Not only socialists and members of the Industrial Workers of the World condemned American participation, but many citizens of German descent and various foreign-born groups as well. The government responded with arrests, deportations, and raids that were considerably more widespread than similar activities during World War II. Mobs of super-patriots smashed windows, broke into the homes of dissenters, and beat them.

The World War I wave of coercion, however, receded rapidly in the 1920's. Liberals and not a few conservatives came to the defense of traditional freedom. Governor Alfred E. Smith pardoned communist leaders, including Benjamin Gitlow, who had been convicted by the courts. Justices Holmes and Brandeis made history with their opinion—a minority at the time, but soon to become the majority view—that speech was free from prosecution so long as it did not "create a clear and present danger." The New York Lusk Bills, strikingly similar to present loyalty oaths and Congressional investigations, were repealed under Governor Smith's prodding. Smith's veto of one of these measures, which called for a committee of probers authorized to question those with revolutionary ideas, is worth repeating in the 1960's: "There is no just cause for providing any different methods for enforcing the criminal anarchy statute from that employed in enforcing the other penal laws of the State—through the agencies of the grand jury, the magistrate and the district attornies of the respective counties of the State. . . . The traditional abhorrence of a free people for all kinds of spies and secret police is valid and justified and calls for the disapproval of the measure." [8] In the relatively placid 1920's, such views represented majority opinion.

During the 1930's, when there were innumerable sitdown strikes, hundreds of unemployment demonstrations, two veterans marches on Washington, and a marked growth in the membership of the Communist party, civil liberties were actually strengthened. The Supreme Court rescinded one suppression of freedom after another: a Negro communist convicted in Georgia under an incitement to insurrection statute; a California citizen who raised a red flag with hammer and sickle; a communist speaker in Oregon; and those who were jailed for peaceful picketing. At the height of the depression, in 1932, many bills were introduced in Congress to control communism. Representative Fiorello LaGuardia commented during the debate that the next thing would be a bill to authorize witchhunting. None of the bills passed.

During World War II, despite the passage of the Smith Act in 1940 and the sedition trial of Trotskyist leaders in Minneapolis, the general tone was milder than in 1917. There were no wholesale arrests, no mob violence, no closing of radical newspapers. Not the least reason for this was the fact that communists and other radicals supported America's war effort. But, by and large, the values of democracy were adjudged important enough not to be overridden by wartime demands for national unity.

It is all the more striking, therefore, that today—when there is so little challenge from the left—there should be so continuing a state of repression. There are few militant strikes; the trade union movement stands with the government. Never has there been less pressure from radicalism. Not even a Populist or Greenback party threatens the establishment. There can be no excuse for any form of suppression, except an attenuated and phobic fear. "Reading what everybody now agrees about the panic-stricken alarmists of 1920, I wonder," says Zechariah Chafee, "what will be said thirty-five years from now about the alarmists of 1950-55." [9]

II

The assault against democratic practice has run parallel to apprehensions about communism. In 1940, shortly after Stalin made his famous pact with Hitler, Congress enacted the first sedition bill since 1798. The Smith Act made it a crime to *advocate* the overthrow of the government by force—whether accompanied by overt action or not. Before that act, the government had had to prove an accused seditionist guilty of *doing* something—organizing, smuggling arms, or conspiring to foment revolt. Writing or speaking in favor of revolution was immune to prosecution. But under the Smith Act, ideas themselves, if adjudged subversive, made the believer subject to a prison term. Further, mere membership in a circumscribed organization became a punishable crime. Thus for the first time, as John Lord O'Brian—adviser to six federal administrations—points out, we "imported into our law the alien doctrine of guilt by association, which up to this time had been regarded as abhorrent and which had never been recognized either by the courts or by the Department of Justice, even during the perils and excitements of the First World War." [10] A rank-and-file member of a subversive group was deemed guilty not for what he himself did or said, but because he associated with *others* who were "dangerous."

The Smith Act did not result in many imprisonments. Eighteen Trotskyists were sent to jail in 1944, and by the end of 1958 one hundred and eight communists had been convicted. Half of these convictions were later reversed by the Supreme Court, which imposed rules making it extremely difficult to prosecute for mere membership in the Communist party. Only one man, Junius Scales, went to jail—later to be freed by President Kennedy. (During the short period of World War I, 1,956 persons were prosecuted and 877 were found guilty.) All in all, therefore, the Smith Act caught few people in its net. Its effect, however, was more insidious, for like the proverbial pebble dropped in water, the doctrine of guilt by association rippled over a much wider area.

The next crisis with communism—Korea—saw the passage of another suppressive law, the Internal Security Act (McCarran) Act. President Truman vetoed it on the grounds "it would put the United States into the thought-control business. It could give government officials vast powers to harass all of our citizens in the exercise of their rights of free speech." [11] Congress, however, was in no mood for this warning; it overrode Truman's veto. The McCarran Act provided for registration with the Attorney General of communist, "communist-front," and "communist-infiltrated" organizations. Such organizations were required to turn over membership lists to the government and to label their written material "communist." Members were prohibited from applying for passports or holding posts with a trade union or in a defense industry. If they were non-citizens they could be deported, and if recently naturalized, de-naturalized. The penalties for non-registration were so stringent—$10,000 in fines and five years in prison for *each day* that a "subversive" leader failed to register his movement—that they can only be explained by the thesis of hysteria.

Under the McCarran Act the Attorney General was empowered, in times of emergency, to detain any person against whom "there is reasonable ground to believe that such person *probably* will engage in or *probably* will conspire with others to engage in acts of espionage or sabotage." (My italics.) Detention camps were provided to house the detainees. This section has never been used, but it is remarkable in its scope. It gives the government and the Federal Bureau of Investigation the right to hold anyone it suspects without trial or any other judicial recourse. J. Edgar Hoover was reported in 1950 as saying that he was prepared to arrest twelve thousand alleged enemy agents as soon as war broke out. Permitting a policeman, no matter how competent or dedicated, to decide who is or who is not a *probable* enemy agent is a dangerous precedent.

The McCarran Act called for a board of five members to hear petitions from the Attorney General designating an organization as subversive. In the first five years, the Department of Justice filed such claims against fourteen "communist-front" organizations. Tens of thousands of pages of testimony were heard. Subsequently there were other hearings. But fourteen years after the Act was passed, not a single organization has yet registered, including the Communist party. In 1963, the United States Court of Appeals reversed the Subversive Activities Control Board in requiring the defunct Labor Youth League and the National Council of Soviet-American Friendship to register as "communist-fronts."

By themselves, therefore, neither the Smith Act nor the McCarran Act have punished many "subversives." But they have provided a machinery for future use, and, more important, they have established a climate for extra-legal suppression of citizens' rights. The so-called "Attorney General's List" of subversive organizations has become a bible for industrialists checking on the "loyalty" of employees, for rightist groups who pillory reputations, and for newspapers. The Attorney General's list is, in effect, an unproven charge by a prosecutor that such and such an organization is subversive. It is not proof per se. Yet it is accepted as such by employers and others who use it. The result is that a man who is a member of a group on the list must prove his innocence—rather than the other way around.

The obvious aim of the McCarran Act was to make leftist

groups illegal *de facto* if not *de jure*, for it made their operations next to impossible. (There was no need for any laws dealing with foreign agents, since there already existed a Foreign Agents Registration Act of 1938 and a law sponsored by Representative Jerry Voorhis in 1940 that applied to organizations under the control of a foreign nation.) Who would subscribe to a publication which was prominently marked "communist?" Who would join a questionable group if his name might be published by the Subversive Activities Control Board, subjecting him to almost certain discharge from his job?

Another, though lesser, harassment was the 1947 Taft-Hartley law requirement that union officers sign affidavits disclaiming membership in the Communist party or other "subversive" organizations. Failure to do so deprived a union headed by such officers of the facilities of the National Labor Relations Board. For the most part, this legislation, too, has resulted in few punishments—less than a dozen persons, in fact, have served prison terms for "conspiring" to evade this section of the law— but it has added to the tense climate within the unions and further inhibited dissent.

III

With the repressive laws there evolved a new practice, virtually a trial by legislative committee.

Under the American system, the only body that can punish a citizen in the final analysis is a court of law. Here an accused has the strongest protection: he must be proven guilty beyond reasonable doubt—he need not prove his own innocence; he is permitted to confront his accusers and to cross-examine witnesses; he can ask for a trial by his peers. Congressional committees, on the other hand, have a different function. Their sole purpose is to hear expert testimony on pending legislation. Since it would be impossible for Congress, sitting as a body of the whole, to evaluate the twenty thousand bills that come before it each session, it assigns the task to forty or so standing committees and many sub-committees. These committees conduct hearings to hear opinions by expert witnesses so as to help them endorse, reject, or amend proposed bills.

But beginning with the House Committee on Un-American Activities (usually referred to as HUAC) in 1938, a number of legislative committees—including the Senate Internal Security Subcommittee and the Government Operations Committee, as well as HUAC—have deliberately used their facilities as an instrument for punishment. Hiding behind Congressional immunity, such committees have stigmatized alleged subversives to the point where they have lost their jobs and their standing in the community. The proponents of these tactics argue that communists are ipso facto agents of a foreign power, and that it is impossible to convict most of them in a court of law. Hence extralegal measures are permissable. Even if this theory were valid, however, it does not explain why so many ex-communists, and so many radicals of different persuasion—non-communists—have been subjected to the same treatment. Nor why trade unionists like James R. Hoffa of the Teamsters have fallen prey to the practice. Once an anxious nation accepted the HUAC doctrine insofar as the communists were concerned, it was inevitable that other unpopular figures would be caught in the same abortion of the judicial process.

The Congressional committees have effectively circumvented safeguards written into the constitution and considered part of the American tradition. They have harmed few communist leaders, because such men are seldom called on to testify, and most of them are not employed by private entrepreneurs—their jobs are not in jeopardy. But the ex-communist or the communist sympathizer has been hurt frequently, even though he has violated not a single law. The committees do him serious damage merely by calling on him to testify. If he admits he is still a leftist, he is almost certain to be fired from his post. Dozens of writers, actors, and factory workers have been discharged after sessions before HUAC. Many had long since quit the Communist party, but they preferred to take the Fifth Amendment of the Constitution, against self-incrimination, because to admit previous membership imposed on them the necessity of naming former associates. The courts have held that once a witness answers one question in a particular area he must answer all others on the same subject. If the witness admits he was a communist in 1928, but quit in 1929, he must still, if asked, provide the names of communists he knew in 1928. The witness who wants to avoid being an informer thus suffers the fate of being called a "Fifth Amendment Communist," with all the attendant reprisals in jobs and status. Congress insists that witnesses before HUAC are not really on trial because they are subject to no prison term if they tell the truth. Yet the loss of a job or of reputation, without trial, is certainly a deprivation of "life, liberty, and the pursuit of happiness."

Democratic tradition is subverted further. The witness is not told what the "charges" are against him. His accuser is faceless, usually an FBI agent, and he is given neither the privilege of preparing an adequate defense nor of cross-examination.

The spy system is pernicious because it gives the police and the FBI an opportunity to recruit men who might otherwise be punished themselves. Thus a foreign-born ex-communist may be threatened with deportation unless he testifies against former associates. One witness, after testifying before HUAC in 1938 that union leader Harry Bridges was a member of the Communist party, signed a statement that he "had committed a number of crimes which came to the knowledge of the Immigration Authorities," shipping companies, and police, and "was induced by these people to give false testimony under the threat that proceedings would otherwise be taken against me." [12] To save himself, the spy frequently lies—or exaggerates. Yet reliance on spies by United States agencies has reached such proportions that, according to former FBI agent Jack Levine in the *Nation* of October 20, 1962, "today, the FBI has nearly 1,500 informants in the Communist Party—a ratio of one informant for every 5.7 members."

Information given to HUAC and its cousin committees is therefore frequently unreliable, un-checked, and un-edited. But the committees have permitted the material to be used for wide-scale private repression. HUAC admitted in 1948 that it had dossiers on 300,000 citizens. [13] A year later the index had grown to one million. The files are not kept secret, for in the ten years from 1949 to 1959 the Committee furnished material on sixty thousand individuals and twelve thousand organizations to inquiring employers. In addition, HUAC published a "Cumulative Index" and supplement, listing some 45,000 individuals and thousands of organizations mentioned in its hearings. [14] This has been a handy reference for blacklisters and has cast a pall over many would-be dissenters. It has strengthened the mood of quiescence and conformity. Before anyone joins even so innocent an organization as the American Civil Liberties Union, he may ask himself whether it is on the proscribed list—or if there is a remote chance it might be someday. Martin Dies, first chairman of HUAC, counselled his fellow Americans to "never participate in anything in the future without consulting the American Legion or your local Chamber of Commerce." Dies's concept of a "dangerous" organization—and this applied to most of his successors as well—was anything as radical as the New Deal. The New Dealers, he said, were "left wingers and radicals who do not believe in our system of free enterprise." They were stooges for the Kremlin: "Stalin baited the hook with a 'progressive' worm, and the New Deal suckers swallowed the bait, hook, line and sinker." [15]

The extent to which America has accepted "legislative trials" is indicated by the decline of opposition to HUAC. When the Committee was first formed in 1938, its chairman asked only for a temporary mandate. He promised to finish his probe of subversive propaganda in a few months, and presumably go out of business. The notion that it was permissible to question citizens as to their political views was averse to American doctrine and had to be presented carefully. When HUAC was promoted to a permanent standing committee in 1945, it barely received majority passage, 207 to 186. But in 1963, when twenty representatives rallied around Congressman James Roosevelt to vote against appropriations for HUAC, the result was considered a great step forward; the previous try a few years before mustered only six votes.

IV

Not only Congress, but the Executive branch of government has vitiated accepted tradition in recent years. Article I, Section 8, of the Constitution gives Congress alone the right to declare war. The President is Commander-in-Chief of the armed forces, but his power is restricted by the provision that Congress must declare actual hostilities. This "check and balance," too, is being circumvented.

President Truman did not bother in 1950 to seek prior approval when he sent troops into Korea. Though it produced four times as many casualties as the Revolutionary War, the War of 1812, the Mexican War, and the Spanish-American War combined, Korea was classed as a "police action." In 1955, Congress passed a resolution giving the President a blank check for the "securing and protection of such related positions and territories of that area [the Pacific] now in friendly hands and the taking of such other measures as he judges to be required or appropriate in assuring the defense of Formosa and of the Pescadores." [16] The President was empowered to make war in the Pacific without consulting Congress or the people. By a vote of 409 to 3 in the House and 85 to 3 in the Senate, Congress abdicated its authority.

It is a natural outgrowth of the thesis of Anti-Communism that the President must have the flexible authority to *threaten* war when he sees fit. The country can no longer wait for a national discussion in Congress or the delaying action of a present-day Senator La Follette. The argument is made that there is no time, missiles and planes are too fast, the nation may be partially or totally destroyed before a Congressional decision is forthcoming. These might be valid objections under the circumstance of all-out attack. But there is adequate time for a full-airing by Congress where *limited* military action is involved. There could have been such a discussion over Korea; it would have delayed matters only a few days at most. There could have been such a discussion over the sending of military "advisors" to Viet Nam and over the 1962 threat to send military forces into Cuba. Chances are that in all three situations the President would have received authorization and would have been able to mobilize public opinion. That no effort was made to do so indicates how far the area of decision is moving away from the control of America's citizenry.

Equally if not more ominous for the democratic process has been a growth of executive secrecy, the withholding of facts from the public, and outright lying. The public is manipulated, not informed, and government by consent of the governed is in danger of becoming a Fourth of July rhetoric. Democracy is impossible without a knowledgeable citizenry capable of weighing the facts. In other peacetime periods, the people have had access to most pertinent information. There was little mania for secrecy. But fear of communist spies reached such proportions after

World War II that tens of thousands of documents, many totally innocuous, were classed "confidential," "secret," or "top secret"— and made unavailable to the people. The Atomic Energy Act of 1946 provided for secrecy concerning data relating to fission and atomic energy. President Eisenhower's Order 10501 of November, 1953, gave seven governmental agencies unrestricted right to classify their documents, and seventeen others power to do so if approved by their directors. According to Walter Millis, "Nearly everyone who has examined the subject has agreed with the Defense Department's own Committee on Classified Information (under Charles A. Coolidge) that there is a tremendous over-classification of documents. But in spite of elaborate regulations for restraint and declassification no one seems yet to have discovered an adequate means for controlling the process." [17]

On the one hand, the government insists it cannot give vital and decisive information to the public; on the other, it urges the public to accept the evaluations of the President and the Secretary of Defense without question because "they have the information." Steuart Pittman, Assistant Secretary of Defense for Civil Defense, warned citizens on June 29, 1962, not to heed the advice of "individuals with scientific background" when they decry fallout shelters, because the President "has taken an oath to do everything he can to protect the American people." [18] On such a premise it is wrong to question the President's judgment on anything.

Secrecy has become a major roadblock to science. The House Special Subcommittee on Government Information noted in 1958 that "the Federal government has mired the American scientist in a swamp of secrecy." It blamed "the nation's loss in the first lap in the race into space" in large measure on the classification of scientific information. Seventeen Nobel Prize winners made the same charge the following year. Dr. H. Bentley Glass, professor of biology at Johns Hopkins, says that at a meeting at Pugwash on the dangers of chemical and biological warfare "no chemists or biologists who had been at all recently associated with such activities could be found to participate (since they could not divulge 'classified' information). The most personally informed scientists in attendance had been dissociated from such work for no less than twelve years." The consequence of the trend to secrecy, commented Dr. Glass, "is that representatives of the military services can make almost any claims they wish without fear of contradiction." [19]

Another break with American tradition has been the establishment of a Central Intelligence Agency, whose budget and activities are in no way subject to popular scrutiny. Even such bodies as the Federal Bureau of Investigation must submit budgets and make reports that are available to newspapers and interested citizens. But the CIA's budget is a secret not only from the people, but from all but a select few members of Congress as well. Its activities are hidden from public purview even though it is a highly important factor in foreign policy; it not only evaluates intelligence information, but subsidizes such activities as sabotage, guerrilla attack, and secret police activity (as in South Viet Nam), which can bring the nation to the brink of war at any time. The CIA's U-2 flights over the Soviet Union were used by Khrushchev as a basis for refusing to hold summit meetings with President Eisenhower.

The CIA, as already related, was deeply involved in the coups in Iran in 1953 and in Guatemala in 1954. CIA agents, according to Stewart Alsop in the *Saturday Evening Post,* were the guiding spirits in "commando-type guerrilla raids on the mainland [of China] . . . in battalion strength." [20] The CIA has been behind the scenes in the fighting in Laos, in subsidizing thousands of Chiang Kai-shek's troops illegally stationed in North Burma, and, of course, in the Bay of Pigs invasion of Cuba in 1961.

All these acts, and many others, involve foreign policy. Presumably they are subject to presidential controls. But when an agency becomes so far-flung and powerful, and when there is no counter-check on its activities, it can flaunt executive commands. Before the Bay of Pigs, for instance, President Kennedy ordered the CIA to remove former followers of Batista from leadership in the exile forces; the order, however, was disregarded.

The CIA is reputed to have between fifteen and forty thousand employees on its staff, and to spend between $400 and $700 million a year (one estimate is $3 to $4 billion).[21] It is the only agency in the history of the United States whose budget is *secret.* The American people are not told how much is involved or how it is spent.

In addition to *not* informing the people of vital facts, the Executive has gone one step further, *mis*-informing. During the

1962 crisis over Russian missiles in Cuba, the Defense Department deliberately released a false story so that the Soviets would not know America's plans. In defending such a policy, Assistant Defense Secretary Arthur Sylvester said: "I think the inherent right of the government to lie to save itself when faced with nuclear disaster is basic." [22] President Kennedy never repudiated this statement. When newsmen accused Sylvester of managing the news, he conceded that government has "no continuing right" to lie, but that it must do whatever is necessary when nuclear war impends. "Information," he says, "is power. In the beginning was the word. It is more powerful than the bomb and the gun." That is undoubtedly true. But what happens to "government by consent of the governed" if the government can withhold some facts from the public and lie about others? How can the people make an objective determination on key issues such as nuclear testing, disarmament, or war and peace, if they are deprived of information and deliberately misled? Democracy degenerates from a "participative" democracy to a "manipulative" one. The people become pawns in a game being played by their "betters."

V

Other Executive departures from the democratic process— again, for the first time in peacetime history—are the loyalty and security programs. Beginning in 1942, the War Department urged the "discharge of subversives from private plants of importance to Army procurement." [23] The "security officer" became a familiar figure in factories across the nation. These procedures, however, were mild compared to what was to happen after the war. The Atomic Energy Act of 1946 required a rigorous screening of employees for "character, associations and loyalty." A year later, President Truman propounded a loyalty program for *all* people in the federal employ. In the first five years thereafter, the FBI, according to J. Edgar Hoover, processed four million applications for government jobs.[24] (By now the number must be astronomical.)

Soon there was a cascade of measures to check the "loyalty" not only of federal employees, but of those in federal housing projects or in private industry. A million tenants in government-sponsored homes had to sign loyalty oaths that they were not communists.[25] Some were evicted for failing to comply, or because they had at one time been "associated" with communists. How a tenant in a government housing unit can hinder national security because of his beliefs has never been explained. It was manifestly an effort to instill conformity. Lieutenant Milo J. Radulovich, whose own loyalty was considered impeccable, was discharged from the Air Force Reserve because his father read a Slavic-language newspaper which was pro-communist, and because his sister associated with "communist-fronts." [26] A policeman in New York was dismissed because he signed a petition for a communist candidate for city council. A Magnuson Act was passed providing that merchant seamen and many longshoremen must be "cleared" for "security." State and local governments took over where the federal government left off. Hundreds of thousands of teachers, professors, and other employees were required to sign oaths that they were not communists or subversives. In Indiana, boxers and wrestlers had to sign loyalty affidavits before they could fight or wrestle.[27] Many, if not most, Americans today take it for granted that a communist or a "fellow-traveler" has no right to teach, to act in a drama, to work in a factory or in the post office.

VI

In recent years there has been a mitigation of the worst evils of the 1950's. A series of Supreme Court rulings has cut the ground from under many prosecutions. Denials of passports to ex-communists have ended. The loyalty and security programs were administered more sensibly under President Kennedy than under his two postwar predecessors. The accused are permitted to confront their accusers and to cross-examine them. This is admitted progress. But it is now an established feature of the "American way" that beliefs and associations are permissable subjects for investigation. As Walter Millis summarizes: "The examination into belief, self-incrimination, punishment for associations became more acceptable as the system was modified to ensure that these sanctions would be applied only against communist believers. . . ." [28]

In two decades, the fears of communism have subtly transformed themselves—as Justice William O. Douglas notes—into "fears of the unorthodox." Discussion and dissent, particularly on foreign affairs and militarism, are muted. "We are passing through momentous times," says Douglas, "where no debate takes place even on crucial issues. Laos is certainly more dangerous to all of us than the Missouri Compromise was to our ancestors. Yet while the Missouri Compromise was thoroughly discussed in and out of Congress and up and down the Nation, no debate on Laos has been held. Why has silence overtaken us? Why has the pattern of no discussion reached into atomic testing, disarmament, Berlin, and other issues that involve the problems of survival or extinction? Is foreign policy—the key to life and death for all forms of life in this nuclear age—beyond the bounds of debate?" [29]

The subsoil of democracy—discussion—has become salinized as a result of the "campaign against communism." Pressures to conform have become so great that many dissenters limit their criticism. By a subtle process, the individualistic élan has been subverted to a considerable extent by mass conformity. It is beside the point to say that many of these things have happened before. They have never happened for so long a period, and with so little opposition.

Alexander Hamilton, writing in 1788, foresaw the danger of overemphasizing "security." "To be more safe," he wrote, "[the nations] at length become willing to run the risk of being less free." [30] The pressing demands of a worldwide policy of Anti-Communism today place us precisely in this position.

X

Anti-Communism Hardens Communism

WE HAVE emphasized thus far the failure of Anti-Communism to win the allegiance of radical nationalism abroad and its negative effects on American democracy at home. But how has it fared against communism itself? What has been its impact, since 1917, on its adversary?

The United States, like all other powers, obviously prefers to deal with governments that are most tractable and least hostile. It is only natural that we help those regimes and those forces within other nations whose interests run parallel to ours or who are, to put it another way, less unfavorable. Though our statesmen would deny "interfering in the internal affairs of another nation," foreign policy actually is a constant interference, at least of an indirect nature. If we impose a quota on butter imports, we are "interfering" in the internal life of Denmark, which exports butter, and affecting the popularity and power of its government. If we make a long-term loan to a Tory regime in Britain which helps to stabilize its economy, we are improving the electoral chances of the Tories *vis à vis* the Labor party. If we send arms to a Spanish dictator, we are strengthening his hand against a possible popular revolt. Conversely, if we withhold aid, cut off loans, increase tariffs, we affect, to some extent, the position both of governing and opposition groups. In itself there is nothing venal about this. It is the normal course of diplomacy. It becomes sinister or useless only when tied to false objectives.

In our relationship with Soviet Russia, then, just as in our relationship with non-communist nations, we and our allies have had many chances to influence its internal life. What we did or did not do was bound, wittingly or unwittingly, to favor one group in the communist world against others. And it is the ultimate irony of Anti-Communism—added to its other miscalculations—that it has helped strengthen those features and those forces of communism that Americans like least, while weakening those that might have drawn West and East closer together.

A policy other than military intervention, in 1918-1920, might have prevented the freeze between East and West and resulted in a more mellow form of communism. An approach to the Soviet Union other than isolation in the 1920's might have short-circuited the most totalitarian form of communism, Stalinism.

Now we are offered still another opportunity. The ideological conflict between Russia and China is the most serious in communism's history. Anna Louise Strong, who publishes an English-language newsletter from Red China, compares the present dispute with that between Stalin and Trotsky, and the earlier one between the Second and Third Internationals. She calls it the third of Marxism's Three Great Debates, and hints that, as in the former instances, it will end in a definitive break. How the United States affects, and is affected by, this disagreement will have wide ramifications.

I

The single image most Americans have of communism is that of the Stalinist monolith which prohibited all dissent and perpetrated so many brutal repressions against real or imagined opponents. Communism seems to most Americans to be a fixed and invariable force. Yet, it is undeniable that the quarrels of communism have been bitter, its path faction-ridden, and its final form uncertain. Its evolution has been like a fishing line—somewhat loose at first, tightening through the 1920's, drawn taut for more than two decades, and now becoming loose once more.

Ten days after Lenin and Trotsky came to power in 1917, they were challenged by Rykov, Nogin, Miliutin, Shliapnikov, and other old Bolsheviks who insisted on a "Socialist Government of all the Soviet Parties"—including the Mensheviks and the two segments of the Social Revolutionaries. The dissenters opposed an all-Bolshevik government, urging instead that Lenin share power with other radical forces. At the initiative of the railway workers, negotiations were actually undertaken with these rivals, but they failed to bring an accord. Eleven of the fifteen People's Commissars and five party leaders, including Zinoviev and Kamenev, resigned their posts, accusing Lenin of "desiring at all costs a purely Bolshevik Government without counting the number of worker and soldier victims it may cost." [1] It took all Lenin's acumen to woo back the dissidents and hold his party together.

Later, when Lenin proposed that German peace terms be accepted at any cost, he was outvoted nine to seven. Trotsky's formula, "cessation of the war, non-signature of the peace, and demobilization of the army," carried. Of the two hundred local Soviets who were consulted, all but two disagreed with Lenin's view. Nikolai Bukharin proposed that the government not only reject German terms, but resume the war as a "revolutionary war." "The internal crisis in the Party was at its worst," writes Boris Souvarine, historian of communism. "Discord amounted to paroxysm." [2] Trotsky and six others resigned from the Council of Commissars, with Bukharin and three of his followers. Only when the Germans seized more Russian territory was Lenin able to win over his detractors and reverse the former majority's position.

There were, in these early days of the Soviet state, many serious abuses, such as the bloody suppression of the sailors and workers of Kronstadt in 1921, or the arrests and executions of political opponents by the Cheka. Even such friends of the Russian Revolution as Rosa Luxemburg, leader of the Polish and later the German working classes, expressed grave concern over some of these acts. Lenin himself decried constantly the ceaseless tendencies toward bureaucracy. But it is undeniable that while Lenin lived there was a considerable degree of latitude for expressing opposition. Immediately after the Bolshevik victory, only rightist journals were suppressed; non-communists of the center and left were permitted to function and to publish newspapers. Only after Lenin had been shot and attempts made on Trotsky's life were the other socialist groups restrained entirely. Even then, however, factionalism and open discussion continued *within* the Communist party. The leaders of Bolshevism argued endlessly over such questions as whether the workers in each factory should operate their own establishments, or whether control should be vested directly in the government; whether unions should play an independent role or be subservient to the state. Communists took opposing sides on these and many other issues, publishing factional documents, debating at conventions, engaging in strident polemic. A dozen factions existed at one time or another, openly and legally—the Workers Opposition, the Opposition for Democratic Centralism, the Workers' Truth group, as well as those led on occasion by well-known leaders such as Trotsky, Bukharin, Zinoviev, Kamenev, and Stalin.

Needless to say, such struggles did not occur in a vacuum. The Soviets' relationship—or lack of relationship—with the West colored every argument and helped to determine which force would win. It was certainly not foreordained either that the Bolsheviks would consolidate their power, or that after a decade Stalin would become the undisputed master of the Soviet Union. Just as the behavior of an employer helps shape the character of a labor organization, so the comportment of the capitalist world became part of the calculus of communism itself.

Had the Allies permitted Russia to leave the war in 1917 and concentrate on internal problems, other radicals might have gained control, or there might have evolved a coalition of all leftist parties. The outcome would have been much different. "The Russian Revolution," writes George F. Kennan, "and the alienation of the Russian people from the Western community for decades to come were only a part of the staggering price paid by the Western people for their insistence on completing a military victory over Germany in 1917 and 1918." [3]

The Allied position at first was ambiguous. While the war was still on, French Marshall Foch proposed military intervention to seize the Trans-Siberian Railway and restore the eastern front. On the other hand, Sir George Buchanan, British ambassador to Petrograd, urged that the Allies gracefully agree to Soviet withdrawal from the war. Lord Lansdowne, in his famous letter, went further. He urged that the Allies themselves accept the Soviet proposal to end all hostilities with the Central Powers. It was an "endless pity," says Kennan, that they did not do it.

A few would have preferred rapprochement with the Bolsheviks, or at least moderation toward them.

Lloyd George stated in 1919: "Personally I would have dealt with the Soviets as the *de facto* Government of Russia. So would President Wilson. But we both agreed that we could not carry to that extent our colleagues at the [peace] Congress, nor the public opinion of our countries which was frightened by Bolshevik violence and feared its spread." [4]

Colonel Raymond Robins, unofficial American envoy to Russia, told Congress, "When we understand what it [the Revolution] is, when we know the facts behind it, when we do not libel it nor slander it or do not lose our heads and become its advocates and defenders, and really know what the thing is and then move forward to it, then we will serve our country and our time." [5]

After the Allies had deployed troops against the Bolsheviks, President Wilson sent William C. Bullitt and the well-known journalist, Lincoln Steffens, to the Soviet Union to seek a *modus vivendi*. The two negotiators met with Lenin and concluded an agreement highly favorable to the West. The Bolsheviks agreed that all governments in Russia, White as well as Red, would retain jurisdiction over the areas they then occupied. Debts owed the Allies would be honored as a joint obligation by all sides, troops would be demobilized, and a general amnesty offered to political prisoners. In return, the West would lift its blockade, withdraw its troops, and re-open communications.[6] Bullitt was triumphant, confident he had found the means to end hostilities. But his plan was never considered. As Lloyd George explained to him, in the face of vitriolic attacks by the conservative press "how can you expect us to be sensible about Russia?" [7]

Time after time the Soviets offered to make peace. In the four months from November, 1918, to February, 1919, Russia sent seven notes to the Allied powers, written—as William Henry Chamberlin says—"in the most conciliatory language." [8] The West, however, refused to be conciliated. Apprehensive that the Bolshevik revolution might upset the delicate balance of power in Europe and spill over to India, China, and the rest of Asia, they were determined, as Churchill put it, to strangle the baby in its crib.

"Never, surely," writes Kennan, "have countries contrived to show themselves so much at their worst as did the Allies in Russia from 1917 to 1920. Among other things, their efforts served everywhere to compromise the enemies of the Bolsheviki and to strengthen the communists themselves. So important was this factor that I think it may well be questioned whether Bolshevism would ever have prevailed throughout Russia had the Western governments not aided its progress to power by this ill-conceived interference." [9]

By 1920, the Bolsheviks had won the civil war and the Allied forces (except for Japan) had been forced to withdraw. After this humiliating defeat, the West might still have repaired the damage with a judicious program of economic aid and normal relations. But the mood that had dictated intervention also produced a policy aimed at isolating the communist nation. France forged its *cordon sanitaire* around the Soviet periphery. The United States withheld recognition for sixteen years. The West generally refused to grant long-term credits to the Soviet Union, without which economic recovery and development was difficult and painful. In 1922, Lenin noted that Russia needed at least 100 million gold rubles to begin reconstruction, but had only one-fifth that amount. The United States, through the mission of Herbert Hoover, did feed ten million people in 1921-1922 who might otherwise have perished. But important as this was to alleviate suffering, it was no substitute for long-term credits. The statesmen of Western Europe and the United States hoped that by squeezing and isolating the Soviet regime they could bring about its downfall. Its economy would collapse, its people would rebel, communism would be overthrown, the "problem" would be solved.

None of this happened. Instead, a form of communism emerged—Stalinism—which turned inward, giving up the dream of world revolution and exacting a fearsome price for rapid industrialization. The Western policy of Anti-Communism was grist for the mill of "hard" communists inside Russia in their arguments with "softer" elements. Stalin might well have told his followers: "There is no possibility of coming to terms with the capitalists. They are trying only to destroy us. We are in a virtual war, without allies, and we must have total national discipline to industrialize ourselves. This is our only defense against an imminent attack." Rapid industrialization, with all its attendant police state measures, was Stalin's response to the Western policy of isolation.

II

After the death of Lenin in January, 1924, a three-cornered struggle wracked the Soviet Communist party for five years. The bitterness of this fight is evidenced by Bukharin's reproaches made in a secret meeting with Kamenev in 1928. "For several weeks," he said, "I have refused to speak to Stalin. He is an unprincipled intriguer who subordinates everything to his appetite for power. At any given moment he will change his theories in order to get rid of someone. . . . Stalin's policy is leading us to civil war. He will be forced to drown the rebellions in blood." [10] In point of fact, there had already been 150 peasant revolts in the short period of six months, and in Moscow a fight had broken out between unemployed workers and militiamen after several shops had been pillaged. The monolith did not evolve without great resistance.

At issue between Bukharin, Trotsky, and Stalin was the question of how the Soviet Union would develop and what help it might expect either from revolutions elsewhere or from the Western world. Bukharin believed that regardless of outside circumstances the Soviet economy must continue to improve living conditions both for its workers and peasants—even if that meant slowing the pace of industrial expansion. Trotsky had no hopes of support from the capitalist states, but his faith in the world revolution was unflagging. In the interim, while awaiting proletarian uprisings elsewhere, Russia must "squeeze" the wealthier peasants for capital so that sufficient industry could be built to satisfy the consumer needs of the rural masses. Stalin, lacking hope both in revolution abroad and Western aid, eventually followed a policy of "squeezing" all segments of the population to provide capital for heavy industry. According to Bukharin, Stalin believed—in his "idiotic illiteracy"—that "the more socialism grows, the stronger will grow the resistance."

Once Stalinism became predominant, and once dissent was choked off entirely, there was little possibility of dislodging it for a long time to come. The West had lost its opportunity.

A tired Russian people, exhausted by war, civil war, hunger, and isolation, was incapable of resisting an "unprincipled intriguer." No one can reassemble the threads of history to say with certainty what might have happened under other circumstances, but it seems reasonably clear that a more understanding Western attitude toward the Soviets in the early years would probably have resulted in a more tractable form of communism. There is merit to the thesis of historian D. F. Fleming, that while the pillars of totalitarian power "may all have been implicit in Marxism . . . it is altogether unlikely that they would have been built as quickly and strongly. Evolution in the Soviet Union would have proceeded much more slowly and, in all probability, with much greater moderation." [11]

III

The elimination of dissent in Russia was not accomplished in a single day, nor did it go totally unchallenged. It took more than a decade for the reel to tighten, and there is some evidence that even after Stalin had abolished formal factionalism he still had to contend for some years with opposition within his central committee. In 1934, Sergei M. Kirov, leader of the Communist party in Leningrad and a member of the Politbureau, was assassinated by a man assumed to be a crank with a personal grudge. But from the famous speech made by Khrushchev in 1956, twenty-two years later, it is now assumed by most experts that Kirov disagreed with Stalin's harsh tactics and evidently commanded a sufficient following in the top communist committees to worry Stalin. "The circumstances surrounding Kirov's murder," said Khrushchev, "hide many things which are inexplicable and mysterious." [12] The implication is that Stalin engineered the assassination of a troublesome rival who opposed his rigid repressions.

Whether or not this is true, the death of Kirov was the signal for a massive purge that solidified Stalin's position until his death. In the following three years, ninety-eight of the 139 members and candidates of the central committee—again, according to Khrushchev—were arrested and shot. This was the final blow to any opposition. With the purges and trials of Bolshevism's Old Guard —Bukharin, Zinoviev, Kamenev, Radek, and Rakovsky—the communist movement of Russia became a full-fledged monolith. The area of decision was narrowed to a single man whose source of power was an omnipresent secret police.

Factionalism in the communist world, however, could not be checked indefinitely, nor the monolithic structure sustained forever. As soon as other communist regimes were formed after World War II, the forces of polycentrism became manifest.

Beginning in 1948, the year Tito and Stalin split, the communist reel began to loosen, the area of decision to widen, dissent to inch forward.

Tito had made his own revolution. He had not been imposed on Yugoslavia by a victorious Red Army, as had the Communist parties in the rest of Eastern Europe. Tito had his own plans for his country, and they clashed sharply with those of Stalin. Stalin wanted Yugoslavia to remain a raw-material producing economy, providing needed supplies for Russia's factories; Tito wanted to industrialize. Stalin preferred Eastern Europe divided into small, weak, regimes; Tito sought to unify them into a strong power. In August, 1947, the Yugoslav and Bulgarian governments agreed at Bled, Yugoslavia, to abolish frontier formalities and form a customs union. "We shall establish co-operation so general and so close," said Tito, "that federation will be a mere formality." [13] Bulgarian leader Dimitrov went further: he urged unity of all six Balkan states, plus Greece. This was anathema to the Kremlin. Stalin insisted on placing the Russian secret police in Eastern Europe; Tito complained bitterly about its behavior in Belgrade and asked that it be withdrawn.

The conflict of interests between two communist states ended finally in the break between Tito and Stalin. Originally it was a pragmatic act, a power play with few ideological overtones. But once the split was consummated, the argument was reduced to philosophical terms. A communist state, said Tito, can move in two directions: toward bureaucratic centralism, as in Russia, or toward democracy as, he claimed, in Yugoslavia. As Titoism evolved, it became a form of communism as divergent from that of Stalin as American capitalism is, say, from that of Portugal.

The rate of capital formation in Yugoslavia, after the split, was cut almost in half, allowing more goods for consumption. Peasants were permitted to leave collective farms and return to their individual plots. They were encouraged to form co-operatives on the Scandinavian model—for buying supplies, selling produce, renting machinery, obtaining credits—but the land itself was individually owned. The hated "buy-up," by which the state forced peasants to sell a quota of their produce at reduced prices, was abolished.

More important, the Titoists formulated a theory of "self-management" which was unique in the communist world. It was a peculiar combination of socialist ownership and capitalist incentive. The workers in each economic unit were organized as a "Workers' Collective." The Workers' Collective, in turn, elected a Workers' Council which decided on production policy, prices, and other matters of management, as the board of directors of a capitalist corporation might do. A sub-committee of the Council, the Management Committee, met with the plant manager on a daily or weekly basis to implement Council decisions. Its goal was to earn as much profit as possible, since any profits above a certain figure went to the workers themselves, to be divided by them as they saw fit—usually a month to six months extra wages, or new housing.

The tight centralist control was loosened. Though the government assigned a "wage fund" to each factory, the Workers' Council, negotiating with the unions, could allocate that fund with considerable flexibility. Thus a tool-and-die maker might earn more in one factory than another, or piece work rates might be higher in one plant than another. Each factory was encouraged to compete with others, to engage in hard selling, to advertise, to cut prices. Yugoslavia is the only communist country where one can buy a pack of cigarettes or a pair of shoes for one price in one store and a lower or higher price in another. Though all factories and all retail shops are socially owned, they compete seriously with each other, each one determined to enlarge sales and profits.

Other operations, too, were decentralized. The state formulated an overall central plan with broad objectives, but the implementation was left to various subdivisions, the federal republics, and the districts. Self-management penetrated every facet of activity. Each school was run by elected representatives of the teachers, mothers, children, unions, and other community groups; the federal education ministry merely co-ordinated efforts and was greatly reduced in status. Each apartment building was operated by the tenants themselves.

This system, it should be pointed out, could function best only if the Communist party itself were decentralized and its discipline loosened. For a time, the reins were actually relaxed. Communists were permitted to disagree in public on all but "major" issues. Federal law provided that at least twice the number of people were to be nominated for various posts as were to be elected. At the lower levels, there was competition for power between party and non-party members. In thousands of instances, old communists were defeated for the Workers' Councils in favor of non-communists. But Tito did not permit this process to be drawn to its full conclusion. When it became clear that the communist movement might fragment, discipline was tightened. The communist movement continued to exercise control. The definition of a "major" issue, requiring that all party members act in unison, was tightened, then relaxed, then tightened again. Power still rests with a single party.

Yet it is undeniable that the forces of dissent have been significantly strengthened in Yugoslavia. The first time I visited Belgrade in 1950, there were forced laborers working in the streets on construction projects with submachine guns at their back. Almost no one would speak to a foreigner for fear of being questioned or jailed. In succeeding trips all this changed. People spoke freely. It was possible to visit with them in their homes. At various Workers' Council meetings, we heard sympathy for the views of Milovan Djilas and a hope they would be implemented.

Here were the birth pangs of a different kind of communism, a "revisionist" communism. It exercised, and continues to exercise, a magnetic attraction to theorists in other parts of the communist world. It was the first nail in the coffin of monolithicism.

Moreover, it was also a backhanded rebuke to the theories of Anti-Communism, for by granting credits and aid to Yugoslavia the United States has made a contribution to a milder form of communism. In the first decade of Titoism, to March 15, 1959, American support totaled $888 million, of which $414 million was in the form of agricultural surpluses, wheat, cotton, and fats and oils.[14] Sensing an important split in the Soviet world, the United States jettisoned its negative Anti-Communism, insofar as Yugoslavia is concerned, and helped build a showcase state divorced from the Cold War.

Denis Healey, British Labor party leader, noted that "two things stand out as the undeniable achievements of the Titoist regime. The first is the consolidation of Yugoslavia as a nation state, composed of people who were slaughtering one another by the hundreds of thousands for racial or religious reasons less than 20 years ago. . . . The second . . . is a rate of economic growth over the last five years surpassing that of every other country in the world except China. But unlike China, Yugoslavia has also enjoyed a staggering increase in personal consumption. Indeed, this is the main reason for its ability to increase investment at a high rate without adopting all the paraphernalia of Communist oppression." [15] American encouragement deserves credit for at least part of this success—and simultaneously offers proof that a policy other than Anti-Communism may reap important results in other sections of the communist world.

IV

Since Stalin's death in 1953, the reel has continued to unwind elsewhere—not evenly or without setbacks and retrenchments, but unmistakably.

Once the dictator was gone, the men of the Kremlin had to share power; no leader was able, immediately, to wear Stalin's mantle. To do so, however, they had to curb the secret police with its unlimited powers. The execution of police chief Lavrentia Beria signified the end of an era and the widening of the area of decision. The new leaders released hundreds of thousands from the labor camps. The purge trials, so characteristic of the 1930's and the period just before Stalin's death, were abandoned. Trials by the secret police, in which the accused were not present, were also abolished. Eddy Gilmore, long-time correspondent for the Associated Press in Russia, could report in March, 1963, that "the biggest change in the Soviet Union since the death of Joseph Stalin ten years ago next Tuesday is the disappearance of police terror from the lives of millions of people." [16] Millions of Russians, repressed for decades, gained courage to make individual demands and take up grievances.

Within the Communist party, a three-cornered factionalism appeared once again. Unlike the 1920's, when conflicting views were published in Soviet newspapers, the issues were confined to inner-party circles. But they were known and discussed generally throughout the land. Malenkov, first Prime Minister after Stalin's death, favored a policy of co-existence with the West and a marked increase of consumer goods. "It was under his premiership," writes Soviet expert Edward Crankshaw, "that the silent debunking of Stalin began . . . that Beria, the police chief, was arrested and executed; that the virtual autonomy of the Security police was abolished, and their sad and evil organization brought to heel; that the slave labor camps were largely done away with; that striking concessions were made to the peasants; that the Soviet leadership started civilizing its contacts with the outside world . . . ; that the emphasis of economic propaganda was switched from heavy industry to the manufacture of consumer goods." [17] At the opposite pole was Molotov, the old dictator's closest associate and a neo-Stalinist to the end, who argued for continuation of the previous policies. In the center was Khrushchev, who eventually isolated both rivals and became Soviet Russia's unchallenged leader. On coming to power he accepted most of Malenkov's doctrine, while rejecting and banishing the man himself.

Many Americans dismiss such charges as irrelevant. Russia, they say, is still a one-party system, lacking in elementary freedoms taken for granted in the West. But this is a mechanistic view. There are dictatorships and dictatorships. It is a matter of considerable importance to the average Russian that he no longer must fear being sent off to jail for making the wrong economic decision, or for being late or absent from his job. The marked decline in fear makes it possible for new social pressures to be generated. Workers take up factory grievances they would have been silent about in the past, sometimes even bringing them to court. Bureaucratic abuses are challenged. Discussions inside the party becomes wider. No organized factions are permitted, but there is an increase of dissent. Factory managers in hundreds of business conferences demand "normalization." Workers argue with their union officials over assignment of housing. Inside the Communist party, Khrushchev himself is sometimes criticized by individual members—as happened, for instance, when he walked out on the scheduled summit talks with Eisenhower. The leaders of the state no longer shoot or imprison opponents such as Malenkov, Kaganovich, Molotov, or Zhukov. Instead they relegate them to minor posts or retire them from public life. But they do not kill them, as they would have in Stalin's day.

The abatement of terror is linked inevitably with an increase in consumer goods. Khrushchev has paid heed to the bitterest grievance of his people, the shortage of housing, by building 21 million dwelling units in seven years. Families who lived in a single room, without private kitchen or toilet facilities, now receive modest apartments. Other necessities, it is generally agreed, are also in greater supply.

The Soviet Union, as it becomes a "have" nation under new leadership, is widening the area of decision. Dissenters may not form factions or publish tracts, but their views are heard in many different ways. A group of textile managers who meet to discuss production problems may also note that poor housing and poor transportation hinders initiative. To improve factory operation, they may recommend political measures such as a greater emphasis on consumer goods. Or a group of writers, meeting to discuss literary style, may argue for more tolerance of maverick subjects, such as the terror under Stalin. The abatement of terror inevitably leads to rudimentary dissent, and rudimentary dissent may some day evolve into legalized dissent with its attendant safeguards.

V

Elsewhere in the communist world, the pressures for change are equally insistent, as the rank and file slowly finds a voice. Even before Khrushchev made his first de-Stalinization speech in 1956, young students in Poland were talking, half-openly, of "Soviet imperialism." Polish writers began to write a little more irreverently. In June, 1956, there were strikes and riots in Poznan. Four months later, demonstrations by students and others brought Wladyslaw Gomulka, a communist moderate who had been jailed in the Stalin era, back to power. The Poles call these events the "October Revolution," and indeed it had many characteristics of a revolution—strikes, demonstrations, and the arming of factory workers. At the peak of the crisis, while the Polish central committee was meeting to confirm Gomulka, Khrushchev and a few associates arrived from Moscow to thwart the plan. Tanks and soldiers, under command of a Russian general who had been born in Poland, Marshall Rokossovsky, stood in readiness near Warsaw. In the factories, workers were given guns and told to remain at their benches ready to resist. When the troops began to move, Gomulka threatened Khrushchev that he would speak to the people over the radio, mobilizing them for defense. The Russians backed down, and a vastly different Poland emerged.

"The most important meaning of Poland's experience," comments Flora Lewis, *New York Times* correspondent, "is that there does seem to be a way for the subjects of the communist states to improve their lot and to restore friendly relations with the West without cataclysmic violence. It is a revelation which was generally unsuspected a few years ago and whose implications even now are not always accepted." [18]

Since "October," Poland has become the freest island in the communist complex. One of Gomulka's first acts was to clip the wings of the hated secret police. Citizens were even permitted to see their police dossiers and destroy them if they saw fit. Here, as in Yugoslavia, there was a return to private farming and a shrivelling of the collectives. Everyone today agrees that there is more freedom and less fear in Poland than in any other communist country, except perhaps for Yugoslavia. Writers and intellectuals have continued to dissent in a way that would have been impossible before 1956. For a while after 1956, legally recognized strikes took place. Plays critical of the Soviets were shown in student theatres. Poland has become a beehive of discussion, and though no organized factions are permitted, individual dissent is not interfered with.

Soon after the Polish October, similar events occurred in Hungary. Led by students and by intellectuals of the Petofi Circle, masses of people demonstrated in the streets and succeeded in ousting the hard communist government of Matyas Rakosi. For a few weeks the former socialist and liberal parties functioned openly, held meetings, and published newspapers. Imre Nagy, a liberal communist of the Tito type, replaced the old leadership and demanded that the Russians remove their troops from Hungary. It appeared at one point that an agreement might be worked out, but, as everyone knows, the Russian response was a barrage of tanks, soldiers, arrests, and the drowning of the revolt in rivers of blood. Imre Nagy was seized and later executed.

The Hungarian experience certainly was a blot on the process of de-Stalinization. It caused many people, including thousands inside the communist parties of the West, to express doubts about Khrushchev's future course. It reinforced the views of many that communism was a tyranny which would never change. Nothing, certainly, can extenuate Khrushchev's actions. Yet, on the other side, it must be noted that there were serious divisions within the Soviet camp relative to Hungary. Khrushchev himself noted four years later that there were "doubts and hesitations." Edward Crankshaw reports that Anastas Mikoyan, plenipotentiary to Budapest, fully believed that the Russian troops were to be withdrawn, and only learned otherwise when he returned to Moscow. There must have been others, perhaps even Khrushchev, who favored a milder approach at first, but changed their minds when it became evident that Hungary would become either neutralist or join the Western camp.

At any rate, it is doubtful that Hungary will be repeated, not only because of its effect on world opinion, but, more important, because it brought the Soviet world itself to a dangerous precipice. Workers in Poznan that fateful month were threatening to go on strike again in support of their Hungarian brothers. Workers in East Berlin pleaded with U. S. representatives to permit them to use the American radio in West Berlin, RIAS, to broadcast a call for a general strike in East Germany.[19] Observers in Czechoslovakia reported that the nation was under extreme tension, expecting some kind of similar action in a few weeks; and in the Hungarian section of Yugoslavia, there was a strong possibility of revolt against Tito, in emulation of Budapest. The victory of Soviet forces was won at great risk; Khrushchev undoubtedly knows that another time he may not be so lucky.

The revolt, in retrospect, was not entirely in vain. Hungary today ranks with Poland and Yugoslavia, as the most liberal countries of the communist world. Conditions have improved, most of the prisoners have been released and are, by all accounts, functioning without hindrance.

VI

Hungary did not, as many feared, signify the end of the process of liberalization within the communist world. Communist parties in every country, on both sides of the so-called Iron Curtain, are today deeply rent between the "hards" and the "softs." Tens of thousands of liberal communists in the United States, Canada, and Western Europe quit their parties because of Hungary. More important, however, has been the emergence of revisionist communism within these parties. The Secretariat of the Italian Communist party now urges greater independence from Moscow. "How was it possible," it asks, "that in the construction of a socialist society there were so many errors and deformations, and what can be done to guarantee that they will not be repeated?" [20] Giorgio Amendola, leading party figure, recently demanded the right of free expression "even if that caused the emergence of factions within the party." [21] The party's press, *Editori Reuniti*, went so far as to republish works by Trotsky, Bukharin, and Zinoviev, which ten years before would have been considered brazen heresy and would undoubtedly have led to expulsions from the party.[22]

The Indian Communist party has divided into four factions, two "hard" and two "soft." The softs seem to have predominated, for as Walter Z. Laqueur reported in 1962: "The Indian Communists now openly support Prime Minister Nehru's anti-Chinese policy. On several recent occasions, they have been even more outspoken in condemning Chinese aggression than the Government in New Delhi." [23] Throughout Latin America, the communist parties are divided between those who follow Khrushchev's "co-existence" policy and those who pursue a more militant and revolutionary course. In Brazil, according to Irving L. Horowitz, the "soft" communist, Luiz Carlos Prestes, seeks to achieve power through elections and through support of the more radical "bourgeois" elements, The "hards," such as peasant leader Francisco Juliao, see no other solution but to organize guerrilla warfare, as in China or Cuba.[24]

These same schisms between hard and soft are evident within the communist countries themselves, for communism is in the most bitter faction fight in its history—more important than the Trotsky-Stalin imbroglio of the 1920's. In each country there is a Stalinist force which is either dominant—as in China and Albania, or is being whittled into insignificance—as in Poland, Hungary, and Russia itself.

"A bitter struggle is emerging in the Soviet Union," writes *New York Times* correspondent Harrison E. Salisbury, "between a powerful neo-Stalinist faction and a broadly based group of 'liberals' for the dominant role in the country's future. . . . [The liberals] stand firmly for the maintenance of the Soviet regime and its fundamental Communist basis. But they believe in a rule of law, of justice as it is known in the West, in freedom of the individual within socially recognized bounds, in freedom for the creative arts and in close and meaningful state and personal relations between the Soviet Union and the West." [25] Publication of such books as *One Day in the Life of Ivan Denisovich*, depicting conditions in a Stalinist forced labor camp, are indicative of the thaw. That it does not proceed smoothly, without spurts and spasms, tells us that the transition confronts serious opposition. But there is no doubt of the trend. "It is not an exaggeration," writes Edward Crankshaw, "to say that the Soviet Union is moving towards a species of democracy." Averell Harriman, former Governor of New York and Ambassador to Moscow, made much the same point in his book, *Peace with Russia?* The pressure for freedom, he said, "will make itself felt as the immediate demand for more material needs is met." This process, he notes, is under way and has been for some time.

The communist spectrum now stretches from Polish revisionist communism, on the liberal side, to hard, traditional communism of the Mao-ist or Albanian type, on the other side. Dr. Adam Schaff, Poland's leading Marxist philosopher and a member of the central committee, criticized his own system not too long ago for failing to grant "bourgeois" democratic rights. Schaff, writing in the literary weekly *Przeglad Kulturalny*, said: "The strongest propaganda trump card against communism and Marxism today in the capitalist world is the problem of the rights to freedom of the individual in the socialist system, the problem of democracy. . . . Experience teaches . . . that we are rather inclined to delay processes of democratization than to accelerate them excessively." [26]

VII

The dispute over democratization is merely a surface expression of something that runs deeper. The fact is that the "soft" communists are today revising Marxism to a greater degree than at any time in the past. Khrushchev dares not go the whole way, unless and until he can come to terms with the West. His thesis that capitalism and communism can co-exist without war needs confirmation in the crucible of life itself before he can elaborate it further. But the implications are already clear.

Standard Marxist-Leninist philosophy holds that capitalism cannot exist without imperialism and colonies, nor can it avoid the impulsion towards war. Reduced to simple terms, it argues that workers produce more goods than they are paid for. The surplus goes to capitalists. Since the worker cannot buy back all he produces and since the capitalist can consume only a part of his largesse, the latter must seek outside markets for his surplus goods and capital. The need for markets propels the capitalist first to invest in and trade with the underdeveloped countries, and then to seize them. Since all capitalist nations, however, are playing the same game, and the areas for exploitation are limited, the imperialist powers reach a point where they must make war on each other for the booty. There is thus an inexorable drive to imperialism on the one hand and war on the other. Capitalism cannot exist without them. This is standard doctrine—very much simplified—which is still promulgated by the Chinese and other hard communists.

Now Khrushchev is saying something very much different. He sees capitalism surviving without its old colonies and without war. The new program of the Soviet Communist party, adopted in 1961, says that war can be banished "from the life of society even before the complete victory of socialism on earth, with *capitalism surviving in a part of the world.*" (My italics.) Past dogma, for the most part, held that capitalism would die in violent revolution. Lenin argued that "we do not seek an agreement with the bourgeoisie, we are going into the last, decisive fight with it." But Khrushchev today says: "The working class, supported by the majority of the people . . . can defeat the reactionary anti-popular forces, win a solid majority in parliament, transform it from a tool serving the class interests of the bourgeoisie into an instrument serving the working people." This new type of popular front can achieve socialism peacefully. It may even pay the capitalist for his factories, rather than expropriate them. "There will arise in certain countries a situation in which it will be preferable for the bourgeoisie . . . to agree to the means of production being purchased from it and for the proletariat to 'pay off' the bourgeoisie." [27]

In another day such concepts would have been characterized as "social democracy," and their adherents branded as hostile to the working class. But the Russian Revolution, like all revolutions, has reached a point of stability. The Soviet Union is rapidly becoming a "have" nation. She is producing seventy or eighty million tons of steel a year. She has a gross national product upwards of $250 billion and is the second most industrialized nation on earth. By 1980, she expects to fabricate 250 million tons of steel. Although it is still in the distance, the basis is being laid for an affluent society. The new Soviet political program, first since 1919, is therefore essentially a reformist rather than a revolutionary document. Though it condemns "revisionism"—along with "dogmatism"—it is itself the most significant revision of Leninist doctrine by a Soviet government.

Previously, any non-communist government was considered hostile to communism. Khrushchev, however, sees a special role for the neutralist nations. "The young sovereign states," says the program, "do not belong either to the system of imperialist states or to the system of Socialist states." They are a progressive force with a special role in the quest for peace: "The joining of the efforts of the newly-free peoples and of the peoples of the Socialist countries in the struggle against the war danger is a major factor for world peace. This mighty front, which expresses the will and strength of two-thirds of mankind, can force the imperialist aggressors into retreat."

Fear of war and what it would do to a stable society has led Khrushchev to modify basically established doctrine. By contrast, China, which is a long way from being a "have" nation, clings tenaciously to standard Leninism. It denies that there would be no victors in a nuclear war. "The result [of war]," say the Chinese, "will certainly not be the annihilation of mankind." "On the debris of a dead imperialism," writes the *Peking Review*, "the victorious people would create very swiftly a civilization thousands of times higher than the capitalist system and a truly beautiful future for themselves." [28]

Perhaps the degree of difference between the two camps of communism can be gauged by this editorial in the *People's Daily* of China, December 31, 1962: "In the final analysis the stand taken by Togliatti and certain other CPI [Italian Communist party] leaders boils down to this—the people of the capitalist countries should not make revolutions, the oppressed nations should not wage struggles to win liberation, and the people of the world should not fight against imperialism." [29] The Chinese are unalterably opposed to this "softness."

It is safe to say that within the Chinese communist movement there exists also a "soft" wing, just as there is a "hard" wing in Russia. But the Chinese liberals are not in power. China is living through difficult economic times, surrounded by an American fleet and threatened ceaselessly by Chiang Kai-shek from Formosa. Such circumstances favor the dogmatic faction. It is not surprising, therefore, that so far it has carried the day. If tensions, world-wide, should relax, it is possible that the Chinese "softs" will make a better showing. At the moment, however, they are in the background.

VIII

No reading of this short review of communist development can escape the conclusion that, in considerable measure, the Leninist world is deeply affected internally by the behavior of the West. What the United States does, therefore, can profoundly influence the faction fight now going on. It can also change the future of· the United States as well.

If international strife should abate, the soft elements in communism would be immeasurably favored. The argument by the hards that there can be no democratic privileges during a "war period" would lose cogency; pressures for liberalization could not be stopped, especially in the European communist countries. To the extent, however, that the United States adopts a hard, militarist policy, casts a network of bases around the communist perimeter, and brandishes the nuclear stick—to that extent the hards will reap a harvest. "When we intellectuals urge the communist leaders to give us more freedom," a non-communist professor in an East European country—once a member of the British Labor party—told me a few years ago, "they argue that it is impossible to have freedom when a nation is at war. We are surrounded, they say, by 950 American military installations.

Under such circumstances, they claim, there must be national discipline and national unity." [30]

It is one of the greatest miscalculations that our Anti-Communist policies have strengthened the hardest aspects of communism and prevented the very kind of moderation that most Americans desired. Anti-Communism has been its own worst enemy.

XI

Latin America: The Final Disaster?

THE SUPREME test for Anti-Communism can be expected in Latin America, almost certainly in the next ten or fifteen years. "There is absolutely no doubt in my mind," writes Milton Eisenhower, brother of the former President, "that revolution is inevitable in Latin America. The people are angry. They are shackled to the past with bonds of ignorance, injustice, and poverty. And they no longer accept as universal or inevitable the oppressive prevailing order which has filled their lives with toil, want, and pain." [1]

Until now it has been the empires of other powers that have been erased by revolution—British, French, Dutch, and Belgian. Beginning with Castro's victory in Cuba on New Year's Day, 1959, however, it is the United States' own fortress that is beleaguered. The upheaval that began in Asia in the 1940's and spread to Africa in the 1950's is now at America's own doorstep.

If the impending revolution should be made, as now seems likely, not only against Latin America's own oligarchy but the United States' as well, it will alter our way of life in a manner we do not yet foresee. One-third of our world investments and one-fifth to one-fourth of our foreign trade will be lost or in jeopardy, requiring important modifications in our economy. Tensions at home inevitably will mount as never before since the Cold War began. The conservatives and rightists almost certainly will call for massive military intervention against "new Cubas"; some may even argue that we should "drop the bomb and get it over with." The pragmatic liberals, as in the past, very likely will accept the military "solution" as the only practical one in the face of a "communist menace."

Such a situation is fraught with dangers. It can provoke actions similar to those taken by France only a few years ago. The Algerian war, it will be recalled, caused such deep schism within the Fourth Republic that it brought General Charles de Gaulle back to power with a new constitution. While de Gaulle was

183

trying to settle the dispute with Algeria's nationalists, he had to contend with rightist French generals like Juin and Salan, who threatened to seize Algeria and perhaps overthrow the regime at home as well. Stung by French setbacks in Morocco, Indochina, Madagascar, Tunisia, and elsewhere, they insisted that Algeria be held no matter what the cost. For a while they fought with arms against the very government they were pledged to defend. There is serious doubt that a lesser leader than de Gaulle could have staved them off.

Should Latin America erupt in revolution and secede from the North American sphere of influence, no one can predict how strong rightist pressure might grow within the United States. That any general would organize a coup d'etat seems highly unlikely, but the full impact of such a situation is not yet at hand. We cannot be sure. It is no exaggeration to say that the issues of war and peace and of democracy within the United States depend in great measure on whether the revolution in Latin America is friendly or unfriendly. "If communism should obtain a permanent foothold in Latin America," said presidential candidate John F. Kennedy on September 14, 1960, "then the balance of power would move against us and peace would be even more insecure." [2] At every point in this coming drama, world war may be a possibility, just as it was over Cuba in October, 1962, for the Latin American revolution will alter the international balance of power more than any event or series of events since the emergence of Communist China.

I

There are some interesting parallels between the history of Latin America during the last 150 years and that of Asia, particularly insofar as the role of the West is concerned. Britain, the main actor on both stages, sought at first only havens of trade, not colonies. Then, as the industrial revolution gained momentum and the need for raw materials and spheres of investment became insistent, Britain found itself in conflict with ancient empires. In its own interests, therefore, it was soon underwriting national rebellion against foreign rule in various areas—in India, for instance, against the Moguls; in Egypt, against the Turks; in Latin

America, against Spain and Portugal. As early as 1789, William Pitt was giving material aid to Francisco Miranda for his grandiose plan to liberate Mexico, Chile, Peru, Argentina, Venezuela, and Colombia from Spanish control. In both Asia and Latin America, the nationalists achieved a measure of victory. But they soon found that Britain's friendship was based on its own desires for commerce and empire, rather than on the needs of the revolutionaries for social change. Britain occupied India and other countries in Asia, reducing them to colonial status. In Latin America she contemplated a similar policy at first, but because she was chary of provoking another dispute with the United States, decided finally on economic imperialism.

The British granted loans to Latin revolutionaries, provided experts for their military staffs, transported rebels on her men-o'-war. But after independence had been won, it was to her advantage to keep the new nations weak, divided, frustrated, and mired in feudalist stagnation. Only in that way was it possible for her bankers to become the creditors of Latin America and her industrialists to gain control over mines, railroads, utilities, and steamship services. Until World War I, Britain was preeminent as trader and investor in the twenty republics, particularly the southern ones such as Argentina.

The United States, much slower to lay its commercial claims and more sympathetic to the goals of the revolutionaries, nonetheless developed no abiding program for helping the Latin Americans complete their revolutions. And as American investors built railroads, established banana plantations, and became financial kings in their own right, the United States too accommodated itself to the policy of working with and buttressing the feudal classes who aborted Latin American hopes for progress. By the time we replaced Britain as the dominant influence on the continent, the policy was firmly rooted. In exchange for economic benefits to our copper, oil, banana, and other interests, we cemented an alliance with Latin American oligarchies and supported their power with loans, military supplies, and, on occasion, direct intervention. We too had a stake in upholding feudal prerogatives.

We helped the Cuban nationalists in 1898 to depose Spain, but, as the price for withdrawing our troops, we forced the nationalists to accept the Platt Amendment in their constitution, which gave us the right on our own motion to occupy the country any time we felt there was danger to life and liberty. Four times in the next two decades the United States intervened to administer Cuba's affairs, once for four years. The social structure remained virtually unchanged. In 1914, the United States Navy bombed and seized Vera Cruz, Mexico; the following year American forces occupied Haiti and a year later, the Dominican Republic. Nicaragua, Haiti, and the Dominican Republic were directly ruled by the United States for the better part of two decades. In none of these countries was the social system changed. Since Franklin Roosevelt's "good neighbor" policy in the 1930's, such acts are usually frowned on. But Latin America, as a North American sphere of influence, has been under little pressure by us, until lately, to make broad social changes. On the contrary, we have been aligned with its oligarchies.

If Latin America today staggers under the load of the past, and if its revolution has never been completed, it is in considerable part because of British-American machinations. It is doubtful that the oligarchies would have survived without this prop to their power. The original weakness of Latin America after the 1820's may have been its own inability to impose a social revolution after the national revolution had secured independence, but the continuation of that condition was abetted by British, and later American, policymakers. The poverty, disease, and illiteracy of the area is a byproduct not of lack of resources or competent manpower, but of a social disease—feudalism—which neither the oligarchies nor we were willing to cure.

At the time of the American Revolution, the Spanish and Portugese colonies of Latin America were more affluent than the thirteen British colonies which became the United States. "In terms of accumulated wealth, large cities, ports, established foreign trade and even technical equipment of plantations," writes economist W. S. Woytinsky, "the liberated Spanish colonies probably had a better start than the United States and Canada." [3] Today, the per capita income of Latin America is only one-eighth that of North America, and even that figure is deceptive because a considerable portion of the people live at a subsistence level of $50 to $100 a year per person—not much higher than that of Asia. One half the people are illiterate—in Haiti, 89 per cent. Five-sixths of the children who enroll in the first grade in Brazil never reach the fourth grade, and less than 2 per cent reach the twelfth grade.

Statistics on disease and death from malnutrition are staggering. According to John Gerassi, former *Time* correspondent, a million people annually die of starvation or lack of proper nutrition. Daily food intake for 52 per cent of the 200 million inhabitants is 500 calories—as against 3,100 in the United States.[4] In Brazil, three of every ten children die before they reach the age of one, and in Guatemala fifty-five out of every hundred die before their fourth birthday. Venezuela and Panama have eight times more tuberculosis per capita than the United States; Brazil fifteen times. Three of every five people in Latin America never drink a glass of potable water, and one thousand children a day die because of it.

Nor is this all. The age-old cry for land, typical of all feudal systems, wracks Latin America from one end to another. In the rural sections where most of the people live, 1.2 per cent own 71.6 per cent of the acreage. Of the 28.5 million farm families, eighteen million have no holdings at all and 5.5 million insufficient holdings.

II

When Father Hidalgo, Bolivar, San Martin, Miranda, and others began the struggle for independence, our Latin neighbors had a singular opportunity to achieve a viable society. In 1824, Bolivar called an "Amphictyonic Congress" at Panama to merge the former colonies into a second American Union, similar to the United States. George Washington's family sent him a locket with the late President's picture and a lock of his hair; Lafayette wrote: "Of all men living and even of all men in history, Bolivar is the very one to whom my paternal friend [Washington] would have preferred to send this present."[5] But the Congress was a failure; Bolivar's efforts at unity collapsed. The Confederation he founded divided into three nations—Colombia, Venezuela, and Ecuador. The Central American Confederation fragmented, between 1833 and 1897, into tiny republics. Though Bolivar was president of both Bolivia and Peru, these two countries also went their separate ways. Even worse than the disunity was the inability of Latin America to deal with feudalism. The peasant, in large part Indian or of mixed blood, did not seize the land from his landlord or force through any legislative land reform. The leaders of the war for independence were the local (Creole) ruling class, whose grievance was against appointees of the Spanish Crown, rather than against feudalism as a social system. The many lower-class soldiers in the armies of independence undoubtedly desired broader changes in their society, but they had been weakened by Spain's repression of Indian revolts some time previously, and were unable to propel their revolution any further. Creole rulers replaced the Spanish rulers—the backward social system remained. "Liberty for most of the Americas," says Carleton Beals, "became a liberty of military chieftains to lord it and liberty of Creole landlords to steal more land." [6] During the next hundred years, there were innumerable struggles of liberals against conservatives to free the peasant from his auto-cratic landlords, to separate church from state, to break the power of the military chiefs. Rivers of blood flowed throughout Latin America, but there was little to show for it by way of social progress.

The second important stage in the travail of Latin America be-gan in Mexico a century after Hidalgo, in 1910. Its significance lies in the fact that it stands midpoint, on the social spectrum, between the original revolutions of the nineteenth century and the recent Cuban Revolution, and that it illustrates some of the problems that such revolutions must contend with.

Mexico, it may be recalled, was invaded by the United States in 1847-1848 and lost one half of its territory, including its best farmland. As if this blow were not enough, France occupied the country while the United States was in the midst of its own Civil War. A liberal regime emerged both before and after this event, led by Benito Juarez. But uniting a country like Mexico, with its large number of illiterate Indians and its poor lines of communication, proved a more formidable task than any govern-ment was able to achieve. From 1876 to 1910, Mexico was ruled by a corrupt and unbridled dictator, Porfirio Diaz.

A desperate revolt broke out in 1910. Just as in Cuba years later, it began as an effort by the middle classes to win political democracy from the dictator. Its slogan, "Effective Suffrage, No Re-Election," gives the moderate tone of its goals. The middle classes were tired of thirty-four years of dictatorship; they demanded a normalization of political life. And, just as in Cuba, the peasants joined with the city well-to-do, seeking their own specific objectives—economic and social democracy. United around men like Emiliano Zapata, they raised a more radical slogan: "Land and Liberty." For them, the upheaval promised a free patch of land, schools, clinics, and other social amenities.

Though hundreds of thousands of people (some say one million) lost their lives in the zigzag civil wars of the next twenty-five years, neither of these aims—political democracy and social democracy—was remotely achieved. In this unhappy annal, one *caudillo* replaced another; the Church often disregarded provisions of the constitution which reduced its power; and the United States issued ultimatums on occasion to prevent Mexico from seizing North American oil holdings. When President Carranza sought to restore subsoil rights to the nation, there was loud talk in the United States of military intervention. It subsided only after the American companies—through a production strike—had forced Carranza to withdraw his threat. On another occasion, the United States seized the port of Vera Cruz. The big stick, used sparingly, was nevertheless always in evidence. For a decade or two, war between the two nations was a distinct possibility. U. S. Ambassador Dwight Morrow was able to negotiate a compromise on the petroleum issue in the 1920's, but in the process the Mexican Church retained its prerogatives, the oil companies remained in American hands, and agrarian reform was abandoned. After a quarter-century, the Mexican people had little to show for their dead. The revolution marked time.

In 1934, finally, a change took place. A new government in Washington, under Roosevelt, moderated American policy. And in Mexico City, President Lazaro Cardenas introduced more reforms than any regime either before or since. Some 45 million acres of land were nationalized and distributed to an impoverished peasantry. Schools, roads, and clinics were built, and irrigation projects were undertaken to make the small amount of tillable land more fertile. Both the Church and the military were reduced in power. As a counter-weight to the army—though he came from its ranks—Cardenas immensely strengthened the mass organizations of peasants, workers, and white collar elements, all of which were combined into his National Revolutionary party (now called Institutional Revolutionary party, PRI). Peasants were enrolled into a peasant movement; workers were unionized on a grand scale and given a modern labor code to encourage their efforts; government employees, professional people, and other members of the middle class were organized into a third popular fulcrum. Together they represented an effective barrier to military ambitions. From that time to the present, Mexican politics has manifested an enviable stability—compared to the rest of Latin America.

Probably the key incident in Cardenas' efforts was the nationalization in 1938 of foreign—mostly American—oil properties. At the time, it was greeted with the same American cries for intervention that were to be heard over Cuba later—and for approximately the same reasons. After two years, however, an arrangement was worked out to indemnify the companies over a twenty-five-year period.

These three measures, land reform, molding a mass "party," and seizure of foreign holdings, were, in historic retrospect, the necessary ingredients of a revolution-in-progress. Without them Mexico would still languish in the torpor of yesterday, its people much worse off even than they are at present, and the nation wracked by civil wars.

The reform measures in themselves were not great successes. Land reform, for instance, was an economic failure. Not enough land was distributed to begin with, and the favored few were able to amass large estates. Sixty-nine per cent of the acreage today is in holdings of 1,200 acres or more. Peasant ownership has tended to fragment or be sold. Not enough credit was made available, nor enough interest shown by the central government. To this day, then, poverty is pronounced in the countryside and the blessings of land reform have been mixed. But as a political measure it did serve its purpose. It weakened the power of the feudal classes and the Church. It gave agriculture as a whole an important push forward and helped it to diversify. According to President Adolfo Lopez Mateos, the value of farm commodities, measured in 1958 money, went up from four billion pesos in 1935 to 23.5 billion a year a quarter-century later. The improvement is particularly pronounced in export crops such as cotton. Staples, such as corn (the main crop), wheat, rice, beans, and sugar, doubled in a single decade. Mexico is now almost self-sufficient in farm commodities, even though the number of farmers continues to decline.[7] By weakening the ancient landlord classes, the Mexican government has been able to prod farming to considerable progress.

The same may be said of the nationalization of the oil industry. Perhaps if Standard Oil and other companies had remained the owners of Mexico's petroleum, production might have been greater. But bare figures cannot tell the story. The industry is now a pivot for developing the *Mexican* economy, rather than a mere source of profits for North Americans. The nationalized company, Pemex, used its resources to initiate the manufacture of fertilizers, insecticides, and paints. It spurred the building of forty thousand kilometers of modern highways. It furthered electrification. Oil and natural gas today provide 90 per cent of the nation's energy. "By supplying fuel below cost," writes the First National City Bank of New York, "Pemex has played an important role in subsidizing agriculture, industry, and public transport." [8] Pemex is now stepping up the development of a petrochemical industry, which no doubt will further boost industrialization.

Mexico's course since Cardenas has not been an even one. Along the way the revolution has faltered. A new breed of men arose, the "political-capitalists," who have accrued to themselves the major benefits of progress. Their affluence was not the result of shrewdness as enterpreneurs or ability as competitors, but exclusively because of political rank. The political-capitalist knew where a road was to be built and bought up nearby property. He profited from government construction contracts. He invested in firms which he knew would get loans from the federal finance corporation, Nacional Financiera. The Mexicans call this "honest graft." By such techniques a former President, Miguel Aleman, has become one of the world's richest men. Thus, while the share of advance by the upper one-tenth of the population has been phenomenal, that of the lowest tenth has been extremely modest. Mexico undoubtedly awaits further struggles and changes. In the aftermath of revolution, the alliance between middle and lower classes sundered, and the former gained the ascendancy.

III

From the Mexican Revolution to the Cuban, there was a hiatus during which the United States jettisoned gunboat diplomacy and proclaimed, under Franklin Roosevelt, the good neighbor policy. The Platt Amendment was abandoned. The Mexican decision on nationalization of oil was accepted, and a program initiated of tariff reduction, special trade agreements, export-import loans, and similar concessions. Important as these were, however, they were not aimed at securing basic change in Latin America. The alliance with feudalism remained the cornerstone of policy not only for North American corporations, but for Washington as well. In making this point we do not mean to suggest that a Latin American revolution can, or should, be made by the United States. On the contrary, only the Latins can liberate themselves. But the support given to oligarchical forces by the United States has been, and remains, a major barrier to change. It is in this sense that American policy must be judged.

By the end of World War II, there were many signs that the good neighbor policy was inadequate, particularly in the context of the Cold War. Preoccupied with "fighting communism" on a world scale, the United States tended to give fulsome support to "safe" allies in this hemisphere, the rightist dictators. Men like Perez Jimenez in Venezuela and Rojas Pinilla in Colombia were welcomed as true friends.

As in Asia and Africa, America misread the signposts of history. Not only was it inevitable that Latin American nationalism would gain courage from its counterparts in the old world, but new forces were emerging in the southern republics that were bound to spur the nationalist cause. During both the First and Second World Wars, when the United States was unable to provide the twenty republics with sufficient manufactured goods, a degree of industrialization took place. The depression of the 1930's also gave impetus to factory development, since the Latin nations were forced to produce for themselves many of the items they normally imported. By 1947, therefore, production of manufactured goods was greater than agricultural production for the first time. By 1952, factories were turning out $11 billion in commodities as against agriculture's $8 billion. From 1937 to 1954, the number of industrial workers in Argentina tripled. What this meant was that new classes were maturing—the working class, the capitalist class—altering the traditional character of Latin America society.

Under such conditions, nationalism began to assert itself in a number of different forms. In Argentina, Juan Peron, and in Brazil, Getulio Vargas, sought to create for themselves bases of political power which included the working masses. Neither were democrats or revolutionaries, but in their own interests they used labor as a counterweight to military and feudal oligarchies. On the eve of the 1946 elections in Argentina, Peron decreed an extra month's pay as a bonus for all workers. He promulgated a welfare program that was more extensive than that of the United States—free medical care, vacations of ten to thirty days a year, pensions at age sixty. In the rural areas, landlords were required to provide showers for their laborers and to pay certain minimum wages. The previous union movement, led by socialists and anarchists, numbered only 300,000 adherents, but Peron's Confederation of Labor, which included agricultural workers, grew to five and a half million. For the first time in Argentine history, labor unions were granted grievance machinery. Discharge of a worker became next to impossible. The laborer gained a dignity he had not possessed before.

Peron and Vargas were dictators and their regimes corrupt, but the reliance on the working class for political support was something new in Latin America.

In Guatemala the dictator, Jorge Ubico, was ousted in 1944 and a democratic-minded former school teacher, Juan José Arevalo, was elected to office. Following his full six-year term, Jacobo Arbenz, a military officer with leftist leanings, became president. Under the two regimes, until Arbenz was ousted by a U. S.-sponsored coup, there were significant social reforms. All men eighteen years or over, whether literate or not, and all women of the same age, provided they could read and write, were granted the right to vote. Presidents were restricted, following the Mexican pattern, to a single six-year term, with no right to succeed themselves. Elections were held by secret ballot, and the freedom of assembly, expression, press, and the like, were unambiguously written into the constitution. Unions, never before legal, were given modern status under a new labor code, and in the short period of nine years grew to five hundred in number and 107,000 in membership. Wages in most sectors went up appreciably. During the short three-year Arbenz regime, some 85,000 peasant families were given plots of nationalized land, and in many areas peasants overran the farms of the *finca* owners and divided the acreage themselves.

In 1952, a deeper nationalist revolution took place in the small landlocked country of Bolivia. It was the closest thing to a "proletarian revolution" since Russia's in 1917. Victor Paz Estenssoro, a politician of the center, was elected president while in exile. When his plane touched native soil, the army refused to permit him to enter. The nationalist movement (MNR) thereupon organized a revolt by dissident members of the military and the police to put their man in his legitimate seat. Their efforts were crushed, however, and MNR leaders sought sanctuary in every embassy available. But at this point the tin miners entered the fray with a sense of discipline and national consciousness unique in so backward a country. Commandeering company trucks and arming themselves with dynamite, they descended on the capital and defeated the army. Three to four thousand died as the battle raged on the craggy hills of La Paz, but the generals were defeated. A feature of the Bolivian uprising, and perhaps a symptom of future ties between the left and nationalism, was the prominent role of the Trotskyists. Though small in number this group had been active among the miners in Potosi, so that when the civil war broke out they were able to provide ideological leadership for the whole movement. It was they who put forth the plan for arming peasants and workers, and for turning the unions into instruments of political power. With the communists, they were decisive adjuncts to nationalism.

Unlike the typical palace revolutions of Latin America, this one brought about deep changes. Only four years earlier, Indians were prohibited from walking the main streets of La Paz in their native clothes. After the revolt, they were given land belonging to large landlords and armed with rifles. At least fifty thousand workers were formed into a labor militia. Old generals were sent into exile. The mines—backbone of the economy— were nationalized.

IV

United States policymakers, imbued with the spirit of Anti-Communism, were incapable of recognizing in such events a portent of the future. They consoled themselves that in the American sphere of influence, unlike Asia and Africa, the past policies would be adequate to sustain hegemony. In June, 1952, the United States quickly recognized General Fulgencio Batista's coup d'état in Cuba. Elections were pending in the Caribbean island, and every poll indicated Batista would run a poor third for President. Without American support he could not have survived, but recognition was proffered him in the mistaken notion he was a "safe" ally. As already noted, Perez Jimenez and Rojas Pinilla were awarded the highest honors by the United States. Our government continued to lavish money on corrupt regimes, such as those of the Somoza brothers in Nicaragua, Duvalier in Haiti, Stroessner in Paraguay, Odria in Peru, and Trujillo in the Dominican Republic.

The most flagrant example of Anti-Communism in the 1950's was the overthrow of the Arbenz regime in Guatemala. There is no question that many communists associated themselves with the Arbenz cause—the Communist party (PGT) had been legalized a few years before by Arevalo—and no doubt rose to prominent position. This became a cause of concern in Washington and for the United Fruit Company in Guatemala. Instead of finding some working arrangement with the Arbenz regime, however, aiding its reforms and drawing it away from communists, the Central Intelligence Agency assumed the task of overthrowing it.[9] Under CIA tutelage, Colonel Carlos Castillo Armas outfitted a small force in neighboring Honduras and invaded his homeland. He did not get as far as the capital, Guatemala City, but he did not have to. Arbenz, fearful of great bloodshed and deserted by old friends in the army, refused to distribute arms to the unions and peasant organizations. No one can tell what might have happened if he had. Many communists in Guatemala to this day cannot forgive Arbenz for his "timidity." But the CIA and Castillo won an easy victory, which no doubt inflated illusions that a few guns and made-to-order army colonels could turn the tide everywhere.

The first acts of Castillo's regime in 1954 were ominous. From June to November, thousands of workers and political leaders were arrested. Employers fired militant unionists with impunity. United Fruit discharged seventy or eighty leaders on the claim they were "absent without permission"—they were hiding; and the railroad which was part of the United Fruit empire fired another two hundred. All unions were disbanded because they were "political." The 85,000 parcels of land that had been given to Indian peasants were taken back and returned to the *finca* owners. Some of these landlords, in a show of strength, marched back to their villages and burned the crops of their serfs. United Fruit was given back much of its holdings. In the next seven years, the Guatemala dictators distributed land to only 4,078 peasants—in a country where 70 per cent of the rural population is landless. The union movement was reduced to sixteen thousand members (from 107,000), no strikes were tolerated, and no wage increases granted—in a nation where 66 per cent of those employed earned less than $30 a month. Illiteracy, 72 per cent in 1954, remained at 72 per cent in 1961. The only "improvement" recorded was that foreign—United States—investment went up by 3,000 per cent! The CIA "victory" turned out to be hollow, for if this were the "American way" no forward-looking Latin American could subscribe to it.

Until Cuba, the United States saw no need to change the old order of Latin America. The alliance with the power elite remained firm; American corporate investors earned profits of 25 to 30 per cent and higher, heedless of the storm that was about to break over their heads

V

Such was the setting when the Fidelista cloudburst descended from the heavens in 1956-1958. No one in Washington was prepared for genuine revolution, or ready to encourage it. Our military men were training Batista's 43,000-man army during his most unwholesome period. While Batista was killing thousands of opponents—the estimate is as high as twenty thousand

—former Ambassador Arthur Gardner still considered him, as he testified later, America's "best friend." [10] Hundreds of millions of dollars were embezzled by Batista and his associates—the word in Havana was that of every dollar invested in public works, 33¢ went to the bureaucracy. At the other end of the social scale, one-third of the working force was unemployed—700,000 people. Three-quarters of the sugar workers labored only three or four months a year, during the *zafra* (harvest) season. More than a third of the population was totally illiterate and another third partially so. In the farm sections, 90 per cent of the people suffered from worm diseases, such as dysentery, or from anemia. Only 9 per cent of the rural homes had electricity, 2 per cent inside piping for water, and 3 per cent indoor toilets. Cuba, however, was a fertile ground for almost a billion dollars of American investment. North American firms owned 40 per cent of the sugar industry; with the Dutch-British firm, Shell, the whole petroleum industry; 90 per cent of the electric and telephone industries; mines and cattle ranches; and 25 per cent of banking facilities. Profits for the large sugar companies ran to 23 per cent of capital, and almost all was repatriated to the mainland rather than reinvested in Cuba.

This favorable situation for foreign companies and native tyrants was gravely disturbed by Fidel Castro and his July 26th Movement. Years later, United States policymakers have tried to erase their own responsibility for Castro's rise by saying he was a "secret communist all along" who had deceived the Cuban people. This was not true, and it was irrelevant under any circumstances.[11] The fact is that "our" side, with 43,000 soldiers, trained by American military advisors, possessing tens of millions of dollars of equipment, and with the whole machinery of government at its disposal, was unable to vanquish a force that began with eighty-odd men and never numbered more than 1,200 guerrillas. If communism, whether "secret" or not, is so formidable that it can open the spigot of revolution under such adverse circumstances, there is little hope that it can ever be challenged successfully.

Deputy CIA Director General C. P. Cabell, testifying before the Senate Internal Security Committee on November 5, 1959, stated that CIA's "information showed that the Cuban Communists do not consider him [Castro] a Communist Party member, or even a pro-Communist. . . . The Communists consider Castro as a representative of the bourgeoisie. . . . We know that the Communists were concerned when, at the time of his trip to the United States, he showed evidence of a friendly attitude toward the United States. . . . Within the 26th of July movement there is considerable evidence of opposition to communism. . . . We believe that Castro is not a member of the Communist Party, and does not consider himself to be a communist." [12]

In his oft-quoted speech of December 1, 1961, Castro actually pointed out that "I had prejudices against their party [the Communist party] originating mainly during the campaigns—I confess it with frankness—but today we are all comrades. We are all socialists." [13] He had considered the communists "sectarian," and he had been "influenced against them by the propaganda of imperialism and reaction."

In Cuba, as in Indochina and China, but with one important difference, a negative Western policy drew non-communist nationalists into the communist camp. But while in Indochina and China the communists had been the leaders of nationalist alliances for some years, in Cuba they had joined Castro's nationalism only a few months before he came to power and had little influence. They had supported Batista in his 1952 election campaign, and they had joined his government after he illegally came to power. Castro, on the other hand, had fought Batista throughout. Viewing all the facts, it is clear that the United States had an opportunity to drive deep wedges between *fidelismo* and communism had it adopted a positive policy toward land reform, American investments, and other facets of the Cuban Revolution. That it did not is testament not to the cunning of communism, but to the folly of Anti-Communism.

The Cuban revolution, like the Mexican, combined within it the objectives of two classes. The middle classes, sick of the illegality of the Batista regime, yearned for normalization, for political democracy. The peasants and workers yearned for land, social reforms, clinics, schools, lower rents, higher wages, and housing. The peasants did most of the fighting; the middle classes provided most of the leadership and money. After Castro came to power, he could have held this alliance together only if given large amounts of aid from the United States, or at least if his sugar trade—82 per cent of all exports—were not hindered. A country of 6.8 million people with a gross national product of only $2.5 billion can hardly put 700,000 jobless to work, distribute land, and build homes and schoolrooms, unless it is assured stability and help.

The United States government was not sympathetic to these problems. On the very day that Batista was preparing to flee, Ambassador Earl E. T. Smith was trying to form a military junta to forestall Castro. Batista has since written a book which gives the details of this incident. After Castro came from the hills to Havana, he requested a $4 million loan for road building equipment and a $1 million barter exchange of Cuban chrome for American corn to meet a food shortage. Both were turned down by the United States. A mission headed by Dr. Justo Carillo came to Washington in February, 1959, and returned empty-handed. The United States was willing to provide military advisers but no aid, and above all no support for land reform. Small planes, piloted by Cuban exiles and based in Florida, made repeated raids on Cuba's cities and sugarfields; but the State Department offered no apologies and the Justice Department took no steps to enforce the neutrality laws which specifically forbade such acts. Pedro Diaz Lanz, an ex-major in the Cuban Air Force, publicly boasted that he had taken part in attacks over Cuba, but the United States Government neither arrested him nor stopped him.[14]

In April, 1959, Castro came to the United States to speak at a meeting of newspapermen. President Eisenhower refused to see him. The State Department did hold a conference with him—in a hotel room; it did not want the meetings to appear as formal negotiations. According to the Cubans, Castro told Secretary of State Christian Herter that while other governments had promised land reform, this one meant to implement it. This would mean that hundreds of millions of dollars in American property might be nationalized; Castro wanted to work out an agreement which would make this step as painless as possible. He urged an arrangement similar to that with Mexico—twenty- or twenty-five-year bonds at stated interest. Regino Boti, Cuba's minister of economics who had once been a United Nations economist in Chile and was present at the talks, told me: "They either did not understand what we were talking about, or did not believe us, or did not want to believe us." [15] The United States insisted on prompt, immediate payment, on our terms. Vice-President Nixon met with Castro privately and concluded—as he reported later—that Castro was a communist and that we must prepare military action against him. He so recommended to President Eisenhower.

From this point on, anti-Castro propaganda began to fill American newspapers. The threat to cut off Cuba's sugar quota became alarming, for sugar was Cuba's lifeline. A nation where sugar constitutes 82 per cent of its exports must either export it or starve. But for the U. S., a billion dollars of investments were at stake. No one can seriously believe that the Department of State was or is disenchanted because "Castro is a dictator," for it has been doing business with dictators, including Batista, for a long, long time.

When the Cubans finally nationalized the sugar industry, the United States protested. We wanted payment for those holdings quickly and based on our own evaluations. As one of the measures to protect itself should trade with the United States end, Cuba ordered oil from the Soviet Union. It could buy a barrel from Russia for about 60¢ less than from American companies in Venezuela, thus preserving precious dollars as well as cutting costs. United States refining companies in Cuba, however, decided at this point to make their own foreign policy. They refused—despite a long-held agreement to refine *all* available oil—to process it. Thereupon Castro seized the refining industry, too.

Now the situation deteriorated unchecked. The Cuban sugar quota was cut and abolished, more U. S. firms were nationalized, diplomatic relations were severed. The Cuban government turned to the Soviet Union for economic sustenance.

In April, 1961, the CIA tried to repeat what it had done so successfully in Guatemala: it armed and trained an invasion force of 1,200 to 1,400 exiles, and spent $45 million for its cause. This time, however, the results were disastrous. Where Arbenz had refused to arm workers and peasants, Castro was prepared not only with his regular army but with a militia of 300,000 to 400,000 members. The exile effort collapsed in three short days. Castro now not only embraced the Soviet Union as an economic ally, but as an ideological guide: he announced his adherence to Marxism-Leninism. For the first time in history, a communist revolution was completed by men who were non-communists to begin with. When Anastas Mikoyan was in Havana in 1960, he had been roundly taken to task by Cuban officials and by radio commentators for Russia's intervention in Hungary in 1956. Such criticisms no longer occur. Cuba is the first communist state in the Western Hemisphere.

For many Americans this closes the book on Cuba and *fidelismo*. A communist country is an undiluted evil that need not be analyzed further. But politics is not that simple, nor can the mistakes of Anti-Communism be swept under the rug. In Latin America the facts are weighed more objectively. Castro has doubtless lost many supporters among the intelligentsia for reneging on his promise to hold elections within eighteen months. Most of the governments of Latin America have been mobilized by strong American pressure to break relations with Havana. But among the youth and the leaders of the workers and peasants, *fidelismo* continues to exercise magnetic attraction.

The reason is not difficult to understand. If you view the Cuban Revolution as a middle-class venture, it has been a total failure. If, however, you think of it in terms of the lower classes, it has accomplished more—certainly in its first few years—than any other Latin American nation.

Castro severed the alliance between middle class and lower class. He needed capital if he were to build schools, clinics, and homes, diversify agriculture, and make credit available to the new co-operatives. Since he could not get outside credits, he sought capital from internal sources—by "squeezing" the middle class. Every revolution in history has squeezed some segment of the population. The American Revolution, which did it much less than most, because there was so much land available westwards, nonetheless pauperized many people whose "continentals" turned out to be worthless. After the Meiji Restoration in Japan, the peasants were virtually robbed of their newly acquired land to form the capital needed for factories. Castro, however, formed capital not at the expense of the lower classes, but primarily of the more affluent elements. He nationalized middle-class and upper-class property, and impoverished its owners. After alienating this force, he refused to grant their demands for political democracy. He reneged on these promises completely. Elections were never held. Habeas corpus became a dead letter. Freedom of the press disappeared, and the right to form opposition parties or groups was repudiated.

Yet this is not the whole story, for Castro did keep most of his promises to the lower classes. In this respect the Cuban Revolution has been the deepest and most significant in Latin American history. With all its faults and shortcomings, it has completed the tasks of Hidalgo and Bolivar better than any other country. It instituted the most significant land reform in Latin American history. All sugar lands and all estates over one thousand acres were confiscated. Sixty-five thousand peasant families received patches of sixty-six acres each. Two hundred thousand more were put into state-formed co-operatives which provided year-round work, rather than three or four months as under the old regime. Tens of thousands of small homes were built for the village and city poor. Rents were cut by one-half, electricity and other services somewhat less. An "urban reform," sometime later, provided for the eventual ownership of apartments and homes by the dwellers themselves. Hundreds of thousands of the unemployed were provided with jobs. The number of classrooms rose in three years from 18,000 to 33,000, and a crash program against illiteracy virtually wiped it out by the end of 1961. Clinics were built in the most remote sections of the country, and though the national supply of doctors decreased as many physicians fled the country, the villages received more medical attention than they had every known before. Discrimination against Negroes was abolished by legal decree. Beach homes, nurseries, and many other facilities that the sons of the poor had never used before, or enjoyed only partially, now opened up for them. The old army was dissolved; the new one built roads, houses, and clinics, and its female members did social work, as well as train in military tactics. Above all, the Cuban Revolution gave the man at the bottom of the social scale a new sense of belonging: this was the first government in Cuban history that was interested in him. It was also the first honest one.

Historians and politicians may argue the merits of Castro's behavior for a long time. My own view is that there should have been more political democracy, that indeed the revolution paid a fearsome price, economically, for not permitting freedom of the press. Many mistakes, particularly in agriculture, might have been avoided if writers had been free to criticize. The regime would have benefited, too, from a normalized judicial system, with all the safeguards; and from dissent, either through opposition parties or factions within the ruling party. These are weaknesses in the revolution that can, under some circumstances, lead to full eclipse of its original humanism. The course of the Cuban Revolution is not yet finally decided; there are too many unknown factors in the equation. It is not a perfect revolution anymore than any revolution in history has been perfect.

The Cuban Revolution, as noted, has failed to live up to many of its promises, some because it could not, some because it would not. It is undergoing severe economic strain as it changes the direction of trade from America to Russia. Yet it is fair to say that most Cubans have benefited from the revolution, some materially, some spiritually, some both. There is a nationalist pride on the island that is not often duplicated. Samuel Shapiro, a professor at Notre Dame University, records that when he "asked the Cuba Libre *cooperativistas* in 1960, the turkey raisers on a state farm in Pinar del Rio in 1961, and the members of a fishermen's cooperative on the Bay of Pigs in 1962 whether they would like to do away with the Castro regime, the response was always an astonished stare, laughter, or an outburst of anger; and the fishermen had proved their loyalty with blood the previous year." [16] Most important, the regime has warded off outside attack and will probably survive for an indefinite period. It may resort to severe repressions—such as forced labor—if its economy continues to falter or if the Soviets reduce aid. It may face vitriolic disputes and factionalism, or it may turn back toward neutralism and a more consistent humanism. Its fundamental changes, however, will not be reversed.

"I would not try to predict," says Herbert Matthews, editorial writer of the *New York Times*, "what will come of the Cuban Revolution or what will remain of it. I only know that it will not die; that for all its faults and excesses it contains ideals and hopes and aspirations for which men and women in Latin America will struggle. However it ends—and all revolutions must end—it will not have been in vain." [17]

Whatever else one can say of the Cuban Revolution, it is a living repudiation of the policy of Anti-Communism. Our

American ego is pierced by this setback "90 miles from home," and we tend to dismiss the Castro victory as a "communist conspiracy," but in the cold glare of history it will be recorded as another example of a nationalist movement that was driven into communist hands by a false strategy.

VI

Washington's reaction to Cuba was similar to the Western reaction toward Russia after 1917—the financing of military attack by an exile group, non-recognition, and isolation. In this respect, the United States seems to have learned little from the past. But insofar as the rest of Latin America is concerned, there has been a significant change in policy, at least verbally. The United States formulated a program in 1961, the Alliance for Progress, that has placed itself squarely in favor of peaceful social revolution. Cuba was to be by-passed while efforts were made to strengthen the other nineteen republics, so as to immunize them against *fidelismo*.

In his inaugural address in January, 1961, President Kennedy said: "To our sister republics south of our border, we offer a special pledge—to convert our good words into good deeds—in a new alliance for progress, to assist free men and free governments in casting off the chains of peverty." [18] The program was spelled out in March as a ten-year plan "to transform the 1960's into an historic decade of democratic progress," and was ratified by the nineteen republics at Punta del Este on August 17, 1961. The United States promised "to furnish development loans on a long-term basis, where appropriate, running up to fifty years and at very low or zero rates of interest." In return, the Latin American countries agreed "to devote a rapidly increasing share of their own resources to economic and social development and to make the reforms necessary to assure that all share fully in the fruits of the Alliance for Progress." The Alliance placed conditions on economic aid—that the recipient nation enact certain social reforms, and especially land reform. The United States would pump $500 million a year additionally into the area, providing the nineteen republics made basic changes that would benefit their lower classes.

In the first year of the Alliance's operation, it became obvious that it was not achieving its goals. A billion dollars was allocated from March 3, 1961, to February 28, 1962, but the social changes were minute. "Latins are slow on basic reform," said the *New York Times.*[19] Teodoro Moscoso, in charge of the program for the United States, was subdued in his claims. There was no reason to celebrate the first anniversary of the Alliance, he said, because its progress had been slow. The following year, United States officials reported gains in the following statistical terms— 168,619 houses built; 18,585 classrooms; 13,354 miles of road (laid or repaired); 27,200 farm loans extended; 16,514 agricultural experts trained; hospitals and health centers opened; 622 water supply systems built.[20] National planning agencies were appointed in seven countries, tax reform laws were passed in ten, land reform measures were on the books in seven (in addition to three others that had had such laws for years, such as Mexico).

These figures, however, are illusory, for they are not correlated with other developments. For instance, while 168,619 houses were built in two years, 1.5 million new families were formed, all seeking shelter—and this must be added to the 60 or 70 per cent that were ill-housed to begin with. The *favelas* and *ranchos* that disgrace the hillsides and outskirts of all large cities were actually growing, not declining.

Education and health improvements were real and substantial, but they raised serious questions. The lifespan in most places is increasing, but so is unemployment. Under President Romulo Betancourt in Venezuela, from 1959 to 1963, joblessness tripled, to the highest level in that country's history. Death from yaws, malaria, and amoebic dysentery declined, but no one can be sure that death from malnutrition was not increasing, since food production and gross national product had barely kept pace with population growth, if not fallen behind. More children were learning to read and write, but there were few new jobs to utilize their talents.

The story of tax reform "in eleven Latin American countries" seems impressive, but some of it redistributes income in favor of the rich, rather than the middle class or the poor—just the opposite of what tax reform is supposed to do. In Guatemala, for instance, a tax law passed in 1962 replaced a business tax of 44 per cent with an income tax that rose to a maximum of 48 per cent. The latter, however, is so full of loopholes, according to American experts with whom I spoke in 1963, that the well-to-do will actually be paying less, while the middle class will be paying more.

Whether reforms elsewhere are more effective is not yet clear. But it is doubtful that the Latin American governments are recouping very much of the $3 billion a year which authorities estimate is denied them by the understated tax returns of the rich; or that the $1 billion to $1.5 billion a year that flees to the vaults of Geneva and New York is being stopped.

The Alliance shows other signs of feebleness. Private investments from the United States and Europe have not come up to expectations; in some places they have declined because investors are fearful of seizure of their properties if a revolution should break out.

Former Brazilian President Juscelino Kubitschek, a moderate and a friend of the United States, complained in 1963 that the program was "headed for failure." Foreign investments in Brazil, he said, had been $900 million in the previous seven years. But during the same period the nation lost $1.5 billion in national income as a result of falling prices for coffee and other exports. The initial United States investment, he said, had been cut from a scheduled $1.1 billion to $600 million, and no funds were being received from other countries or financial institutions that had been expected to contribute.[21] Many, if not most, of the nineteen republics were having severe financial problems trying to save their currency from inflationary trends and their treasury from bankruptcy. Luiz Carlos Prestes, leader of the Brazilian Communist party, could report to Moscow that communist strength had doubled in two years and was rising dramatically in the "ranks of the Brazilian army."

VII

The fundamental weakness of the Alliance seems to be that it cannot and will not remodel the power structure of the Latin countries. Here, as elsewhere, we have operated through the power elite. Washington has been underwriting a revolution from the top down—through the very feudal oligarchies which have impeded it for years—rather than from the bottom up.

Caught in the vise of Anti-Communism, it has feared that disruption of these power structures might lead to *fidelismo*. A "responsible, senior U. S. official" told Frederick Kuh of the *Chicago Sun-Times:* "Presumably in the Alliance for Progress we're trying to put distance between the United States and reactionary regimes of Latin America, such as those of Paraguay, Nicaragua and Haiti . . . [but] our Cuban problem militates against this. For instance, in January, 1962, at the conference of Punte del Este, we were working to create hemispheric solidarity against Fidel Castro. Lining up some Latin American states with center-left governments was difficult. They have sympathy with the original aims of the Cuban revolution, though they tend to regard Castro as the betrayer of his own revolution. . . . And yet when the U. S. delegation went to Punta del Este, it found itself counting votes, and in order to get the desired anti-Castro majority it had to woo Haiti and other Latin American nations with reactionary regimes." [22]

To woo an "anti-Castro majority," the United States shut its eyes to fraudulent elections in Paraguay, Haiti, Nicaragua, Guatemala, and Salvador; it overlooked military coups in Peru, Guatemala, and Ecuador, and military pressures which forced elected governments out of power in Argentina and Brazil. In 1962 and 1963 alone, there were six military coups. On the one hand the United States was urging Latin America to make needed reforms; on the other it was propping the military institutions that stood as a bastion *against* reform. Military assistance by the United States to Latin America rose from $200,000 in 1952 to $11 million in 1953 and $92 million in 1961. It is conceded, says James Reston of the *New York Times,* that little of this can be used for "hemispheric defense." "Our arms are now intended to maintain internal order, [and] President Kennedy has formally authorized their use in that way." [23] What the military of Latin America consider to be "internal order" was more than abundantly evident as they toppled one regime after another from 1961 to 1963, because these regimes were too "radical," or because the military feared an honest election. Thus, on March 30, 1963, Colonel Enrique Peralta seized the reins of government in Guatemala because it was obvious that Juan Jose Arevalo, a non-communist and former president of the country, would easily defeat his rivals in the impending presidential election. And the Argentinian military, some time before, vitiated elections and placed President Frondizi under house arrest, because the Peronistas had gained too many seats.

Certainly the most disturbing military coup of the first three years of the Alliance for Progress was the one in the Dominican Republic in mid-1963. The President of this small country, Juan Bosch, a writer, humanist, and democratic socialist, offered perhaps the best counterweight to *fidelismo* of any leader in the nineteen republics. The answer to communism, he told me in the summer of 1963, was to do a better job for the peasant and laboring masses. He refused to outlaw the communists and *fidelistas* unless they acted illegally. "If I suppress the left," he said, "I must lean on the right. In that case there is no chance for my reform program." Bosch contemplated distributing land to 70,000 of the 98,000 families who are landless or have inadequate holdings. His program, only partly worked out, called for a $150 million project at Puerto Plata in the north that would have supplied jobs for forty thousand workers; the building of one thousand schools in four years; considerable electrification and irrigation, as well as other improvements. In a country which produces only $800 million of goods and services a year, this would have been a substantial advance.

But Bosch was overthrown by the military after only a half-year in office. The army made the usual claims that he was "soft on communism," but in actuality the issue was economic. Leaders of the opposition, the Union Civica, told me a few weeks before Bosch fell that their main objection to his regime was that he refused to de-nationalize $500 million of properties that belonged to the former dictator, Rafael Trujillo. To the credit of the United States, Ambassador John Bartlow Martin opposed the coup and gave Bosch fulsome support. But the military officers of the United States Mission encouraged both the opposition and the military coup by openly speaking of Bosch either as a "communist" or "soft on communism." [24] A union federation close to the American labor attaché published an advertisement in *El Caribe* urging the people to rely on the army, as well as themselves, in the fight against communism.[25] In reality, the American policy faced both ways, with many embassy officials endorsing the usual policy of Anti-Communism.

VIII

By all odds, the greatest need of the southern republics is change in the land-owning structure. In Brazil, 5 per cent of the rural population owns 95 per cent of the land; in Venezuela, 2 per cent owns 74 per cent of the land, while 300,000 families are landless; in Chile 9.7 per cent owns 86 per cent of the acreage. Of the seven countries that have enacted land reform legislation since the Alliance, only two had actually settled anyone on their own land by the end of 1962. In Venezuela, the four-year program was expected to settle 200,000 peasant families, but in the first three years (1960-1962) only fifty thousand were settled. "This means," writes Oscar Delgado, "seven percent of the active agricultural population, as opposed to forty-one percent in Mexico and thirty-two percent in Cuba (as a result of their land reforms)." [26] Of the 1.5 million hectares of land distributed to peasants, only a half-million came from the larger landowners—and they received full pay for it, and sometimes better. Before "land reform" the landlords owned 22 million hectares; afterwards 21.5 million—still three-quarters of the tilled acreage of all Venezuela. Their power was untouched and that of the peasantry has improved only minutely, if at all.

Venezuela, it should be noted, has done more than all the other Latin adherents to the Alliance put together, except for Mexico and Bolivia. Chile's government decided to divide only "abandoned" land. In proposing this measure, Minister of the Economy Luis Escobar said that Chile must consider "political reality." The political reality is that many in the government coalition are themselves big landowners. In Guatemala, landowners have been buying marginal land for the past few years, against the possibility that "land reform" will force them to sell some holdings.

In Brazil, the most important country of Latin America, land reform has been discussed in parliament for a decade, but only in 1914 were some decrees invoked. A few thousand peasants, encouraged by men like Leonel Brizola, former governor of Rio Grande do Sul, have seized some land on their own, but this hardly begins to make a dent in the problem.

Under any circumstances, land reform as presently conceived under the Alliance for Progress is actually "parcellization," not true reform. The peasant is usually granted a strip of ten or twelve acres, from which he can earn only a small sum—in Cunday, Colombia, where one such program is underway, for instance, between $60 and $300 a year. This is better than what he had before, but a true land reform not only must transform agriculture more drastically, not only must change the social relationship between peasant and oligarch, but must decisively alter the character of the city economy as well.

Consider Colombia. There are now 1.8 million families living on the farm. They cultivate 7.5 million acres, an average of four each. According to Dr. Enrique Pena Losa, who heads the agrarian reform organization, Colombia has a surplus of at least a million families. With 800,000 farmers, the same amount of land, and semi-modern methods, he claims the nation could produce more than at present.

"If you gave me all the money I wanted to buy land, to irrigate, build dams, provide credit, and so on," says Dr. Pena Losa, "and if I had an absolute free hand, without political restrictions, I still couldn't reclaim more than a few million acres, nor utilize more than 800,000 families on our farms." [27]

But what do you do with a million extra families? Twelve years from now the figure will be two million, and by the year 2000 it will be four million. In the United States the process of de-ruralization took a century and a half. Meanwhile, the country accumulated the capital and found the consumers so that it could provide jobs. But Colombia has only fifteen million people. Of these, only one-third are consumers; the rest do not enter the money market, except episodically. Since Colombia cannot compete on the world scene with the advanced nations, all its manufacture must be for internal use. But this is limited when you have only five million customers. How, then, do you create jobs for one, two, or four million redundant peasants?

"You Americans," says Dr. Pena Losa, "are entranced by statistics. If I were to distribute 500,000 acres to 50,000 landless families you would publish it in your papers back home as a grand achievement. But what good would it do? They'd be living in penury, and if they produced more coffee than we do now it would only drive the price down. What we need is *less* farmers, but farmers who have a middle class standard of living and can buy commodities from the city."

The bottleneck in Colombia's economy, says Pena Losa, is in the balance of payments. Three-quarters of Colombia's exports are coffee, but coffee has declined in price since 1955 from 85¢ a pound to 40¢. On the other hand, the commodities Colombia buys from the United States have gone up appreciably. These unfavorable terms of trade create ceaseless crises, devaluations of currency, and political tensions. The temporary solution is to reduce imports and increase exports. But there are not too many imports that can be dispensed with. Most are necessary food, trucks, and machinery. Each year Colombia buys from abroad $70 million worth of food; by 1970, this figure will rise to $135 million, and by 1980 to $250 million. The only way to reduce these sums is to diversify agriculture—produce vegetable oils, cocoa, wheat, etc., at home. Again, however, this is not possible under the present social structure. The small farmer *cannot* diversify because his holding is uneconomic and he does not have the credits or the know-how. The large, feudal farmer *will not* diversify because he does well enough now. He is accustomed to sending capital out of the country, and if he does invest internally, it is in something where the risk is minimal and the profit astronomical.

Should the state, then, launch large state farms, Russian-type collectives, or Scandinavian-type co-operatives? This might work, but it would take great sums of capital, and anyway the oligarchs of Colombia will not permit their government to engage in "socialist" experiments. Dr. Pena Losa feels that if he had a billion dollars over the next fifteen years he could reclaim another three million acres of land and settle 200,000 to 300,000 families in middle-class agriculture. But this would still leave two million redundant families in the villages. Where Colombia can find the jobs for them, he does not know—particularly since city unemployment now is going up by fifty thousand a year.

Meanwhile, Dr. Pena Losa's agrarian reform limps along as best it can. When he is under political pressure—as in Cunday, where there has been much violence for more than a decade— he buys a few thousand hectares and distributes it to a hundred or so families. For the rest, everything is in suspended animation. "When I realize," Dr. Pena Losa says, "there are 1,000 new rural families each week, I can't sleep nights."

The Alliance for Progress does not meet this problem in its full complexity. It does not because it dare not tamper either with the power structure in Latin America or the private enterprise addiction at home. When a country is near bankruptcy, the Alliance loans it money to meet the balance of payments deficit and sustain its currency. It provides loans to factory owners, agricultural middlemen, sometimes farmers. It fashions a stronger "infra-structure"—roads, electricity, dams, railroads. It helps develop new export industries (the vogue right now is sugar, cotton, and cattle). It tries to lure American business south of the Rio Grande and stimulate local capital formation. The result is that some jobs are created in new industries, and that commercial farming exports increase to make up in part for cuts in coffee and other prices. The crisis is mitigated. But the deeper problems are not solved: the balance of payments remains adverse, and tens of millions of villagers remain at the point of destitution. Unemployment increases, and the total feeling—except in Mexico, which is a story apart—is one of continued stagnation.

IX

To generalize about Latin America is fraught with peril, because each nation has its own special problems, based on history, tradition, resources, and leadership. Yet there is a common denominator to the travail of the nineteen republics, for in varying degrees they are held back by the residues of feudalism and foreign economic control. Their oligarchies seek to preserve ancient privileges; their military forces, for the most part, are servants of this oligarchy; and their U. S. corporations have a stake in keeping things as they are. The oligarchies send large sums of their money out of the area, to banks and vaults in Geneva and New York; the foreign corporations take out ordinarily more than they put in. In 1960, for instance, U. S. firms invested $267 million in Latin America, but sent home to the United States $641 million of their profit; the following year they invested $500 million but remitted $770 million. By contrast, American corporations in Western Europe during these same years shipped back to the United States only a third as much as they were investing.[28]

Alliance for Progress loans and gifts do not and cannot compensate either for the outflow of capital and profits, or the unfavorable terms of trade. What inhibits Latin America is a social structure that is incapable of capturing its resources for its own use. In theory, no doubt, the Alliance would prefer that the oligarchies be curbed, but because North America's own corporations are so linked with those oligarchies, it has been unable to exert the required pressures—economic and political— to alter the situation.

Consider the plight of former President Romulo Betancourt of Venezuela. Betancourt was honest, dedicated, and hopeful of introducing basic changes. But when he took office in February, 1959, he carried two millstones around his neck—the American-owned oil industry and the American-trained and supplied army. Venezuela's economy depends on oil. It produces 90 per cent of the exports and its tax payments provide three-fifths of the national budget. It is a law unto itself, for if the government tried to nationalize it, it would face an international boycott—as Iran did in the 1950's. It would be unable to secure tankers to transport its petroleum, or customers to buy it. What the oil interests decide in Rockefeller Plaza, therefore, is more important for the development of Venezuela than most of the decisions in Caracas. The petroleum interests, for instance, reduced new investment from $590 million in 1957 and $579 million in 1958 to $167 and $178 million respectively in 1961 and 1962. Betancourt's best laid plans, even if they confronted no other obstacles, would have difficulty overcoming so great a loss of capital investment. Unless he were ready to "squeeze" the oil companies—impose higher taxes, illegalize the remittance of profits, or take other measures—he could do very little. He could, of course, press the oligarchy more vigorously for needed capital, but there he would confront the opposition of the top military leaders. Unless Betancourt were ready openly to oppose Washington, which supports the oil firms, and his own military, his desire for fundamental change was bound to lie in abeyance. And if he did tackle the problem at its roots, he could only do so by calling on the city and rural masses to act as a counterweight to the oligarchs and the military. Here, however, he would face the hostility of the communists, who had considerable working class support, so long as he was pro-Washington and anti-*fidelista*. His position was an endless circle of frustration, which began—not as commonly assumed—because of "communist subversion," but because of Venezuela's power structure and the inherent role of foreign investors.

Almost from the beginning, therefore, Betancourt confronted a crisis. Though he plodded along and produced many improvements, particularly in education and health programs, he was unable to cure or significantly lay the groundwork for curing the economic problems of the people. The first two and a half years of his term were depression years. In 1962, because of a rise in petroleum production, conditions improved but per capita production remained slightly lower than when he came to power four years before. In the 1950's, gross national product grew by 8 per cent a year; in 1960, by only 1.4 per cent; 1961, 1.7 per cent; and 1962, 6 per cent. Net investment declined from 16 per cent of the gross product in 1959 to 6 per cent in 1961. The promise of jobs—Betancourt's main plank in 1958—failed to materialize. Unemployment in 1963 was 13.6 per cent of the labor force, and partial unemployment twice that figure. In this respect, the situation was three times worse than it had been five years before.

Concomitant with this economic problem was an inevitable political one. The communists naturally used the situation to try and build a larger mass base. They found fertile ground among the disaffected masses, especially in the large cities. Betancourt's response was to suppress many unemployed demonstrators, as well as the communists. During half of his term in office, he imposed a "state of suspension of constitutional guarantees." Thousands were arrested without the right of habeas corpus, the press was censored (and in 1963, two newspapers close to the communists were prohibited entirely from publishing), political activity by opposition groups—including noncommunists—was seriously hindered, union protests were circumscribed, and the nation was reduced to dictatorial status for varying periods.

So long as Washington takes no affirmative steps to change the *power structure* of Latin America, the Alliance for Progress is doomed to impotence, and men like Betancourt, to frustration. Under these circumstances, the Latin American revolution will tend more and more to violent solution. The most likely results will be either *fidelista* guerrilla campaigns or rebellions by young officers in the armies who model themselves after Nasser in Egypt. Only a small hope remains for a non-violent revolution by the Latin American equivalents of Martin Luther King.

By seeking to make a revolution from the top down—through the oligarchies—the Alliance for Progress has failed in its mission. Unless it reorients its policy, it promises to isolate the United States once again from radical nationalism and to drive it, as in Cuba, China, and Indochina, into the hands of the communists.

The United States, we must repeat, cannot *make* revolutions in Latin America. It should not, for this is the task of native leaders. But through its aid program it can discourage and weaken the dictators, while encouraging the nationalists. By eliminating all military help, for instance, some dictatorships would collapse in quick order. Without American guns and military training, the dictators of Nicaragua and Guatemala—to name only two—would have difficulty surviving. If, in addition, the United States would exert economic pressure, by refusing aid and loans where reform does not take place, the hopes of the old classes would be shattered, perhaps beyond repair.

If, however, the present reliance on the oligarchies continues, Latin America will present problems for the United States as difficult—if not more so—as those faced by Britain, France, and the imperial powers in Asia and Africa. Latin America can be the final disaster for the policy of Anti-Communism.

XII

The Futile Crusade

THROUGHOUT history, nations which have misjudged the effects of technological or social change have lost wars or have been eclipsed as important powers. Carthage was vanquished by Rome in the Punic Wars because she mistakenly believed that her mercenaries, quinqueremes (boats with five banks of oars), and elephants were invincible. They had been for a long time. But the Romans used free citizens as soldiers, added a corvus to their ships which hooked enemy boats and prevented them from ramming, and learned how to disperse the elephant brigades. Carthage was destroyed; Rome began her long career as the world's most powerful nation.

France was overrun by Nazi Germany in World War II because she relied on the strategic principles of World War I. The earlier campaign had been a "war of position." Armies dug deep trenches, shot at each other across the lines, and, when they had decimated the enemy sufficiently, went over the top to capture his position. Movement was limited to a few hundred yards each time, or, during strategic retreats to better lines, a few miles. In preparing for the second war, France adhered to the same concept of "position." Her Maginot Line of "impregnable" forts, built with thousands of tons of steel and concrete, was like a long trench that could not—or so it was believed—be pierced. But technology now made possible a different type of military effort, a "war of movement," with fast tanks and high speed stuka planes. Using these weapons, Germany quickly encircled fortified areas and made them impotent. The Maginot Line proved useless; it fell with hardly a shot.

The intervention in Russia by the Allied powers, from 1918 to 1920, was based on an even more serious miscalculation. The Allies conceived of the struggle in purely military terms: if enough soldiers were placed on Russian territory and enough money and arms donated to the counter-revolutionary forces, the Bolshevik regime would be smashed. Such strategy had worked against nationalist revolt in the colonies and had worked in the World War; it was bound to succeed here, too. But this time military considerations were far less important than social ones. The Bolsheviks, though able to throw only a rudimentary army into the fray, depended mostly on propaganda, guerrilla tactics, and world-wide support in their behalf. They rallied innumerable people in and out of Russia who felt—rightly or wrongly—that by supporting the Bolsheviks they were supporting an idealistic cause. The Allies and the White Russians were unprepared for this kind of conflict, and so they actually paved the way for the Soviet victory.

Lenin distributed land to poor peasants. The White armies, on the other hand, restored these holdings, wherever they could, to the large landowners who traveled with them. The mass of Russia became convinced that a White Guard success would bring back Czarism or its equivalent—and joined Red guerrillas. Lenin also made concessions to the middle peasants and small handicraft workers, consolidating them behind his regime. "The rapid collapse of [rightist generals] Kolchak and Deniken," writes Walter Duranty, former *New York Times* correspondent, "was greatly aided by guerrilla activities behind their front lines, in which middle peasants and artisans took a vigorous part." [1] The Soviets appealed to foreign soldiers and foreign workers to help them. "Comrades," they said in their leaflets and propaganda, "why are you fighting us? We don't want to fight. We want to be let alone. You go home and we'll go home." [2] Their efforts bore fruit among tired soldiers, sick of war and confused by the realignment of friends and enemies. American troops sang "Home toot sweet" and staged a near mutiny to force their withdrawal. A mutiny by the French fleet in Odessa caused France to evacuate that key city. All over Europe and America there were demonstrations for "hands off Russia," not only by communists, but by mild socialists and liberals as well. Longshoremen and sailors refused to load or man ships carrying munitions to the enemies of the Soviets. The Allies were defeated because they failed to reckon with the appeals of land reform, national patriotism, and social revolution. Militarily and financially they were far superior, but their false analysis of the situation caused their setback.

It is interesting to note that the weight of opinion in the

West from 1918 to 1920 was that the Soviets could not hold out—but they did. And the weight of opinion in 1938, as any survey of the press will prove, was that France would be able to restrain Germany—but she did not. Yet in both cases, policy-makers clung tenaciously to policies of the past, incapable of comprehending that technology or social change had outdated them.

I

The same sort of mis-estimates today hinder the United States. Its policy-makers and experts operate on the thesis that national security is essentially a military question—as in the past. If planes and nuclear bombs could assure security in 1941-1945, bigger planes and bigger bombs can do the same today. Washington recognizes that the world revolution is a reality, but it does not consider this to be *decisive*. It agrees that much has changed, but behind the facade of "fighting communism" its main motivations are still trade, investment, and business-as-usual. It does not, or will not, recognize that technology and radical nationalism have not merely modified the world of yesterday but created a new *kind* of world, with new sources of power.

It is understandable that this should be so, for the United States has suffered no severe shocks since the mid-1930's. Even the war did not break its stride—no American cities were bombed; American casualties, though grave, were far less than those of European nations; and the hardships of 1941-1945 were relatively minor. The unemployed, that still numbered nine million in 1939, had been absorbed into the economy. There were billions of dollars of war bonds to be converted and spent on postwar automobiles and other gadgets. Most Americans wanted nothing else than to be left alone to enjoy material benefits. Anything at home or abroad that challenged the established order seemed to threaten their own status. The agitation of dependent people for independence, the demands of socialists in Germany or Britain for nationalization of basic industry, the guerrilla fighting in Greece or Indonesia, disturbed the conservative mood of the nation. Americans were resigned to the fact they had a new responsibility in international affairs, as the leading nation in the world, but they hoped to confine that responsibility to relief programs such as UNRRA. They sympathized with the nationalist aspirations of the people of Asia and Africa, but their sympathy was a remote and dispassionate one, not easily converted into deed. In Europe, the political shift was to the left—the British Labor party replaced the Tories, communists and socialists became part of coalition governments in Italy, France, Belgium, and Holland. But in the United States the trend was to the right. The smashing victory of the Republican party in 1946 wiped out much liberal influence. Liberalism and radicalism were beginning an uninterrupted decline that would last for many years.

Under these circumstances, as James P. Warburg puts it, "the great crusade for human freedom degenerated into an effort to restore as much as possible of the prewar world." [3] The status quo was preferable to new experiments and new realignments of power. Thus, while Americans abhorred colonialism, they were less outraged by British, French, and Dutch efforts to sustain old spheres of influence than by Russian moves to carve out a new sphere for themselves in Eastern Europe and East Germany. A new factor, radical nationalism, had been added to the international equation, while the Western Allies were playing by the old rules. Given its conservative frame of mind and the lack of decisive leadership by liberalism, America became prey to the manipulations of a burgeoning military and industrial complex whose goal was to maintain privileges and prerogatives gained during the war.

The war was over, but militarists and important segments of industry insisted on maintaining a military stance. To do so they played up the Soviet disavowal of promises made at Yalta, while downplaying the British and French disavowals of promises made during the Atlantic and other meetings. Soviet behavior in Eastern Europe was certainly harsh and a transgression on the Atlantic Charter. But in Greece, France, Italy, China, and the French colonies, communism took a moderate and accommodative position. Yet the American military-industrial complex overlooked the latter and emphasized the former. The military stance needed an enemy, and communist Russia offered a convenient target. The growing dislocation of the international balance of power was attributed not to the diseased social order which was spewing forth a wave of revolutions, but to "communist aggression," which could be checked only by a refurbished militarism. It had worked before; it had brought victory to the United States in World Wars I and II; it would inevitably succeed again. America had a monopoly on the atomic bomb, and it could be brandished at the Soviets to "hold the line."

II

This thesis overlooked two fundamental changes in the character of the postwar world:

1. Radical nationalism was on the march in Africa, Asia, and Latin America, and it could not be stopped regardless of what the Soviets did or did not do.

2. A technological and scientific revolution was under way which was making military power itself obsolete.

The colonial world, quiescent and defensive for a century, was now on the offensive. It would upset the world balance of power whether the West liked it or not, and whether the communists aided it or not. Its aspirations could no longer be squelched, even by superior military power. A combination of nationalist fervor and such rudimentary tactics as demonstrations, strikes, and guerrilla warfare was proving itself more formidable than modern planes, tanks, and even the implicit threat of nuclear bombing. The measure of change could be gauged by the fact that in the 1850's Britain could conquer all of India with only fifty thousand troops, but that in the 1950's a half-million French forces, spending $1 billion a year and armed with the latest weapons, was unable to defeat 45,000 Algerian guerrillas. The underpinnings of diplomacy were being changed from trade, investment, and spheres of influence, to liberation and establishment of viable societies. But with eyes riveted on the past, America either could not see this fact or downgraded its importance. It was mired in a Maginot Line complex.

Nor was this all. The national and social revolution was joined by a technological and scientific revolution that made victory in a total war impossible. "Always in the past," wrote Walter Lippmann, "war and the threat of war, whether it was aggressive or defensive, were usable instruments. They were usable instruments in the sense that nations could go to war for their national purposes. They could threaten war for diplomatic reasons. Nations could transform themselves from petty states to great powers by means of war. They could enlarge their territory, acquire profitable colonies, change the religion of vanquished populations, all by means of war. War was the instrument with which the social, political and legal systems of large areas were changed. Thus, in the old days before the nuclear age began, war was a usable—however horrible and expensive—instrument of national purpose. The reason: Old wars could be won." [4] But new world wars cannot. No matter what nation emerges as "victor," it will suffer so many casualties and have so much of its industry destroyed that it will cease to be a viable state.

In 1959, the Joint Committee on Atomic Energy of the United States Congress estimated that if the Soviets dropped 1,446 megatons of bombs on American soil, most of them in non-urban areas, there would be fifty million dead and twenty million wounded.[5] Fourteen hundred and forty-six megatons is only 10 per cent of the Soviet stockpile, according to conservative estimates, and 4 per cent of the American stockpile. Three years later, President Kennedy estimated that had the crisis over Cuba escalated to nuclear war, it would have resulted in 300 million deaths—100 million each in Europe, Russia, and the United States. In such a war, he said, no matter how it started or by whom, "all we have built up, all we have worked for, would be destroyed in the first twenty-four hours." [6] So rapid is the march of technology and the storing of nuclear arms that with each passing month such figures must be revised upwards, so that in the not too distant future the death toll can be total, no matter which nation strikes the first blow.

Bertrand Russell, writing in the *Minority of One* for February, 1964, asserts that "the United States has, at the moment, a stockpile of 130,000 aerosol nerve gas bombs. This non-nuclear stockpile is as deadly as its nuclear counterpart. Each nerve gas bomb is capable of extinguishing life in an area of 3,500 square miles. The total stockpile is capable of eliminating life in an area of 455 million square miles. This is eight times the total land area of the globe and 151 times that of the United States of America."

Yet, while Rusk and other policymakers concede that world wars can no longer be won, they believe that nuclear weaponry is needed for psychological reasons—to *deter* an enemy. For the first time in history, neither side in a war can defend itself from a destruction that would make it un-viable, but both sides rely on a "balance of terror" to prevent total war while they concentrate on "brush-fire" or limited wars. The arguments against this policy have been made so often we need not repeat them here in any detail. Military deterrence is invalid as a strategy to contain international conflict, because war can break out anyway if one side or the other becomes irrational—as happens all too often in history, or because a bomb explodes by accident, or because the escalation of the arms race itself makes it necessary to paint the enemy as all-black, thus impeding reconciliation and negotiation. The strategy of deterrence disregards the fact that small wars tend to pyramid into big ones, that nations in battle tend to lose all restraint, and, above all, that most of the battles of our time have been revolutionary ones by nationalist guerrillas.

Furthermore, the military theorists fail to consider adequately the *political* prospects of their course. What does militarism do for democracy at home? What kind of life will America lead even if it "prevails" after the holocaust? Almost everyone concedes that we would be forced into a military dictatorship for many years; the very phenomenon against which America is fighting—totalitarianism—would become our own lot for a long time, even assuming we survived. And what of the machinations of other powers? Wouldn't a prostrate United States be an open invitation to the Chinese to seize all of Asia, and perhaps invade this country as well? Could this country, weakened by unparalleled catastrophe, continue to exercise power in the Western Hemisphere? No matter how optimistic our policymakers can be about military prospects, the political and social possibilities are more dire. Our strategy since 1946 has been unrealistic, because even if it succeeded it could not possibly keep the United States strong or preserve it as a first-class power.

The policy of Anti-Communism has failed to recognize today's circumstances—the social revolution, the scientific revolution. Its role is negative. It relies primarily on military power, as in the past, while social power has become the determinant of world affairs. It gropes for an elusive absolute weapon, in the hopes that it can deliver the final ultimatum to the Soviets, while underplaying the social weapon which is the only means by which America can be sustained. And while doing this it warps the democratic process at home, so that our appeal to other countries and other peoples has seriously declined.

To compensate for these fallacies, the American public is fed the propaganda—particularly by the ex-radicals who have associated themselves with the Anti-Communist goals of the military-industrial complex—that the revolutions in progress throughout the world are not really succeeding. Indonesia's Sukarno has arrested many of the best leaders of the Indonesian revolution. Nkrumah has incarcerated his political opponents and has made a mockery of the multi-party system. Nasser permits no political democracy. Algeria outlaws opposition. Cuba is reeling under heavy economic burdens and the Castro regime may fall. The Indian revolution has failed to stamp out untouchability after nearly two decades and is moving at a slow pace generally. China is an unvarnished dictatorship.

All of this is true for the most part, yet it is only an episodic phase of the world revolution. No revolutionary nation can fulfill its promises without great difficulties, without setbacks, without spurts and spasms. The American Revolution in 1775, if we would only look back at our own history, needed many years of adjustment. It was followed in 1783-1788 by the "critical years," in which men like Daniel Shays of Massachusetts sought to overthrow the government because it had not achieved its aims, and because many people had been temporarily pauperized. During the early days of the Republic, Hamiltonians and Jeffersonians smashed each other's presses and imposed beatings on their opponents. For a few years under the second President, John Adams, the Alien and Sedition laws subverted democracy. Property qualifications for voting remained for decades after the Revolution, as well as imprisonment for debt, Negro slavery, and other blots on the democratic process. And this was a revolution with far more favorable possibilities than the present ones: there were millions of acres of land to the West, there was a competent and educated leadership, and the capital needed to industrialize was small compared to today. America finally solved its problems after many decades. The new nations of Asia, Africa, and Latin America, despite much more formidable difficulties, will eventually do the same. Their revolution is in transition, but it no longer can be—or should be—stopped. It is moving, haltingly but persistently, from the national liberation phase to the social transformation phase. Nothing short of total war can prevent its continuation.

This revolution is the central feature of our epoch, but Anti-Communism, while paying lip service to it, does not make it the central theme of strategy. Instead it concentrates *first* on "defeating communism," and *then* adjusting to the revolution's need for social reforms. It mistakes communism for the cause, rather than an effect of the world's instability. And it is so consumed by fear and anxiety that it does not properly evaluate the softening process within communism itself. It is fighting the wrong war with the wrong weapons.

If the debacle of American Anti-Communist policy is not entirely visible it is only because we are mid-point in the game. Communism has won only in China, North Viet Nam, and Cuba, so far. But as the revolution continues and accelerates, other nations will turn to communism, other nations will become more unfriendly to the United States. The balance of world power we defend so rigorously by military means will have altered more drastically—against us—because of social changes. Unless we can make our own society much more attractive, and unless we can convince the radical nationalists elsewhere that we are not interested in them primarily for military bases and spheres of investment, but because we truly want to help *them,* the pendulum will swing further away from us. Even assuming that the world can escape nuclear incineration, the United States can be eclipsed as a great nation without a single hydrogen bomb falling.

Leaving aside the moral issue—U.S. spending of $650 billion dollars on the arms race since the war, while so many people lived in slums, earned low wages, and did without the necessary hospital facilities, mental clinics, and schools—leaving that aside, the negative policy of Anti-Communism is not only futile but self-defeating.[7] "If, under the courses we are now following," observes Walter Millis, "the free society is not destroyed in the nuclear fires; if it is not corrupted from within by the illiberal and immoral implications of its basic foreign policy, it will still face a third peril. Simply stated, this is that the Russian Communist empire will win the world from us by those non-military means which our own policies and attitudes have done so much to facilitate." [8]

Americans have been disoriented by the continuing crises in foreign affairs. No sooner is the loss of China recorded then a "problem" arises in Indochina, and after Indochina, Algeria, South Viet Nam, Laos, the Congo, Cuba, and others. There is a momentary respite, and trouble looms in Panama or Cyprus. Africa seems quiescent, almost fully independent, when outbreaks occur in Zanzibar, Tanganyika, Kenya—nations that are already free.

Our statesmen are caught short by such events because they fail to recognize that there *is* a double revolution underway. This double revolution will not end, despite setbacks and some counter-revolutions, until the dependent nations become independent. And the independent nations will not be free of tensions unless and until they proceed in an orderly fashion to the promised better day. Independence does not solve all problems; it is only a prerequisite to begin solving them. Some nationalist leaders quickly become opportunists. Power begets corruption, especially amongst those whose idealism is tenuous. Cabinet members in Nigeria build lavish homes (one for each wife) and cabinet ministers in Ghana become rich as real estate speculators. For their personal gain they are willing to delay the pace of social change. But the masses of such countries insist that the promises of land, schools, hospitals, and higher living standards be kept. And, given the impetus of their original revolution, they prod it ever forward.

Thus a conservative sultan in Zanzibar is overthrown because the people feel that independence without broad social change is not enough. Guerrillas renew action in the Congo because they feel their government is moving too slowly. Not only is there a colonial world revolution in progress, but it moves inexorably from the national to the social phase.

Here, again, the communists seize on opportunity. They not only join with nationalism, but simultaneously attempt to deepen it. Though they scarcely had any following in Black Africa a few years ago, their ranks are swelling significantly as pressures mount for revolutions to pay off their promissory notes. If the United States, on the other hand, finds itself with new "problems," it is because it is not doing all it should to help the revolutions advance in an orderly and peaceful fashion. No one can argue that the United States has tried to prevent independence for the countries of Black Africa—though its record in the Union of South Africa leaves much to be desired. Yet the emphasis of American planning is some vague theme of "containing communism." There is no affirmative conception of how to make the revolutions fruitful. We prefer the moderate to the more radical —the Adoulas in the Congo, for instance, to the Lumumbas. We prefer a slow, rather than a rapid, tempo of change. Radicals and rapid tempos, we fear, may pave the way for the communists.

III

But if a negative policy is hopeless, what constitutes a positive policy in this period? How, in fact, does a nation join the revolution of rising expectations?

To start we must divest ourselves of some myths. The most important of these is the one, drummed into the national consciousness day in and out, that if we stop relying on our weaponry the Soviets will invade Western Europe and eventually the United States. "In barely a generation," writes FBI chief J. Edgar Hoover, "Russia had moved swiftly forward in its campaign of world conquest. . . . Such a dictatorial empire grows out of the very nature of Marxist thought and is inevitable wherever it is applied. In the Kremlin the dream of world conquest still persists. It threatens free peoples everywhere." [9] Awesome as this statement sounds, it actually begs the question. What must concern us is not that the Soviet Union wants to enlarge its sphere of control—all nation-states have similar impulses, and if they do not yield to them it is only because the opportunity is not at hand. What is really at issue is *how* the Soviets intend to spread their system. So far, except for Eastern Europe, the Soviet offensive has been ideological and social, rather than military. The Russians did not commit a single soldier to the victory of communism in China, Indochina, or

Cuba. They did use arms against the Hungarian Revolution in 1956, but this in our opinion runs against the trend. It is highly doubtful that it will be repeated, because the whole Soviet empire hung in the balance for a fleeting moment during those eventful days. Even in Eastern Europe today, it appears that Russia is anxious to bend to the winds of liberal communism.

More important are other considerations. It is inconceivable that should the United States disarm—a process that would take at least five or ten years—Russia could resist pressures at home for a similar course. Most Soviet families recognize that their dreams for a private apartment and more consumer goods are tied to de-escalating the arms race. The United States may be able to afford guns *and* butter, but the Soviets cannot. Most Russian citizens know that if the Cold War came to an end, their chances for a better life would improve greatly. And while Russia may be a dictatorship, even dictatorships must respond to such overwhelming desires of its people—particularly when the adversary removes the threat to its security.

Nothing in history is certain, but it is probably as close to certainty as we can get that the Soviets would respond to American disarmament initiatives with initiatives of their own. It has not happened so far only because the negotiations for disarmament have, by and large, been part of the arms race. The Soviets ask us to give up a key item that America considers vital for its security—such as foreign bases—while giving up nothing comparable of their own. And the United States asks the Soviets to yield what it considers decisive—secrecy—while failing to make a comparable concession. Russia can give up foreign bases because, except perhaps for Cuba, it has none; and the United States can afford large scale inspection because it is overwhelmingly superior in nuclear arms. When the Russians, therefore, ask for both sides to give up all foreign bases or the American negotiators ask for both sides to open their borders to inspection, they are not really negotiating but propagandizing. Only when each side is willing to give up something that "hurts" can true negotiations begin. At that point, tensions in both nations will relax, and pressures within the Soviet Union (as well as in the United States) for full disarmament will mount.

Then there is the question of "Soviet occupation" of Western Europe and/or the United States. Many Americans think of this as a likely possibility, once the West divests itself of armaments. But this argument is based on three weak assumptions: first, that the Soviets hope to achieve the world-wide victory of communism through military, rather than social, action; second, that American disarmament can take place without momentous pressures within the Soviet Union for similar disarmament; and third, that physical occupation of hostile countries with millions of square miles of territory can be achieved at whim. The fact is that so long as the American people maintain a basic loyalty to their society, Russian attempts to rule the United States would be so costly in men and materiel as to render such efforts hopeless.

Strikes, demonstrations, guerrilla warfare, and non-violent resistance would so plague an invading force that the fruits of its victory would be dissipated. An American colonel, expert in guerrilla warfare, George M. Jones, has estimated that it takes fifteen regular soldiers to contain an irregular guerrilla, and that the guerrilla exacts ten casualties for every one he suffers.[10] The Soviets would need millions of troops to offset American youths who "took to the hills" or engaged in non-violent resistance. Each crossroads, each village, each hillside in this enormous country would become a trap for occupation soldiers; and so long as national patriotism imbued the American people, they could not be vanquished.

Under any circumstances, assuming the worst, we must weigh not a "good" alternative—the arms race—as against a "bad" alternative—disarmament, The choice is between two possibilities, both of which involve great risks. But on balance the risk in the former, militarism, is infinitely greater than that in the latter, disarmament and a social offensive. The arms race can lead us nowhere except to isolation from potential friends and to war. Disarmament and a social offensive at least offer the hope of defending our security. The danger is that a myopic Anti-Communism makes it virtually impossible for us to make an objective evaluation. In our anxiety we become immobilized and impotent, resorting to myth and cliché to cover our tracks.

There are other myths, too—for instance, the facile cliché that it is "better to be dead than red." Throughout history noble men have given their lives in the cause of freedom, so that their children and grandchildren might enjoy the results of their efforts. If by the martyrdom of a few hundred or a few thousands we could avoid totalitarianism, then indeed this conventional wisdom might have meaning. But this is not the choice at all. Martyrdom will not produce freedom, for even in "victory" the American nation would become a dictatorship for many years at least. And man's most bestial characteristics would reassert themselves as he scrounged for food and shelter in a society of scarcity. Not the least of militarism's harmful effects has been the elaboration of capsule slogans that appeal to a frustrated national ego but cannot stand up under objective analysis. The jettisoning of myth and facile cliché is a first prerequisite of turning back to sanity.

IV

Beyond that, a positive policy would fashion a strategy to deal with three problems:

1. Relative to the communist world, including China and Cuba, a strategy for competitive co-existence.
2. Relative to the world revolution, a strategy of exchanging aid, know-how, and other support for social reform and international integration.
3. Relative to our own society, a strategy of completing the American Revolution so that we might become, as we were in 1775, an attractive polarizing force for other nations.

The communist world is here to stay. It cannot be undone, and if it could be, it would only be replaced by another form of radical society and radical ideology. The Soviet system is approaching our own in stability. Whatever disquiet exists within it is a disquiet over method, not content. Russian, Polish, Hungarian, Rumanian, Bulgarian, North Vietnamese, North Korean, Albanian, East German, Chinese, and Cuban citizens may be unhappy over this or that facet of communism. They undoubtedly want more freedom, more consumer goods, more participation in meaningful decisions, but, as anyone who has ever traveled in these areas knows, they would not give up nationalized industry, planning, or the welfare state. Given a choice they would probably prefer co-operative stores, farming on the Scandinavian model, and limited private enterprise in small industry and the services, as well as a multi-faction or a multi-party political system. But they cannot be won back to feudalism, or be brought to accept capitalism. To think of the communist world as a *permanent* enemy, therefore, is to alienate ourselves not only from its governments, but from its people. Communism will be altered, changed, modified, and revamped, but its essential structure will survive. We cannot conquer or occupy its territory any more than it can conquer or occupy ours. Our only hope is to co-exist and compete with it on the social plane, not the military one.

Co-existence involves de-escalating and then abolishing the arms race, confining our conflicts with communism as well as with other societies to social issues. "The real competition," says George F. Kennan, "is to see who moves most successfully to the solution of his own peculiar problems." [11] After two decades of Cold War, it seems difficult to view communism in another light, but as U Thant, Secretary-General of the United Nations, has observed: "No country has permanent friends or permanent enemies, but only permanent interests." Our interests—to defend and enlarge our own democracy—demands at this stage in history that we change our competition with Russia and China from a military to a social form.

Once co-existence becomes American policy, the nation can look to the revolution beyond our borders from another focal point. Our aim will no longer be to exchange aid for military bases and alliances, but to shore up the economies of developing countries and guide them, insofar as we can, to true social change. To those who think in the business-as-usual terms of the past, this may seem like unrealistic utopianism. What, they ask, do we get in return? The answer is, international stability. A positive strategy, unlike the negative one, will not produce visible *quid pro quos*, such as military bases or investment opportunities. We may, in fact, have to give up some of the commercial and investment advantages we now enjoy, say, in Latin America. In the long run, however, this is the only *practical* course, for if we continue to be aligned with the oligarchies, and if we continue to support the conservative elements who abort their revolutions, we will eventually lose our prerogatives anyway. A revolutionary Latin America, for instance, will expropriate many of our investments and refuse to accept the present unfavorable terms of trade.

It makes no sense to pour hundreds of millions of dollars into Iran or Pakistan because they grant us bases and are military "allies," if their regimes are about to fall and be replaced by neutralists or communists. We have seen this policy fail over and over again—for example, in Iraq, when our "friend" Nuri Said was overthrown by the neutralist Kassem. All our military plans for that part of the world were immediately disrupted.

Thus, what appears to be an "impractial" policy is in actuality the only practical one. It is better to adjust in advance to the demands of the revolution of rising expectations than be shocked by its future restrictions upon us.

A positive policy would aim at helping the developing nations proceed as smoothly as possible to democratic and non-violent social change. We would withdraw all military aid immediately, not only because militarism cannot protect our own security, but because such aid helps dictators everywhere to crush nationalism. By the same principles, we would withhold economic aid to leaders and nations who tolerate economic and social stagnation so long as their own personal power is enhanced. The amount we give in grants and loans is far less important than the purpose for which it is given. In some cases, the elimination of aid is more beneficial to the people of certain countries than continuation. The monies we allot now to Guatemala, Taiwan, Spain, Portugal, Nicaragua, Paraguay, Thailand, and other rightist dictatorships is not only wasted, but is harmful to American security because it strengthens the hand of world reaction. It would be far better to do away with *this* aid. Many of these nations would then, it is true, suffer economic distress, but their people do not benefit from our gifts and loans anyway. It is not converted into effective development; it remains primarily with the upper classes. By weakening these oligarchical forces—and a refusal of both military and economic aid would have that effect— we would be simultaneously encouraging the masses below to change their governments.

V

The test of a positive policy is not what it gains for us, in material terms and in the short run, but how it helps in the democratic development of poor nations. The implementation of such a program would not be simple or automatic. It would require a keen sense of judgment to gauge the direction of developing nations. Are they moving *toward* democracy, or away from it? We would have to reconcile ourselves to the fact that not only will democracy take different forms, but that it is a process rather than a finished product. It includes not only the right to vote and honest elections, but more importantly, social and economic democracy, such as land reform, education, and health facilities. We would therefore offer aid to all nations, including communist nations that are developing, and apply certain guideposts to judge the direction in which they are moving:

1. Have they instituted a true program of land reform?
2. Are they organizing marketing, machine, and credit cooperatives?
3. Do they have village development plans which involve the people in decision making?
4. Are they taking positive steps against feudal and tribal autocracy?
5. Are they initiating educational, health, and housing programs?
6. Are they increasing the area of dissent and reducing police restrictions?
7. Are they abating terror?
8. Are they advancing toward economic viability?
9. Are they reducing the gap between the upper and lower economic strata?

Our friendships would be judged by how quickly governments were willing to climb the steps of a democratic ladder. By such criteria, it would be clear that as of today India deserves far more aid, absolutely and relatively, than Pakistan; Ghana more than Liberia; Guinea more than Sudan; Poland more than Ethiopia; Yugoslavia more than Turkey. The effectiveness of our policy would be reviewed periodically to determine how effectively it is being translated into social reform.

In addition, the positive policy would evolve many forms of aid that are now unknown or seldom used. One that comes to mind is the organization of fifty-fifty companies, by which the United States (as well as our allies and the Soviets, if we could enlist them) would put up the capital, provide the supervisory manpower, and operate various industries of developing nations. The local government would own 50 per cent of the stock but have no voice in management for a number of years. We would manage the facilities—say a steel mill or an electrical plant—withdraw a certain amount of our investment each year and a small profit of 1 or 2 per cent, train native engineers and administrators to take over operational functions, and after ten, fifteen, or twenty years withdraw and turn the companies over to the home government. This is a better system of aid for industrial development than to have private enterprise do the job, because it would be co-ordinated with the planning of such countries and it would leave most of the profits at home for new investment. It is also superior to nationalized industry, because it would provide both capital and know-how immediately, whereas the nationalized firm would have difficulty securing both and would have to undergo a long period of "shakedown" to become efficient. This type of aid has not been tried extensively as yet, but there are examples to draw on. Israel and Ghana had such an arrangement for the shipping industry of Ghana, and Britain and Burma had one for the mining industry of Burma. Perfection of fifty-fifty plans would go a long way to help developing nations make the transition to industry, without which land reform and other reforms would be sterile.

Another form of aid would stimulate customs unions, common markets, and eventually single inter-nations. Few of the countries now reaching independence can exist on their own resources and with their own limited markets. Of the fifteen million citizens of Colombia, only five million are "in the market"; of the eight million in Venezuela, only three million regularly buy merchandise. Small nations with only one, two, or five million citizens find it unfeasible to build mass production industries. They are hindered by tariffs, quotas, and other restrictions placed on their exports by other nations. Self-interest dictates that they take steps to amalgamate with other nations, but they cannot do so without considerable dislocation and difficulties.

The common market in Western Europe already proves that. One nation with an efficient beer industry can take over the market of another nation with an inefficient one. In the period of transition, help must be given to the latter country so that the long-term benefits of a common market or a common nation are not erased by short-term hardships.

Finally, more and more functions should be transferred to a strengthened United Nations. Technical aid, medical aid, educational aid, budget and statistical aid, and labor union development can be turned over to the United Nations now, if only the great nations would make more money available to it. If the United States and Russia were to agree to terminate the Cold War, both could, in their newfound security, channel much of their material and technical aid through the world organization.

The benefits would be two-fold: first, international aid avoids the criticism of national aid—that it is given only for self-interest; second, the world must move toward an eventual single state. In a few years the trip from New York to London will take only two hours; Telstars will be used for regular international broadcasts and communications; men will travel to the moon. Technology is knitting our world into one, and politics must follow apace. The population explosion and the need to grow more food will drive the various nations, in self-defense, toward common citizenship and common purpose. The rich nations cannot exist as an island in a sea of hunger, without being engulfed by the poor nations. To facilitate an orderly progress toward "one world"—a process that will take many decades—it is necessary, therefore, to turn over as many functions as possible, as quickly as possible, to the world organization.

Such, in brief, would be a positive strategy toward the world revolution now in progress. We do not offer it as a blueprint, but solely as an approach that would be modified by the strictures of practice and experience. We recognize that it seems "different" and "dreamy," that many will reject it as a moral solution rather than a "practical one." But we submit that today more than ever in history the moral is the only practical path. The Judaeo-Christian goal of brotherhood, so disregarded by Judaeo-Christian societies, has become the essence of pragmatism.

VI

The most important step we Americans can take to implement a positive strategy is to complete our own revolution begun in 1775. As the late President Kennedy stated so often, nothing we do overseas can be effective unless our own country begins to "move forward." Translated into practical terms, that means eliminating the pockets of poverty that still exist, ending discrimination against Negroes and other minorities, restoring the liberties lost in the Anti-Communist period, and offering each citizen a minimum of security from the cradle to the grave. It is only insofar as we prove to the world by ineradicable deed that we are willing to travel a humanist path at home, that they will respect our foreign policy goals abroad.

Again, the moral and the practical coincide, for if we are to disarm we must find some means of absorbing into peaceful pursuit the $50 billion annually spent on arms. Otherwise there will be depression and unemployment. Such sums can be beneficially expended today only on social improvements. America, rich as it is, has an enormous social deficit. It needs at least 700,000 schoolrooms and better pay for teachers. It needs at least one million more hospital beds and national health insurance, so that every person will not only be assured medical help when he is sick, but can take advantage of the benefits of preventive medicine. It needs $100 billion to provide more water facilities, and many billions to wipe out slums. It needs billions more for adequate mental clinics, higher pensions for the aged, more unemployment insurance for displaced workers. The backlog of social needs, according to the National Planning Association, is at least $350 billion.

Needless to say, nothing will change in America or in American policy unless there is a severe shift in the power structure, away from the military-industrial complex. Many communists and other leftists argue that this is impossible under the capitalist system, that indeed capitalism must be overthrown before any progress can be made. This is the subject for another book, but we are not convinced that the argument is valid. Changing our power structure without violence will be difficult, but it has happened before in history—in Denmark in the eighteenth and early nineteenth centuries, during the Meiji Restoration in Japan in 1868, and in a few other situations.[12] Those who dream of a revolution in America which will topple the present institutions at one fell blow are thinking mechanistically, by past precepts of radicalism. America will change as more people engage in the civil rights movement, as more unionists prod their unions to be vigorous in the fight for jobs, as more citizens join the peace movement, as all these forces combine in a new political alliance to force political realignment. The process is dual: insofar as a new insurgent impulse in America draws us to co-existence, to joining the world revolution, to completing our own revolution at home, so will the power relationship alter; and insofar as the power relationship changes, momentum will be available for more fulsome co-existence, for joining the world revolution and completing our own.

The United States, sidetracked and repressed by a negative Anti-Communism, is rapidly approaching the most critical moment in its history. It is being called on to respond to the most dire challenge it has ever faced. It can follow the principles of the past, toward futility and eclipse, or it can chart a new, positive course that will renew its vigor. If it chooses business-as-usual, the status quo, militarism, and all the other regressive features of Anti-Communism, there is little hope either for itself or for Western civilization. On the other hand, if it correctly analyzes the national, social, technological, and scientific revolutions now underway, and seeks the path based on this analysis, all of mankind will applaud.

NOTES

Chapter I—*A Half-Century of Fear*

1. Alan Barth, *The Loyalty of Free Men,* New York, 1952, pp. 38-39.

2. Lewis Broad, *Winston Churchill, A Biography,* New York, 1958, p. 183.

3. Isaac Deutscher, *The Prophet Armed,* New York and London, 1954, p. 443.

4. Walter Lippmann and Charles Merz, "A Test of the News," *New Republic,* August 4, 1920.

5. George Seldes, *World Panorama 1918-1933,* Boston, 1933, p. 127.

6. A. Mitchell Palmer, "The Case Against the Reds," *Forum,* February, 1920.

7. It is interesting to note that after the American Revolution the Russian Czars refused to recognize the United States for thirty-three years. Almost a century and a half later, the tables were turned: the United States refused to recognize the Soviet Union from 1917 to 1933.

8. Alan Barth, "Report on the 'Rampageous Right," *New York Times Magazine,* November 26, 1961.

9. John W. Fulbright, "The Fatal Obsession in U.S. Foreign Policy," *Progressive,* September, 1958.

10. *Chicago Sun-Times,* June 17, 1962.

11. *Time,* August 23, 1963.

12. D. W. Brogan, "A Historian Questions Our Mood," *New York Times Magazine,* December 3, 1961.

13. Quoted by Alan Barth in "Report on the 'Rampageous Right,'" *New York Times Magazine,* November 26, 1961.

14. James P. Warburg, "Our Obsolete Foreign Policy," *Progressive,* January, 1959.

CHAPTER II—*The Anatomy of Anti-Communism*

1. James F. Byrnes, *Speaking Frankly*, New York, 1947, pp. 35-36.

2. Elliott Roosevelt, *As He Saw It*, New York, 1946, pp. 24-25.

3. John W. Spanier, *American Foreign Policy Since World War II*, New York, 1960, p. 14.

4. Walter Millis, ed., *The Forrestal Diaries*, New York, 1951, p. 22.

5. Clifton Brock, *Americans for Democratic Action*, Washington, 1962, p. 46.

6. Sumner Welles, *Where Are We Heading?*, New York and London, 1946, p. 371.

7. Brock, *op. cit.*, p. 20.

8. Walter Reuther, "A Total Peace Offensive," pamphlet published by the United Auto Workers, Detroit, n.d.

9. Brock, *op. cit.*, p. 138.

10. *Ibid.*, pp. 63-64.

11. *Ibid.*, pp. 85-87.

12. The use of such terms as "tribalism" and "feudalism" presents certain semantic difficulties, for there were periods in history when both were progressive forces. We are referring here to the latter stages of these social systems, in which they had become stagnant societies inhibiting economic development. Admittedly, there are features of tribalism which to this day are highly attractive—such as the co-operative spirit and mutual concern among members of the same tribe.

13. V. I. Lenin, "The Attitude of Social Democracy Towards the Peasant Movement" (written September 1905), *Selected Works*, New York, n.d. III, 146.

14. Sidney Hook, *Political Power and Personal Freedom*, New York, 1959, pp. 106, 109-115.

15. Barry Goldwater, *Why Not Victory*, New York, 1962, p. 39.

16. The Editors of Fortune, with Russell W. Davenport, *U.S.A.: The Permanent Revolution*, New York, 1951, p. 240.

17. *China, White Paper*, State Department Document No. 3573, Washington, 1949, pp. 176-177.

18. Nathaniel Peffer, "Close-Up of China in Travail," *New York Times Magazine,* May 4, 1947.

19. John F. Kennedy, in a speech in the U.S. Senate, April 16, 1954.

CHAPTER III—*Cold War and New Credo*

1. *New York Times,* May 30, 1948.

2. Adam Ciolkosz, *The Curtain Falls,* edited by Denis Healey, London, 1951, pp. 38, 41, 44, 46.

3. Robert E. Sherwood, *Roosevelt and Hopkins,* New York, 1950, I, 440.

4. Elliott Roosevelt, *op. cit.,* p. 41.

5. Dean Rusk, before the U.S. Senate Hearings on the Test-Ban Treaty, August, 1963.

6. John W. Fulbright, before the U.S. Senate Hearings on the Test-Ban Treaty, August, 1963.

7. Robert E. Sherwood, *op. cit.,* II, 475.

8. *Ibid.,* II, 478.

9. L. S. Stavrianos, *Greece, American Dilemma and Opportunity,* Chicago, 1952, p. 85.

10. Elliott Roosevelt, *op. cit.,* p. 222.

11. Winston Churchill, quoted by D. F. Fleming in *The Cold War and Its Origins 1917-1950,* New York, 1961, p. 182.

12. Byrnes, *op. cit.,* p. 45.

13. Sumner Welles, *op. cit.,* p. 106.

14. Sherwood, *op. cit.,* II, 516.

15. D. F. Fleming, *The Cold War and Its Origins,* 1917-1950, p. 1060.

16. Hugh Seton-Watson, *From Lenin to Malenkov,* New York, 1954, p. 223.

17. For further details, see my book, *A World in Revolution,* New York, 1956, the chapter "Big Stick, Little Stick."

18. Spanier, *op. cit.,* p. 37.

19. Joseph Alsop, *New York Herald Tribune,* July 12, 1946.

20. James P. Warburg, *The United States in a Changing World*, New York, 1954, p. 399.

21. *Ibid.*, p. 399.

22. *Ibid.*, p. 390.

23. Frank Gervasi, "Watchdog in the White House,," *Collier's*, October 9, 1955.

24. Welles, *op. cit.*, p. 106.

25. Winston Churchill, in a speech at Fulton, Missouri, quoted in Warburg, *op. cit.*, p. 416.

26. Henry A. Wallace, quoted in Spanier, *op. cit.*, pp. 24-25.

27. Edgar Ansel Mowrer, *The Nightmare of American Foreign Policy*, New York, 1948, p. 237.

28. Stavrianos, *op. cit.*, pp. 135-136.

29. *London Times*, April 17, 1945.

30. Quoted by Stavrianos, *op. cit.*, p. 148.

31. *Ibid.*, p. 150.

32. Hanson W. Baldwin, *New York Times*, February 26, 1948.

33. Milovan Djilas, *Conversations With Stalin*, New York, 1962, pp. 181-182.

34. John P. Capsis, "Report from Greece," *New Leader*, November 10, 1958.

CHAPTER IV—*The Alliance of Conservatives and Ex-Radicals*

1. *Wall Street Journal*, October 12, 1956.

2. Donald Nelson, quoted in Fred J. Cook, "Juggernaut, The Warfare State," *Nation*, October 28, 1961, p. 284.

3. Bureau of the Budget, *The United States at War*, Washington, 1946.

4. Cook, "Juggernaut, The Warfare State," p. 285.

5. *Ibid.*, p. 289.

6. *Ibid.*, p. 290.

7. *United States News & World Report,* May 14, 1948.

8. Arthur A. Ekirch, Jr., *The Civilian and the Military,* New York, 1956, p. 275.

9. Cook, *op. cit.,* p. 287.

10. William H. Neblett, *No Peace With the Regulars,* New York, 1957, p. 13.

11. Charles E. Wilson, quoted in Cook, *op. cit.,* p. 299.

12. *Chicago Daily News,* November 14, 1961.

13. Fred J. Cook, "The Ultras," *Nation,* June 30, 1962, p. 585.

14. David A. Shannon, *The Socialist Party of America,* New York, 1955, p. 119.

15. Theodore Draper, *The Roots of American Communism,* New York, 1957, p. 115.

16. Max Ascoli, *Reporter,* April 29, 1952, p. 24.

17. *Free Cuba News,* published by the Citizens Committee For A Free Cuba, Washington, June 1, 1963.

18. Irwin Suall, *The American Ultras,* pamphlet published by New America, New York, n.d., p. 38.

19. AFL Convention Report, New York, September 15-23, 1952.

20. Irving Brown, *Vital Speeches,* October 1, 1952, p. 752.

21. *Free Trade Union News,* AFL-CIO publication, January, 1963.

CHAPTER V—*Pax Americana in Europe*

1. John Fischer, *Master Plan U.S.A.,* New York, 1951, p. 84.

2. Millis, *The Forrestal Diaries,* pp. 10-11.

3. Ernest Bevin, in a speech before the House of Commons, October 22, 1946.

4. *London Economist,* April 6, 1946.

5. Millis, *The Forrestal Diaries,* p. 273.

6. Harry S. Truman, in a speech, March 5, 1947.

7. See Richard Sasuly, *I. G. Farben,* New York, 1947.

8. Howard K. Smith, *The State of Europe,* New York, 1949, pp. 127-128.

9. John Gunther, *Inside Europe,* New York, 1961, p. 23.

10. James P. Warburg, *Germany, Key to Peace,* Cambridge, 1953, pp. 119, 121.

11. Quoted in Howard K. Smith, *op. cit.,* p. 134.

12. Stuart Gelder, *London News Chronicle,* May 10, 1947.

13. Joseph and Stewart Alsop, "Must America Save The World?" *Saturday Evening Post,* February 21, 1948.

14. Spanier, *op. cit.,* p. 35.

15. Theodore H. White, *Fire In The Ashes,* New York, 1953, p. 69.

16. From a mimeographed release by ECA, gathered in a trip to Italy, 1950.

17. Spanier, *op. cit.,* p. 46.

18. Thomas K. Finletter, *Power and Policy,* New York, 1954, p. 41.

19. Welles, *op. cit.,* p. 1.

CHAPTER VI—*Nationalism and Communism in Asia*

1. Achmed Sukarno, quoted in James Tracy Crown and George P. Penty, *Kennedy in Power,* New York, 1961, p. 69.

2. *New York Times,* July 5, 1963.

3. Quoted in *Monthly Review,* October, 1963, p. 296.

4. Adlai Stevenson, "Extend Our Vision . . . to All Mankind," *Life,* May 23, 1960.

5. Quoted in Kumar Goshal, *People in Colonies,* Kingsport, Tenn., 1948, p. 218.

6. Frederick E. Crockett, "How The Trouble Began in Java," *Harper's,* March, 1946.

7. David Anderson, dispatch from The Hague, *New York Times,* February 14, 1947.

8. Quoted in Anna Louise Strong, *One-Fifth of Mankind,* New York, 1938, p. 46.

9. Lynn Thorndike, *A Short History of Civilization*, New York, 1930, p. 533.

10. Aitchen K. Wu, *China and the Soviet Union*, New York, 1950, p. 315.

11. Graham Peck, *Two Kinds of Time*, New York, 1950, p. 69.

12. D. F. Fleming, *op. cit.*, p. 549.

13. Foster Hailey, *Half of One World*, New York, 1950, p. 51.

14. Joseph W. Stillwell, *Stillwell's Papers*, New York, 1948, p. 320.

15. Hailey, *op. cit.*, p. 64.

16. *Ibid.*, p. 53.

17. Dean Acheson, quoted in Hans J. Morgenthau, *Defense of the National Interest*, New York, 1951, p. 257.

18. Theodore H. White, "Indo-China—The Long Trail of Error," *Reporter*, June 22, 1954.

19. Vladimir Dedijer, *Tito*, New York, 1953, p. 322.

20. For more detail on this subject, see my book, *The Counterfeit Revolution*, Boston, 1952, the chapter "First Round in Asia."

21. *Ibid.*, p. 178.

22. Hailey, *op. cit.*, p. 67.

CHAPTER VII—*Their Side and Ours: People Versus Arms*

1. Vo Nguyen Giap, quoted in Jerry A. Rose, "The Elusive Viet Cong," *New Republic*, May 4, 1963, p. 21.

2. Dwight D. Eisenhower, *Mandate for Change*, New York, 1963, p. 372.

3. A. Roselli, "Guerrilla Warfare As It Really Is," *Harper's*, August, 1953.

4. Lanniston Sharp, *The Far Eastern Survey*, December 18, 1946, p. 196.

5. William Worthy, Jr., "Our Disgrace in Indo-China," *The Crisis*, February, 1954.

6. Virginia Thompson and Richard Adloff, *The Left Wing in Southeast Asia*, New York, 1950, footnote p. 36.

7. *Ibid.*, p. 37.

8. Interview by the author with nationalist leaders of the French colonies in the office of *Franc Tireur*, Paris, 1950.

9. *Solution in Indochina*, pamphlet published by the American Friends Service Committee, Philadelphia, n.d., p. 8.

10. *Ibid.*, p. 7.

11. D. A. Graber, *Crisis Diplomacy*, Washington, 1959, p. 280.

12. *New York Times*, January 22, 1955.

13. Jerry A. Rose, "The Fading Strength of Viet Nam," *New Republic*, November 13, 1961.

14. *Le Figaro*, February 9, 1961.

15. *Chicago Sun-Times*, February 14, 1956.

16. Thomas R. Phillips, quoted by O. Edmund Clubb in *Progressive*, April 1962, p. 17.

17. *Time*, November 28, 1960.

18. *New Republic*, March 23, 1963.

19. *National Review*, March 26, 1963.

20. Jerry A. Rose, "Dead End In Vietnam," *New Republic*, October 12, 1963, p. 15.

21. *New York Times*, September 25, 1963.

22. Owen Lattimore, *The Situation in Asia*, Boston, 1949, pp. 96-97.

23. E. Grant Meade, *American Military Government in Korea*, New York, 1951, p. 55.

24. *Chicago Daily News*, March 29, 1963.

25. Maurice Goldbloom, *New America*, January 24, 1961.

26. Andrew Tully, *CIA, The Inside Story*, New York, 1962, p. 88.

27. *Ibid*, pp. 97-98.

28. *Ibid*, p. 89.

29. See *Christian Science Monitor*, August 13, 1963.

30. Ali M. S. Fatemi, "The Shah's Democracy," *Minority of One*, November, 1963.

CHAPTER VIII—*Burma: Case History of a Positive Policy*

1. Very little has been written on the struggle between Burmese Socialists and Buddhists against the communists. My own information comes from a stay in that country in 1953, interviews with two key government officials at the time, Ba Swe and Kyaw Nyein, and packets of material accumulated while in Rangoon.

2. Virginia Thompson and Richard Adloff, *op. cit.*, p. 81.

3. *Ibid*, p. 86.

4. *Ibid*, p. 87.

5. A. Leonidov, "Labor Imperialism's Colonial Strategy in Burma," *New Times* (Moscow), February 9, 1949.

6. See my book, *A World in Revolution*, New York, 1956, p. 157; also Ba Swe, *The Burmese Revolution*, pamphlet published by the Information Department Union of Burma, 1952.

CHAPTER IX—*Anti-Democracy at Home*

1. John F. Kennedy, State of the Union Message, January 30, 1961. "Foreign Affairs," pamphlet, published by the Department of State, Washington, 1961.

2. Woodrow Wilson, quoted in John L. Heaton, *Cobb of the World*, New York, 1924, p. 270.

3. Harry Cain, *Freedom Equals Security*, pamphlet published by the Trade Union Program on Civil Liberties and Rights, Washington, n.d., p. 19.

4. C. T. Lanham, *Infantry Journal*, January, 1949.

5. Zechariah Chafee, Jr., *The Blessings of Liberty*, Philadelphia, 1956, p. 87.

6. Charles A. Beard and Mary R. Beard, *The Rise of American Civilization*, New York, 1930, I, 376.

7. Quoted in Chafee, *op. cit.*, pp. 116-117.

8. Henry Moskowitz, ed., *Progressive Democracy: Addresses and State Papers by Alfred E. Smith*, New York, 1928, pp. 270-284.

9. Chafee, *op. cit.*, p. 67.

10. John Lord O'Brian, *National Security and Individual Freedom*, Cambridge, 1955, p. 28.

11. Chafee, *op. cit.*, p. 137.

12. *A Quarter of a Century of Un-Americana*, New York, 1963.

13. Frank Donner, "HUAC: The Dossier-Keepers," *Studies on the Left*, Madison, Wisc., I, 4 (1961), pp. 12-13.

14. Frank J. Donner, *The Un-Americans*, New York, 1961, p. 263.

15. Quoted in *A Quarter of a Century of Un-Americana*, p. 15.

16. D. F. Fleming, *op. cit.*, p. 707.

17. Walter Millis, *Individual Freedom and the Common Defense*, pamphlet published by the Fund for the Republic, November, 1957, p. 68.

18. Information Bulletin, Department of Defense, Office of Civil Defense, June 29, 1962.

19. Quoted in *Progressive*, October, 1962, p. 38.

20. Stewart Alsop, "The Story Behind Quemoy: How We Drifted Close to War," *Saturday Evening Post*, December 13, 1958.

21. Tristram Coffin, "Probing the CIA," *New Leader*, May 15, 1961.

22. *Chicago Sun-Times*, December 7, 1962.

23. Millis, *op. cit.*, p. 34.

24. *The McCarthy Record*, pamphlet published by the Wisconsin Citizens Committee on McCarthy's Record, p. 85.

25. Chafee, *op. cit.*, p. 99.

26. *Look*, September 7, 1954.

27. Chafee, *op. cit.*, p. 99.

28. Millis, *op. cit.*, p. 53.

29. William O. Douglas, in a speech July 1, 1962, published by University of Judaism, Los Angeles, p. 4.

30. Alexander Hamilton, quoted in Walter Millis, "How to Compete With the Russians," *New York Times Magazine*, February 2, 1958.

CHAPTER X—*Anti-Communism Hardens Communism*

1. Boris Souvarine, *Stalin*, New York, 1939, pp. 191-192.

2. *Ibid*, p. 216.

3. George F. Kennan, *Russia and the West Under Lenin and Stalin*, Boston, 1961, p. 32.

4. *Ibid*, p. 124.

5. *Ibid*, pp. 62-63.

6. Walter Duranty, *USSR, The Story of Soviet Russia*, Philadelphia, 1944, pp. 57-58.

7. Kennan, *op. cit.*, 133.

8. William Henry Chamberlin, *The Russian Revolution, 1917-21*, New York, 1935, II, 156.

9. Kennan, *op. cit.*, p. 117.

10. Souvarine, *op. cit.*, p. 483.

11. Fleming, *op. cit.*, p. 32.

12. Nikita Khrushchev, quoted in "The Crimes of The Stalin Era," *New Leader* Special Supplement, July 16, 1956, p. 22.

13. For further details, see my book, *The Counterfeit Revolution*, Boston, 1952, pp. 75ff.

14. Norman E. Isaacs, "$1 Billion Aid to Tito—Has it Paid Off?" *Chicago Sun-Times*, September 27, 1959.

15. Denis Healey, "Yugoslavia 1960," *New Leader*, October 31, 1960.

16. Eddy Gilmore, "Russia 10 Years After Stalin: The Terror Is Gone," *Chicago Sun-Times*, March 3, 1963.

17. Edward Crankshaw, *Khrushchev's Russia*, Baltimore, 1959, pp. 59-60.

18. Flora Lewis, *A Case History of Hope*, New York, 1958, p. xii.

19. Interview with Rainer Hildebrandt in 1957. Hildebrandt, author of many articles and a book on communism, was the leader of the Fighters Against Inhumanity, headquartered in West Berlin, and had innumerable contacts in East Germany. He was made aware of this incident by contacts in East Berlin.

20. *New York Times,* November 29, 1961.

21. *New Leader,* January 8, 1962, p. 14.

22. *The Militant,* May 20, 1963, p. 3.

23. Walter Z. Laqueur, *New Leader,* January 8, 1962.

24. Irving L. Horowitz, "Latin America and the Sino-Soviet Split," *Liberation,* May, 1963.

25. *New York Times,* February 6, 1962.

26. *New York Times,* October 19, 1961.

27. *New York Times,* August 1, 1961.

28. *New York Times,* May 27, 1960.

29. Quoted in *National Guardian,* January 24, 1963.

30. Interview with the author in 1960, in an East European capital.

CHAPTER XI—*Latin America: The Final Disaster?*

1. Milton Eisenhower, *The Wine is Bitter,* New York, 1963, p. xi.

2. *Chicago Sun-Times,* May 26, 1963.

3. W. S. Woytinsky, "The U.S. and Latin America's Economy," *New Leader* Supplement, November 24, 1958, p. 12.

4. For a statistical picture of Latin America, see John Gerassi, *The Great Fear,* New York, 1963, especially Chapters 1 and 2.

5. Carleton Beals, *America South,* Philadelphia, 1937, p. 11.

6. *Ibid,* p. 213.

7. Adolfo Lopez Mateos, *The Economic Development of Mexico During a Quarter of a Century,* pamphlet published by Nacional Financera, S.A., Mexico City.

8. *Mexico Today,* pamphlet published by First National City Bank, Mexico City.

9. For a description of the CIA role in Guatemala, see Andrew Tully, *op. cit.,* pp. 60ff.

10. Quoted by Samuel Shapiro in *New Republic,* March 13, 1961.

11. For a good summary of the subject, see Maurice Zeitlin and Robert Scheer, *Cuba: Tragedy In Our Hemisphere*, New York, 1963, Chapter 10.

12. Cited in Samuel Shapiro, "Cuba, a Dissenting Report," *New Republic*, September 12, 1960, p. 15.

13. The text of this speech by Castro was reprinted in the *National Guardian*, December 25, 1961.

14. Samuel Shapiro, *New Republic*, September 12, 1960.

15. This material is based on two interviews by the author with Regino Boti in Havana in December, 1960, and August, 1961.

16. Samuel Shapiro, *Invisible Latin America*, Boston, 1963, p. 91.

17. Herbert L. Matthews, *The Cuban Story*, New York, 1961, p. 279.

18. *The Alliance For Progress, What You Should Know About It*, brochure published by the Pan American Union, Washington.

19. *New York Times, March* 12, 1962.

20. *Chicago Daily News,* April 16, 1963.

21. *Chicago Daily News,* March 19, 1963.

22. *Chicago Sun-Times,* February 10, 1963.

23. *New York Times,* August 3, 1962.

24. The information here is based on my own observations in Santo Domingo in July and August, 1963, and on talks with an Agency for International Development official, who asks to be anonymous, and a highly-placed AFL-CIO official, in Washington in November, 1963. The *New York Times* of October 5, 1963, carried similar information, as did the socialist paper, *New America*, the following month.

25. The advertisement was given me by a leader of CONATRAL, in August, 1963.

26. Oscar Delgado, "Revolution, Reform, Conservatism: Three Types Of Agrarian Structure," *Dissent*, Autumn, 1962.

27. Interview by the author with Dr. Enrique Pena Losa, Bogotá, Colombia, August, 1963, published in *Progressive*, September, 1963.

28. John Gerassi, *The Great Fear*, New York, 1963, based on a 1961 release of the U.S. Department of Commerce and an estimate by *U.S. News & World Report* economic unit.

CHAPTER XII—*The Futile Crusade*

1. Duranty, *op. cit.*, p. 63.

2. Seldes, *op. cit.*, p. 113.

3. Warburg, *The United States in a Changing World*, New York, 1954, pp. 380-381.

4. Walter Lippmann, *Chicago Sun-Times*, January 14, 1962.

5. Summary of Analysis of Hearings, June 22-26, 1959, Joint Committee on Atomic Energy, U.S. Congress, Biological and Environmental Effects of Nuclear War.

6. *Chicago Daily News*, June 10, 1963.

7. The world as a whole has spent $1.5 trillion on arms since the end of World War II—which, by liberal estimates, is four times as much as *all* the underdeveloped nations earn in one year.

8. Millis, "How to Compete With the Russians," *New York Times Magazine*, February 2, 1958.

9. J. Edgar Hoover, *Masters of Deceit*, New York, 1961, p. 40.

10. George M. Jones, quoted in *New Republic*, May 22, 1961.

11. Quoted by Millis in *New York Times Magazine*, February 2, 1958.

12. For more detail on this subject, see my pamphlet, *Revolution and Cold War*, published by the American Friends Service Committee, Philadelphia.

Index

Acheson, Dean, 110, 112
Adams, John, 125, 146, 223
Adenauer, Konrad, 82, 85
Adloff, Richard, 119
Africa, 18, 29, 57, 79
Albania, 177
Aleman, Miguel, 191
Algeria, 47, 131, 184, 223
Alien and Sedition Acts, 125, 146, 223
Alliance for Progress, 204, 205, 206, 207, 208, 209, 210, 212, 213, 215
Allied Control Council, 53
Alsop, Joseph, 50, 51, 86
Alsop, Stewart, 50, 86, 157
Alter, Victor, 28
Amendola, Giorgio, 177
American Federation of Labor (AFL), 75
American Federation of Labor and Congress of Industrial Organizations (AFL-CIO), 74
American Legion, 68
American Revolution, 65, 79, 94, 116, 125, 201, 223, 229
American Security Council, 71
Americans for Democratic Action (ADA), 27, 31, 32, 72
Amphictyonic Congress, 187
Anti-Communism, first phase, 15-17; post-World War II, 17-20; and liberals, 26-32, 36-37, 38; and militarism, 37, 39, 87; formalized by Truman, 57-58; and failures in Asia, 97-112, 120-122; and domestic injustice, 143-160; effect on communism, 161-182; in Latin America, 195-196
Anti-Fascist People's Freedom League (AFPFL), 138, 139, 140, 141
Arbenz, Jacobo, 193, 194, 195, 200
Arevalo, Juan José, 193, 195, 207
Argentina, 193, 207
Ascoli, Max, 74
Asia, 18, 29, 57, 79, 94, 97, 185
Atlantic Charter, 22, 43, 44, 47, 99, 219
Atomic Energy Act, 156, 158
Attorney General's List, 150
Aung San, 138

Ba Swe, 103, 139
Bao Dai, 113, 118, 121
Barth, Alan, 13
Baruch, Bernard, 73
Batista, Fulgencio, 113, 114, 157, 195, 196, 197, 198, 199, 200
Bavaria, 15
Beals, Carleton, 188
Belgium, 45
Beria, Lavrentia, 172
Betancourt, Romulo, 205, 213, 214, 215
Bevin, Ernest, 83

Bolivar, Simon, 187, 202
Bolivia, 187, 194, 209
Bosch, Juan, 208
Boti, Regino, 199
Boun Oum, 129
Bowles, Chester, 27, 31
Boxer Rebellion, 105
Boy Scouts, 68
Bradley, Omar, 67
Brandeis, Louis D., 147
Brazil, 177, 186, 187, 193, 207, 209
Bridges, Harry, 153
Brizola, Leonel, 209
Brogan, D. W., 18
Brown, Irving, 75
Brussels Pact, 91
Buchanan, George, 164
Bukharin, Nikolai, 73, 163, 164, 166, 167, 168, 177
Bulgaria, 51
Bullitt, William C., 165
Bureau of the Budget (U.S.), 66
Burke, Arleigh A., 74
Burma, 22, 136, 137, 138, 139, 140, 141, 142, 233
Burma Independence Army (BIA), 137, 138
Burnham, James, 73
Byrnes, James F., 47, 82

Cabell, C. P., 197
Cain, Harry, 144
Capsis, John P., 62
Cardenas, Lazaro, 189
Carranza, Venustiano, 189
Carthage, 216
Castillo Armas, Carlos, 195
Castro, Fidel, 122, 183, 197, 198, 199, 200, 201, 202, 203, 204, 223
Central American Confederation, 187
Central Intelligence Agency (CIA), 37, 40, 65, 74, 77, 96, 97, 132, 134, 157, 195, 196, 197, 200
Chafee, Zechariah, Jr., 144, 148
Chamber of Commerce (U.S.), 68
Chamberlin, William Henry, 65, 165
Chiang Kai-shek, 19, 38, 39, 50, 71, 104, 107, 108, 110, 111, 112, 113, 114, 117, 130, 157, 181
Ch'ien Lung, 104
Chile, 209
China, 37, 38, 50, 79, 103, 104, 105, 106, 108, 109, 110, 111, 112, 119, 131, 139, 140, 162, 172, 177, 180, 181, 205, 223, 229
China Lobby, 71
Chinese Revolution of 1911, 105
Chou En-lai, 120
Christian Democratic Union (Germany), 82, 85
Christian Democrats (Italy), 50
Chu Teh, 110
Churchill, Winston, 15, 21, 23, 24, 40, 42, 43, 45, 46, 47, 49, 50, 55, 56, 57, 165

Citizens Committee for a Free Cuba, 74
Clay, Lucius, 67, 70, 85
Clinton, Henry, 116
Clos, Max, 121
Cold War, roots of, 21-26, 41-63
Collins, J. Lawton, 66
Colombia, 210, 211, 233
Committee of Military Action, 49
Committees of Preparation for National Independence, 127
Communism, fear of, 13-15; and nationalism, 33-36, 40, 94-112; in Asia, 95-96; pressures for change within, 174-182
Communist International, 73, 106
Communist party, Brazil, 206; Burma, 136, 138; China, 106; Cuba, 198; France, 51; Germany, 86; Guatemala, 195; India, 177; Indochina, 136; Indonesia, 102; Italy, 177, 180; Soviet Union, 163, 179; United States, 13, 17, 32, 72, 147
Confederation of Labor (Brazil), 193
Congo, 225
Congress of Industrial Organizations (CIO), 27
Conspiracy Act, 146
Cook, Fred, 67, 71
Coolidge, Charles A., 156
Cornwallis, Lord, 116
Court of Appeals (U.S.), 150
Crankshaw, Edward, 172, 176, 178
Crockett, Frederick E., 99
Cuba, 79, 183, 184, 188, 189, 195, 197, 198, 199, 200, 201, 204, 209, 215, 223, 229
Cuban Revolution, 188, 192, 198, 201, 202, 203, 207
Czechoslovakia, 52

Daley, Richard J., 69
Davies, Joseph E., 55
Dayton, Lee, 89
De Gasperi, Alcide, 86
De Gaulle, Charles, 46, 47, 49, 50, 53, 183, 184
Debs, Eugene V., 146
Decembrists, 33
Declaration of Independence, 94, 116
Defense Department (U.S.), 68, 156, 158
Delgado, Oscar, 209
Deniken, A. I., 217
Denmark, 236
Department of Justice (U.S.), 16, 149, 150, 199
Diaz, Porfirio, 188
Diaz Lanz, Pedro, 199
Dies, Martin, 154
Dillon, Read & Company, 85
Dimitrov, Georgi, 169
Djilas, Milovan, 62, 171
Dodd, Thomas J., 18
Dominican Republic, 186, 208
Dong Minh Hoi, 117
Donitz, Karl, 85
Doolittle, Hooker, 47
Douglas, William O., 160
Draper, William H., 85
Dulles, John Foster, 119, 121, 129, 143

Duncan, Isadora, 73
Duranty, Walter, 217
Dutch East Indies, 98
Duvalier, François, 195

EAM (National Liberation Front, Greece), 45, 46, 51, 58, 59
East Germany, 53, 82, 176
Eastern Europe, 17, 23, 28, 46, 52, 88, 169, 227
Eastman, Max, 73
Economist (London), 83
Ecuador, 207
EDA party (Greece), 62
Eden, Anthony, 46
Eisenhower, Dwight D., 23, 41, 67, 69, 71, 113, 120, 156, 157, 173, 188, 200
Eisenhower, Milton, 183
Ekirch, Arthur A., Jr., 67
ELAS (National Popular Liberation Army, Greece), 46, 58, 59, 62
Emmanuel, King Victor, 45
Engels, Friedrich, 34
Erhard, Ludwig, 85, 89
Erlich, Henryk, 28
Escobar, Luis, 209
Espionage Act, 146
Europe, 19, 79, 82

Federal Bureau of Investigation (FBI), 65, 145, 153, 157, 158
Fellowship of Reconciliation, 74
Ferguson, John, 153
Finland, 15
Finletter, Thomas K., 92
First National Bank of New York, 191
Fischer, John, 79
Fleming, D. F., 49, 108, 167
Foch, Marshal Ferdinand, 164
Foreign Affairs Committee, House of Representatives, 41
Foreign Agents Registration Act, 151
Foreign Policy Association, 16
Formosa, 97
Forrestal, James, 82, 83, 85
Fortune, 37
Fourth Army (China), 108
France, 15, 17, 33, 36, 42, 51, 52, 53, 77, 88, 89, 105, 117, 119, 120, 128, 137, 146, 166, 183, 188, 216, 217, 218
Franco, Francisco, 19, 58, 82
Free Cuba News, 74
Free Trade Union News, 76
French Revolution, 34
Frondizi, Arturo, 208
Fulbright, J. W., 18, 44

Gandhi, Mohandas K., 48, 90, 102, 103
Gardner, Arthur, 197
Garibaldini, 49
Gelder, Stuart, 86
General Dynamics Corporation, 70
Gerassi, John, 187
Germany, 15, 33, 50, 53, 82, 83, 86, 88, 216, 218
Gervasi, Frank, 55
Ghana, 225, 233

Gibbons, Harold, 89
Gilmore, Eddy, 172
Gitlow, Benjamin, 147
Glass, H. Bentley, 156
Goldbloom, Maurice, 129
Goldwater, Barry M., 36, 70, 120
Gomulka, Wladyslaw, 174, 175
Government Operations Committee, 152
Graber, D. A., 120
Graham, Frank P., 94, 100
Great Britain, 15, 17, 21, 23, 25, 33, 42, 45, 50, 51, 52, 53, 58, 59, 77, 81, 87, 88, 90, 104, 105, 116, 123, 131, 138, 184, 185, 220
Greece, 22, 45, 46, 57, 58, 60, 61, 62, 63, 169
Griswold, Dwight, 60
Groves, Leslie R., 67
Guatemala, 187, 193, 195, 205, 207, 209, 215
Guillain, Robert, 111
Gunther, John, 85

Hailey, Foster, 108, 110, 112
Haiti, 186, 207
Hamilton, Alexander, 146, 160
Harness Committee (U.S. Congress), 66
Harriman, Averell, 178
Hatta, Mohammed, 98, 100
Healey, Denis, 171
Henderson, Loy, 60
Herter, Christian, 199
Hidalgo y Costilla, Miguel, 187, 188, 202
Hilldring, John H., 84
Hitler, Adolph, 23, 24, 44, 47, 58, 60, 76, 83, 85, 92, 148
Ho Chi-minh, 36, 113, 117, 118, 119, 122, 125, 137, 140
Hodge, John R., 126, 127, 128
Hoffa, James R., 152
Holland, 33, 42, 98, 99, 101
Holmes, Oliver Wendell, Jr., 147
Hook, Sidney, 35, 73
Hoover, Herbert, 166
Hoover, J. Edgar, 13, 150, 158, 226
Hopkins, Harry, 48, 51, 52, 54
Horowitz, Irving L., 71, 177
House Committee on Un-American Activities (HUAC), 75, 152, 153, 154
Hull, Cordell, 84
Humphrey, Hubert, 31
Hungary, 15, 175, 176, 177
Hungarian Revolution, 227
Hunt, H. L., 71
Hurley, Patrick, 50

I. G. Farben Trust, 84
Ickes, Harold, 27, 30
Independent Citizens Committee of the Arts, Sciences and Professions, 27
India, 48, 90, 97, 103, 131
Indian Revolution (1947), 34, 223
Indochina, 30, 39, 113, 114, 117, 118, 120, 128, 136, 137, 138, 139, 140, 142, 215
Indonesia, 99, 100, 101, 102, 103, 118

Industrial Workers of the World (IWW), 147
Institutional Revolutionary party (PRI), 190
Iran, 54, 132, 134, 135, 213
Iranian party, 134
Israel, 233
Italy, 23, 33, 45, 49, 50, 89

James, Daniel, 74
Japan, 22, 23, 98, 105, 106, 107, 117, 128, 137, 138
Jefferson, Thomas, 116, 146
John Birch Society, 19, 71
Johnson, Lyndon B., 41
Joint Committee on Atomic Energy, 22
Jones, George M., 228
Juarez, Benito, 188
Juin, Marshal, 184
Juliao, Francisco, 177

Kaganovich, L. M., 173
Kahn, Herman, 71, 72
Kamenev, Leon B., 162, 164, 167, 168
Kassem, 231
Kempeitai, 99
Kennan, George F., 164, 165, 230
Kennedy, John F., 39, 41, 130, 149, 157, 158, 159, 184, 204, 207, 221, 235
Kenya, 131
Khrushchev, Nikita, 76, 157, 168, 173, 174, 175, 176, 177, 178, 180
King, Martin Luther, 215
Kirchwey, Freda, 31
Kirov, Sergei M., 168
Kolchak, A. V., 217
Korea, 30, 127, 155
Korean War, 113, 126
Kubitschek, Juscelino, 206
Kuh, Frederick, 207
Kun, Bela, 15
Kuomintang, 35, 38, 49, 104, 106, 107, 108, 109, 111, 117, 139
Kyaw Nyein, 139

Labor party (Great Britain), 82, 90
Labor party (Indonesia), 102
Labor Youth League, 150
Lafayette, Marquis de, 187
LaFollette, Robert M., 16, 155
LaGuardia, Fiorello, 148
Lanham, C. T., 144
Lansdowne, Lord, 164
Laos, 120, 128, 129, 130
Laotian Independence Movement, 128
Laqueur, Walter Z., 177
Latin America, 26, 57, 79, 183-215, 231; history of travail, 184-191; Good Neighbor policy, 192; and nationalism, 192-194; Alliance for Progress, 204-213; land problem, 187, 209-212
Lattimore, Owen, 126
Latvia, 15
League of Nations, 17
Leahy, William D., 56, 67
Lend-lease, 52, 54, 55

Lenin, V. I., 16, 17, 33, 34, 72, 107, 162, 163, 165, 166, 179, 217
Levine, Jack, 153
Lewis, Flora, 175
Lippmann, Walter, 16, 221
Lloyd George, David, 15, 164, 165
Lockheed Aircraft, 70
Loeb, James, 28
Lopez Mateos, Adolfo, 190
Lovestone, Jay, 73, 74, 75, 76, 77
Lusk Bills, 147
Luxemburg, Rosa, 163
Ly Vinh Khuon, 119
Lyons, Eugene, 73

MacArthur, Douglas, 53, 67, 70
McCarran Act, 149, 150
McCarthy, Joseph, 144
McNamara, Robert S., 18
Madagascar, 46
Maginot Line, 216
Magnuson Act, 159
Malaya, 130
Maleki party, 134
Malenkov, Giorgi, 172, 173
Mao Tse-tung, 49, 50, 103, 108, 109, 111, 112, 119, 122, 139, 140
Marshall, George C., 38, 67, 88, 91, 109
Marshall Plan, 19, 32, 79, 82, 88, 89, 90, 91, 92
Martin, John Bartlow, 208
Marx, Karl, 33, 34
Masjoemi party, 102
Mathews, J. B., 73, 74
Matthews, Herbert, 203
Mau Mau, 123, 131
Maximos, M., 60, 61
Meade, E. Grant, 127
Meany, George, 75
Meiji Restoration, 201, 236
Mendès-France, Pierre, 120
Merz, Charles, 16 .
Mexican Revolution, 192
Mexico, 33, 186, 188, 189, 209
Mikoyan, Anastas, 176, 201
Miliutin, Paul, 162
Millis, Walter, 156, 159, 224
Minor, Robert, 73
Miranda, Francisco, 185, 187
Mission for Aid to Greece, U.S., 60
Molotov, Vyacheslev, 56, 172, 173
Moreel, Ben, 70
Morgenthau, Hans J., 122
Morgenthau, Henry, Jr., 27, 31, 82
Morrow, Dwight, 189
Moscoso, Teodoro, 205
Mossadegh, Mohammed, 132, 133, 134, 135
Mowrer, Edgar Ansel, 58
Mussolini, Benito, 58

Nagy, Imre, 175
Napoleon Bonaparte, 146
Nasser, Gamal Abdel, 223
Nation, 31
National Citizens Political Action Committee, 27
National Council of Churches, 16
National Council of Resistance, 49

National Council of Soviet-American Friendship, 150
National Planning Association, 235
Nationalism, and communism, 33-36, 40, 94-112; in Asia, 95-96; and popular support, 113-135; in Latin America, 192-194
Ne Win, 142
Neblett, William H., 66, 68
Nehru, Jawaharlal, 22, 103, 118, 177
Nelson, Donald, 66
New Leader, 62
New Republic, 31
New York Herald Tribune, 60, 84
New York Times, 16, 118, 205
Ngo Dinh Diem, 39, 114, 121, 122, 123, 124
Ngo Dinh Nhu, 124
Nguyen Van Tam, 118
Nicaragua, 186, 207, 215
Nigeria, 225
Nixon, Richard, 119, 200
Nkrumah, Kwame, 223
Nogin, V. P., 162
North American Aviation, 70
North Atlantic Treaty, 91
North Atlantic Treaty Organization (NATO), 91, 92
North Korea, 126, 128
North Viet Nam, 79, 125
Nuri Said, 231

O'Brian, John Lord, 148
Odria, Manuel A., 195
Opposition for Democratic Centralism (Soviet Union), 164
Organization of European Economic Cooperation (OEEC), 91
Osgood, Charles, 72

Paine, Thomas, 116
Pakistan, 97
Palmer, A. Mitchell, 16, 73
Palmer Raids, 16
Panama, 187
Papandreou, George, 59
Paraguay, 207
Park, Chung Hee, 128
Pathet Lao, 128, 129
Patton, James, 27
Paz Estenssoro, Victor, 194
Pearson, Drew, 56
Peck, Graham, 107
Peffer, Nathaniel, 38
Peking Review, 180
Pemex, 191
Pena Losa, Enrique, 210, 211, 212
People's Daily, 180
People's Volunteer Organization (PVO), 139
Peralta, Enrique, 207
Perez Jimenez, Marcos, 192, 195
Perkins, Frances, 31
Peron, Juan, 193
Peru, 187, 207
Petofi Circle, 175
Phillips, Thomas R., 122
Phoumi Nosavan, 129
Pishevari, Jafar, 132
Pitt, William, 185
Pittman, Steuart, 156